"*Stand Firm* is a fresh, integr: ᵁˢ⁻
tian apologetics. Rather than ᵉˡ⁻
lectualized, it is insightful, th ₙd
this lively, readable resource!"
— **Paul Copan**, Pledger Family Chair of Philosophy and Ethics, Palm
Beach Atlantic University

"Separating this volume from a plethora of titles that treat similar topics, Gould, Dickinson, and Loftin move directly to the core of each subject, beginning with the most up-to-date explications. The responses that follow are directed straight to the heart of each quandary, providing the reader with a grasp of the most crucial components. Introductory and advanced topics alike are expressed in easily-grasped language, helped along by charts, high-lighted insights, the best scholarly references, and discussion/study questions. One will look long and hard to find so many of the very toughest issues, solutions, and special features addressed thoroughly in a sophisticated manner within the covers of a single text."
— **Gary R. Habermas**, distinguished research professor of apologetics
and philosophy, chair, Department of Theology and Philosophy,
Liberty University

"The French polymath Pascal once remarked that those who hate or fear Christianity are difficult to persuade by direct argument. Here is a book that follows Pascal's strategy. The authors take pains to show their readers how Christianity is both good and beautiful—to make skeptics *wish* that it were true—and then to show them that it is."
— **Timothy McGrew**, chairman, department of philosophy, and
professor of philosophy, Western Michigan University

"This volume seeks not only to offer a reasonable case for the veracity of Christianity, but also for its goodness and beauty by appealing to our longings in reason, conscience, and imagination. The authors appeal to the apologeti-cally suspicious, the enthusiastic, and the intimidated by offering a winsome apologetic for apologetics for a contemporary culture. *Stand Firm* is good for laymen and well-trained apologists alike."

— **Corey Miller**, president and CEO, Ratio Christi campus
apologetics alliance

"I give my highest endorsement to *Stand Firm*. It covers the central apologetics topics, but I have never seen an apologetics text that, chapter after chapter, makes an effort to connect apologetics with evangelism, the gospel, and devotion. This will be an excellent text for undergraduate and seminary students."

— **J. P. Moreland**, distinguished professor of philosophy,
Biola University

"As a Christian case-maker, I travel the country training Christians to make an adequate defense of their Christian worldview. My audiences repeatedly ask for resources to help them understand the evidence for Christianity and the relationship between making the case and sharing the Gospel. *Stand Firm* fits the bill perfectly. *Stand Firm* offers an excellent overview of the case for God's existence, the reliability of the Bible, and the truth of Christianity. More than just a book, *Stand Firm* also provides readers with brief, engaging assignments and a complete list of additional reading options. If you want to learn how to make the case for Christianity, *Stand Firm* is an excellent place to start."

— **J. Warner Wallace**, cold-case homicide detective, and senior fellow,
Colson Center for Christian Worldview, and adjunct professor of
apologetics, Biola University

STAND FIRM

APOLOGETICS

STAND

AND THE BRILLIANCE

FIRM

OF THE GOSPEL

PAUL M. GOULD / **TRAVIS DICKINSON** / **R. KEITH LOFTIN**

ACADEMIC

NASHVILLE, TENNESSEE

To our students

Contents

Acknowledgments

Apologetics is best done in community. We've had the pleasure of writing this book and teaching this material together within an institution that values the life of the mind and the defense of the gospel. Each of us has benefited from the friendship, teaching, and mentorship of many. Special thanks to J. P. Moreland, William Lane Craig, J. Warner Wallace, Timothy McGrew, Doug Geivett, Scott Rae, David Horner, Garry DeWeese, and Steve Cowan.

The process of writing the book also involves the sacrifices of many. To our families, thanks for putting up with our relentless asking of many oddball questions and forcing fine-grained distinctions—especially at the dinner table. Seriously, we love you. And by "love" we mean . . .

To our artist and illustrator, Judith Dickinson (Hi Mom! From Travis) and Wayne Miller, thank you for an incredible job of adding beauty to our words. To Amy Davison, Audrey Greeson, and the B&H team who saw us through the editorial stages, thank you for all the help. We clearly needed it.

To our friends, Aristotle is right: some of you are merely useful. Oh, and please buy this book; we are poor. Finally, to Ross D. Inman, *you complete us*, and so we can't wait to write the next book with you.

CHAPTER 1

An Invitation
to Apologetics

What comes to mind when you hear the word *apologetics*? What emotions surface when you think about *doing* apologetics? For some, apologetics is all the rage. It's fun, exciting, cutting-edge, essential. For others, the idea of apologetics elicits little enthusiasm or perhaps, worse, some suspicion or even disdain. It's "head over heart," too intellectual, passé, irrelevant. For most, however, apologetics is something they know to be important, something they want to learn more about, and something that may be a little intimidating.

We write this book with all three camps in mind—the enthusiast, the suspicious, the open but intimidated—hoping to show the relevancy and importance of apologetics to evangelism, spiritual formation, and indeed, all of life. In fact, what we find in Christianity is a perfect joining together of reason and romance. Nowhere in Scripture is there a call to separate head (reason) and heart (romance) in our love of God and man. This is good news! Christianity does not require us to abandon the intellect or emotions. Christianity is both true and satisfying. Consider C. S. Lewis's description of himself before conversion: "The two hemispheres of my mind were in the sharpest conflict. On the one side a many-island sea of poetry and myth; on the other a glib and shallow 'rationalism.' Nearly all that I loved I believed to be imaginary; nearly all that I believed to be real I thought grim and meaningless."[1] Lewis discovered that it was only in Christianity that his two hemispheres could be brought together into a coherent whole. In Christianity he had found a place to stand and a story that understood his longing for both

---

1. C. S. Lewis, *Surprised by Joy* (New York: Harcourt, 1955), 170.

1

how things are (truth) and how things ought to be (goodness and beauty). Christianity is *true myth*. That is why the first book Lewis wrote as a Christian, *The Pilgrim's Regress*, was subtitled *An Allegorical Apology for Christianity, Reason, and Romance*.[2] Lewis's point in writing the allegory, which is also partly autobiographical, is that Christianity and Christianity alone affirms and honors reason without falling into a kind of calculating disembodied rationality as well as romance without falling into a kind of narcissistic and base sentimentality. What encouragement! God wants us to be whole people who love him with all of our being—which includes our minds, hearts, and wills—and likewise, to love others with our whole being too (as Jesus himself calls us to in Matt 22:37–39). In this introductory chapter, we hope to whet your appetite and set the stage for what follows by clearly articulating what apologetics is and why it matters.

What Is Apologetics?

Apologetics is not about apologizing to someone for being a Christian. The English word "apologetics" comes from the Greek word *apologia*, which means "defense." The idea of presenting a credible defense of one's position is nothing new.[3] For example, in Plato's *Apology* we read of the ancient Greek philosopher Socrates's "apology," or defense of his innocence, before a jury of Athenians against the charge of atheism and the corruption of youth. On April 16, 1963, Martin Luther King Jr. wrote his famous "Letter from Birmingham Jail," in which he defended his nonviolent approach to opposing racism. Today, the so-called New Atheists, such as Richard Dawkins, Sam Harris, and Lawrence Krauss, are vocal apologists for atheism, as defended in best-selling books such as *The God Delusion*, *Letter to a Christian Nation*, and *A Universe from Nothing*.[4]

So, what is apologetics? We define apologetics as *an attempt to remove obstacles or doubts to, as well as offer positive reasons for, believing that Christianity*

---

2. C. S. Lewis, *The Pilgrim's Regress: An Allegorical Apology for Christianity, Reason, and Romance* (Grand Rapids: Eerdmans, 2002).

3. This point and the idea for the following examples are from Douglas Groothuis, *Christian Apologetics: A Comprehensive Case for Biblical Faith* (Downers Grove, IL: InterVarsity Press, 2011), 23–24.

4. New Atheism is a recent movement of activist atheists. There is nothing too new about New Atheism in terms of their arguments or claims. In fact, many of their arguments tend to make high-blown rhetorical points rather than careful philosophical objections.

is true and satisfying. In making a defense, the Christian apologist makes no explicit Christian assumptions; for example, she doesn't assume Scripture is true and simply appeal to chapter and verse in defense of Christianity's claims. Sometimes doubts or obstacles to faith will be intellectual, and sometimes they are due to a failure to imagine a world wherein Christianity is good and beautiful. Christian philosopher Peter Kreeft speaks of three prophets of the human soul: reason, which longs for truth; the conscience, which longs for goodness; and the imagination, which longs for beauty.[5] All of these longings—for truth, goodness, and beauty—are fully satisfied in Christ. Thus, part of our job as apologists is to awaken these universal longings in those we seek to reach for Christ and point them, through reason (e.g., the deliverances of philosophy, history, science, and even commonsense observation), the conscience (e.g., through a life well lived and the pursuit of justice), and the imagination (e.g., through the use of literature, music, and art) to the One who is the ultimate object of our longings. This definition of Christian apologetics is broader than typical definitions, which focus merely on the rational defense of Christianity and the demonstration of its fundamental truth.[6] Our suggestion is more holistic. By focusing on the whole person, we seek to provide a credible witness not only to the truth of Christianity but to its goodness and beauty as well. Additionally, our definition of apologetics is meant to be inclusive of both unbelievers and believers. Christians are not immune from struggling with doubts, misplaced desires, or failed imaginations. Apologetics, as we shall discuss momentarily, is beneficial to the believer as well as the unbeliever in helping to show the relevance of Christianity to all of life.

---

5. Peter Kreeft, *Back to Virtue* (San Francisco: Ignatius Press, 1992), 49.

6. For example, William Lane Craig states, "Christian apologetics involves making a case for the truth of the Christian faith." William Lane Craig, *On Guard* (Colorado Springs: David C. Cook, 2010), 13. Presumably, Dr. Craig would not disagree that there is more to Christian apologetics, but his discussion of the apologetic task mostly consists of providing arguments to establish the truth of theism (again, a necessary component of apologetics), not necessarily its goodness or beauty. Douglas Groothuis's definition is closer to ours: "Christian apologetics is the rational defense of the Christian worldview as objectively true, rationally compelling and existentially or subjectively engaging" (*Christian Apologetics*, 24). We think this definition is in the main correct, but what it means to be "existentially or subjectively engaging" needs to be further clarified. Finally, James Sire speaks of Christian apologetics as "an intellectually and emotionally credible witness to its fundamental truth." Sire, *Little Primer on Humble Apologetics* (Downers Grove, IL: InterVarsity Press, 2006), 26. Again we agree but want to urge apologists to think more holistically about how truth, goodness, and beauty all converge in Christ.

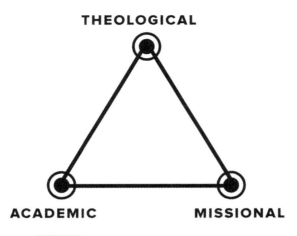

FIGURE 1.1 The Three Themes of Apologetics

Philosopher Greg Ganssle pushes toward this more robust view of apologetics when he speaks of three different sets of issues to consider in the *doing* of apologetics.[7] First, there are theological issues, such as the nature and scope of common grace, the nature of man, the effects of sin, and the nature of general revelation, that inform our understanding and practice of apologetics. For example, in his speech to the god-fearing Greeks in Lystra (Acts 14:15–17), the apostle Paul appealed to the goodness of God and the common grace available to all: ". . . although [God] did not leave himself without a witness, since he did what is good by giving you rain from heaven and fruitful seasons and filling you with food and your hearts with joy" (v. 17). This is an example of what Randy Newman calls "joy-based apologetics": appealing to the goodness and joy of life, available to all, as evidence for God.[8] It also encourages us to think about our evangelism in terms of all that "we" share as humans, instead of the differences between "you" and "me."[9]

Second, according to Ganssle, apologetic issues include the academic or intellectual. This area encompasses most of what people think of when

7. Gregory E. Ganssle, "Making the Gospel Connection: An Essay Concerning Applied Apologetics," in *Come Let Us Reason: New Essays in Christian Apologetics*, ed. Paul Copan and William Lane Craig (Nashville: B&H Academic, 2012), 3–5.

8. Randy Newman, *Bringing the Gospel Home* (Wheaton, IL: Crossway, 2011), 55–59.

9. Newman, 65–68.

they think about apologetics. Staples include arguments for God's existence, discussions of the problem of evil and hell, a defense of the historicity of the Bible, and the resurrection of Christ. Often what begins as a brief comment on some topic quickly turns into detailed discussions related to history, philosophy, science, archaeology, New Testament studies, sociology, mathematics, and more. This demonstrates that apologetics is very much a multidisciplinary field of study. This is as it should be. Since God is the creator of all distinct reality, it follows that all truths discovered (all knowledge gained) in every academic discipline somehow connect back to and illuminate the divine. Everything points to God!

Finally, there are missional issues relevant to the nature and task of apologetics. This area involves seeking to build bridges from a particular audience to the gospel. We must become "cultural exegetes," learning about those we seek to reach—their beliefs, values, and emotional response patterns—so we can identify relevant starting points, adequate bridges (using the planks of reason, conscience, and imagination), and the various barriers to belief to be cleared so the gospel will get a fair hearing. One helpful diagnostic tool, suggested by Ganssle, is the idea of a spiritual mapquest.[10] Just as you can input your current location and any desired destination into the website Mapquest and directions will pop up, so too we must learn accurately to diagnose where an unbeliever is spiritually—his or her "current location"—so we can accurately discern the stages and processes the person must go through in order to grasp and apply the message of the gospel—the destination. Something like the Diagnostic Scale provided by Ganssle will help us think more carefully about the spiritual, intellectual, and emotional condition of those we seek to reach with the gospel.[11]

In this book we hope to bring together all of these considerations related to the nature and task of apologetics in such a way that a person, as a whole person, will, with the help of the Holy Spirit, *see* and *believe* that Christianity is true and satisfying.

---

10. Ganssle, "Making the Gospel Connection," 12–16.
11. Ganssle, 12–13.

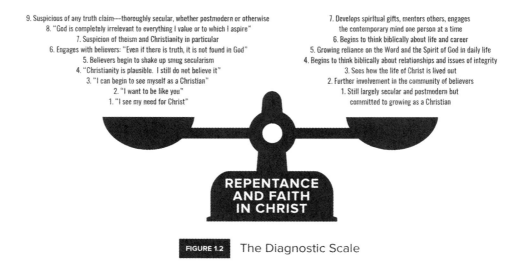

9. Suspicious of any truth claim—thoroughly secular, whether postmodern or otherwise
8. "God is completely irrelevant to everything I value or to which I aspire"
7. Suspicion of theism and Christianity in particular
6. Engages with believers: "Even if there is truth, it is not found in God"
5. Believers begin to shake up smug secularism
4. "Christianity is plausible. I still do not believe it"
3. "I can begin to see myself as a Christian"
2. "I want to be like you"
1. "I see my need for Christ"

7. Develops spiritual gifts, mentors others, engages the contemporary mind one person at a time
6. Begins to think biblically about life and career
5. Growing reliance on the Word and the Spirit of God in daily life
4. Begins to think biblically about relationships and issues of integrity
3. Sees how the life of Christ is lived out
2. Further involvement in the community of believers
1. Still largely secular and postmodern but committed to growing as a Christian

REPENTANCE AND FAITH IN CHRIST

FIGURE 1.2   The Diagnostic Scale

Is Apologetics Biblical?

Part of our goal in this book is to offer a more robust view of apologetics. Apologetics is a rational enterprise, but it is not merely a rational enterprise. It is much more. We think apologetics is essential to faithfulness unto Christ. It points us to the brilliance, beauty, and truth of the gospel. Still, there are some who think apologetics is unbiblical. The idea behind the "apologetics is unbiblical" charge is that our job as Christians is simply to preach the gospel, or merely repeat the words of Scripture, and to sit back and allow the Holy Spirit to work in the unbeliever's heart. Any appeal to a rational defense (as apologetics is often characterized) is to put the case in man's hands instead of God's. We reject this dichotomy. We believe that it is the Holy Spirit that moves in a person's heart in response to the gospel message—yet God has called us to be faithful witnesses, sometimes even expert witnesses, and part of faithfulness, as we shall now argue, includes providing reasons for belief in Christ.

In Exodus 20 we learn that apologetics is grounded in the existence and nature of the one true God.[12] "Then God spoke all these words: I am the LORD your God, who brought you out of the land of Egypt, out of the place of slavery. Do not have other gods besides me" (Exod 20:1–3). Apologetics,

---

12. Groothuis, *Christian Apologetics*, 30.

it seems, *is rooted in our desire to represent faithfully the reality of God*. Part of what it means to flourish as humans is to be rightly related to reality. Apologetics can help by pointing to the One who stands at the center of reality as its Creator, Sustainer, and Redeemer.

Moreover, *apologetics is commanded in Scripture*. Peter implored, "In your hearts regard Christ the Lord as holy, ready at any time to give a defense to anyone who asks you for a reason for the hope that is in you. Yet do this with gentleness and respect" (1 Pet 3:15–16). Peter specifically instructed believers to make a reasoned case for their beliefs. Believers are to give a "defense" (*apologia*) by providing a "reason" (*logos*) for the hope within.

Peter also instructed us to engage with a proper attitude toward both the unbelievers *with whom* we are speaking and the Lord *about whom* we are speaking. We are to be gentle and respectful toward those we seek to reach for Christ. Further, we are to conduct our defense of the faith with an attitude of reverence or holy fear toward Christ, whom we honor as Lord. We are not to be "gunslinger apologists." We have seen gunslingers in our day; in fact, we've engaged in gunslinging ourselves. Let us explain. Often, we take arguments for God or replies to objections to belief in God and load them like bullets into a pair of imaginary Colt .45s, which we place, like those proud and brave cowboys of the Wild West, into the double holsters around our waists. We then walk around town, like Wyatt Earp, with our hands at our sides, looking for an atheist, a skeptic, or a doubting believer—a bad guy—in need of correction. When we find the hapless unbeliever (or doubting believer), in the blink of an eye we draw, unload both guns, blow away the smoke, re-holster, and move on in search of our next victim. The unbeliever, riddled with imaginary bullet holes, is left standing speechless and shaking his head. This imaginary story of the gunslinger apologist is tragic but unfortunately all too close to reality at times. We must resist the temptation to be gunslinger apologists. We are to engage unbelievers in the way we would want to be engaged if we were in their shoes: with gentleness and respect. We can do this without compromising on truth.

Finally, *apologetics is demonstrated in Scripture*. In fact, in the New Testament there is not a single person who does not give a defense for his faith (especially given a proper and broad understanding of evidence, as we develop in chapter 2). Jesus pointed to miracles and fulfilled prophecy to validate his claims.[13] In John 14:11, Jesus states, "Believe me that I am in the Father and the Father is in me. Otherwise, believe because of the works themselves." In effect, Jesus was saying, "Look, if you don't believe me based on what I am telling you, at least believe in light of the evidence of the miracles I've performed." Jesus appealed to evidence to support the reasonableness of the belief that he is the Messiah. Moreover, the disciples used fulfilled prophecy, Jesus's miracles, and the resurrection to prove that Jesus is the Messiah (when engaging fellow Jews) as well as the evidence from nature (when engaging non-Jews).[14] We've seen the apostle Paul's appeal to nature before the god-fearing Greeks in Lystra. When Paul reasoned with his fellow Jews, he "reasoned with them from the Scriptures, explaining and proving that it was necessary for the Messiah to suffer and rise from the dead." Paul concluded: "This Jesus I am proclaiming to you is the Messiah" (Acts 17:2–3). It is apparent from these examples, and many more like them, that neither Jesus nor the disciples hesitated to use evidence in making their case. Did they trust in their arguments to win unbelievers to God? Not at all. As William Lane Craig puts it, "they trusted the Holy Spirit to *use* their arguments" to draw unbelievers to God.[15]

Why Does Apologetics Matter?

Apologetics is not only biblical; it is vital for a vibrant faith and witness. We offer three reasons why apologetics is important.[16] First, *apologetics addresses the ideas and values embraced by a culture that shape its receptivity to the gospel*. As Tim Keller has helpfully pointed out, every culture, and every individual within culture, has a set of "defeater beliefs" that, if true, rule out or "defeat"

---

13. Craig, *On Guard*, 15.
14. Craig, 15.
15. Craig, 15.
16. These three reasons loosely follow Craig, 15–24.

belief in Christianity.[17] Moreover, this set of defeater beliefs is culturally or individually relative. For example, in the West the belief that "all religions are equally valid" is a defeater belief for Christianity. This defeater is an obstacle to faith that needs to be addressed in helping others see the truth and beauty of the gospel. In the Middle East, however, no one believes that all religions are equally valid. Instead, the belief that "everyone in the West believes in Christianity" is an obstacle to the gospel.[18] Whatever the nature of the defeater beliefs, the apologist must address these beliefs so that the gospel will get a fair hearing. This further underscores the importance of being diagnosticians of an individual or culture in order to address the actual obstacles to faith for the unbeliever, as well as the doubts and challenges to faith for the believer.

Second, *apologetics contributes to our spiritual formation unto Christ.* Knowing both *what* you believe and *why* you believe it helps you grow into Christlikeness. The apostle Paul highlighted the importance of the mind in the process of spiritual formation when he implored believers to "be transformed by the renewing of your mind" (Rom 12:2). What you believe about God, the world, and the self will, in a large part, determine the course of your life and the shape of your soul. As J. P. Moreland puts it, "beliefs are the rails upon which our lives run."[19] Apologetics can help you think more deeply about the content of your mental life in order to root out error, strengthen beliefs, and bring a deeper appreciation of the lure and enchantment of Jesus and the gospel.

Finally, *apologetics helps win unbelievers to Christ.* Speaking personally (Paul), God used apologetics in my own journey toward faith in Jesus. As a freshman in college, I was confronted with the gospel message for the first time in a clear and concise way. I realized, again for the first time, that the half-hearted and half-baked religiosity of my youth was not sufficient. I was trying to be "religious," effectively trying to earn salvation by being a (mostly) good person. I realized that I had misunderstood the essence of the

---

17. Timothy Keller, *The Reason for God* (New York: Dutton, 2008). See especially the introduction, where Keller discusses how a "set of alternative beliefs" provides reasons for doubt regarding Christianity.
18. Keller, xvii.
19. J. P. Moreland, *Love Your God with All Your Mind*, 2nd ed. (Colorado Springs: NavPress, 2012), 86.

gospel. I further realized that I was a sinner and that nothing I could do on my own would earn me salvation.

Yet I hesitated. I had doubts. *If* Christianity was true, then I should give my life to it.[20] But, was it true? A friend invited me to a class taught at his church. I was stunned on the first day of this class. The teacher stood before the group of serious-looking students, with a stack of books on the table, and began to unpack the evidence for the historicity of the resurrection of Jesus. I had stumbled into an apologetics class! I continued to attend this class my freshman year and eventually came to the point of realizing that Christianity was indeed true. Apologetics had had its way with me. God used apologetics to remove my intellectual doubts and some of my emotional doubts regarding Christianity. I saw its truth. I believed it would satisfy, and I realized that the choice was before me. Finally, later that year, I bent my knee and placed my faith in Jesus. God uses apologetics to help win unbelievers to Christ. Thanks be to God that he calls us to himself as whole persons! How about you? How has God used apologetics in your own life, or in the lives of those you hope to reach for Christ?

Apologetics: An Invitation to Come Home

The story of Saint Augustine is both fascinating and encouraging. You can read about it in his spiritual autobiography, *Confessions*.[21] If someone as bad as Augustine could find Christ and change, then there is hope for us. If someone as broken as Augustine could become whole and live as God intended, then there is hope for us. Augustine's story provides a helpful

Saint Augustine

---

20. I sensed what Lewis more eloquently put in his address to a group of youth leaders and priests in 1945 in Wales, "One must keep on pointing out that Christianity is a statement which, if false, is of *no* importance, and, if true, of infinite importance. The one thing it cannot be is moderately important." C. S. Lewis, "Christian Apologetics," *God in the Dock*, ed. Walter Hooper (Grand Rapids: Eerdmans, 1970), 101.

21. Saint Augustine, *Confessions*, trans. Henry Chadwick (Oxford: Oxford University Press, 1991).

metaphor of how we are envisioning the apologetic task. Let's consider in detail his journey to Christ.

FIGURE 1.3 *Exitus-Reditus*

Augustine thought all of life could be made sense of in terms of wander and return to God. His *Confessions* begins with this wonderful statement: "You stir man to take pleasure in praising you, because you have made us for yourself, and our heart is restless until it rests in you."[22] His younger years are aptly characterized as restless. At an early age Augustine was captivated by the pursuit of pleasure.[23] Born in AD 354 in the small town of Thagaste in modern-day Algeria, the younger Augustine lived a life straight out of a contemporary Hollywood magazine. His mom was a devout Christian, torn between the noble desire to see her son become a Christian and her hope that he would find secular success as a professor/teacher of rhetoric. At seventeen, Augustine, already immersed in sexual promiscuity, was living with a girl of low standing. He was also a very bright young pupil, classically educated in Greek and Latin (although he hated Greek!).

One day, at the age of eighteen, he was reading Cicero's philosophical dialogue *Hortensius,* now lost to antiquity, in which he learned that happiness is not found in physical pleasures but in the pursuit of truth. He tried reading the Bible, but it seemed simplistic to him. Still, he said, he knew that somehow, any book that doesn't mention Christ falls short of the truth.

Attracted to the philosophy of Mani, the founder of Manicheism, Augustine followed the Manichee teachings for the next decade of his life. He began teaching rhetoric by opening his own school at Thagaste, then

22. Augustine, 1.1.1.
23. This summary of Augustine's life draws from the excellent introduction to *Confessions* by Henry Chadwick found in Augustine, ix-xxv.

moved to Carthage, Rome, and finally Milan. By the time he arrived in Milan, Augustine was among the high and wealthy educated class. He had also become skeptical of the Manichean faith, paving the way for his conversion to Christ.

He came under the teaching of Ambrose, who was then Christian bishop of Milan. Augustine was impressed with his rhetorical skills, his faith, and his exposition of the Bible (it suddenly made sense). He came to believe that Christianity was true. (One of his biggest intellectual doubts had been whether an immaterial substance was possible, and that last doubt had been removed by his decade-long reading of the Platonist books.) Yet, he did not convert.

He believed with his mind what his will would not assent to. The internal struggle was intense. He said, "I had discovered the good pearl. To buy it I had to sell all that I had; and I hesitated."[24] Why the hesitation? "The burden of the world weighed me down with a sweet drowsiness such as commonly occurs during sleep," and yet, he admitted in prayer, "every day I sighed after you."[25]

This internal struggle between mind and will reached a fever pitch one day while he was walking in a garden at the back of a home. He wanted his will to bend to what his mind had already assented to, yet he could not. And the main reason was that he did not know how to change. He could not envision how his desire for illicit sex could be overcome. He was afraid. Then he heard a voice say, "*Tolle lege, tolle lege*" ("Pick up and read"). He looked down and saw a Bible on the ledge next to him. He picked it up, opened it, and read, "'Not in riots and drunken parties, not in eroticism and indecencies, not in strife and rivalry, but put on the Lord Jesus Christ and make no provision for the flesh in its lusts' (Rom 13:13–14)."[26] When Augustine read these words, "all shadows of doubt were dispelled."[27] He immediately bent his knee to God. At that moment, he realized God was the one who would change him. All that was required was to "put on the Lord Jesus Christ."

---

24. Augustine, 134.
25. Augustine, 141.
26. Augustine, 153.
27. Augustine, 153.

Augustine had returned home. He had found Christ. And he was soon to become one of the most important leaders of the Christian church.

There are at least four lessons from Augustine's story that we can learn about our apologetic task. First, *our highest good and greatest need is Christ.* Our hearts are restless until they find rest in Christ. Only Jesus is worthy of our allegiance and affection. Only Jesus will ultimately satisfy. Only Jesus can forgive our sins, redeem us, and make us whole. This is as true of us as it is of those we seek to reach.

Second, *God draws people to himself as whole people—the mind is not left behind.* God began to rouse Augustine through his mind: it was his reading of Cicero's *Hortensius* that awakened Augustine to seek truth, and he knew, probably because of his mother's influence, that truth ultimately cannot be found apart from Christ.

Third, *defeater beliefs must be addressed before a person is willing to consider Christ.* Augustine thought that the concept of an immaterial substance was impossible—and God used the Platonic books, books that opened him up to a world of nonphysical reality, to help him see the possibility of an immaterial substance.

Finally, *assent to the truth of Christianity is not enough*—the heart of the issue is one of the will—as C. S. Lewis stated in *The Great Divorce*, "There are only two kinds of people in the end: those who say to God, 'Thy will be done,' and those to whom God says, in the end, '*Thy* will be done.'"[28] Apologetics can clear away the intellectual obstacles that keep people from Christ so they can see clearly that it is at bottom a moral issue.

Our desire is that you, like Augustine, will find your rest in God. Stand firm in the glorious truth, the marvelous goodness, and the majestic beauty of the gospel. We want you to see Jesus for who he is: the fount of all truth, goodness, and beauty, and the only hope in this life and the next. As you are captured by this vision of Christ, it can only help spur you on to share this gift of life with others. This book is designed to help you along on the journey.

---

28. C. S. Lewis, *The Great Divorce* (San Francisco: HarperCollins, 2001), 75.

Assignments

Assignment 1-1: Making Gospel Connections

Ask your nonbelieving friend what he or she thinks about Christianity. What are the reasons that are keeping him or her from belief in God? Listen. Try to discern whether the obstacles to faith are intellectual, or a failure of imagination, or a moral issue (or all of the above). Respond accordingly.

Assignment 1-2

Discuss the "gunslinger apologist" example. Have you ever been a gunslinger? Have you witnessed gunslinging? How did it turn out?

Assignment 1-3

Answer the following questions:

1. Before reading this chapter, what was your preconception of apologetics? How has that changed?
2. Does the thought of doing apologetics excite or scare you? Discuss.
3. How is Christianity a perfect blending of reason and romance?
4. What did you find interesting about the story of Saint Augustine? Can you relate?
5. What area of apologetics are you most interested in?
6. What area of apologetics do you think is most relevant to the objections and doubts of those with whom you are in relationship?
7. How can the church incorporate apologetics into its ministry?
8. What is the next step for you with respect to apologetics?

Suggested Reading

Craig, William Lane. *On Guard*. Colorado Springs: David C. Cook, 2010.

Davison, Andrew. *Imaginative Apologetics: Theology, Philosophy and the Catholic Tradition*. Grand Rapids: Baker, 2012.

Groothuis, Douglas. *Christian Apologetics: A Comprehensive Case for Biblical Faith*. Downers Grove, IL: InterVarsity Press, 2011.

Lewis, C. S. *Mere Christianity*. New York: HarperOne, 2001.

Newman, Randy. *Bringing the Gospel Home*. Wheaton, IL: Crossway, 2011.

CHAPTER 2

Truth, Knowledge, and Faith

Before going any further, it is important to make some distinctions. This is a book about standing firm. But upon what are we firmly standing? One answer is that we firmly stand on the *truth*. This seems right as far as it goes. However, saying just this is not sufficient, since there are a number of ways to understand the notion of truth in today's marketplace of ideas. Moreover, it can't just be truth in general upon which we stand. We will argue that it should be certain truths of which we enjoy *knowledge*. But even knowledge is arguably not the full picture for our cognitive stance as Christians. Standing firm will also require *faith*, but this is an extremely misunderstood concept and needs clarification. So there's truth, there's the knowledge of truth, and then there's having faith in what we know is true. That's a mouthful, but unpacking this is our task in this chapter. Let's take each of these in turn: truth, knowledge, and faith.

Truth

The task of giving a robust definition of truth has caused many philosophical headaches for some of the best minds, as it is a notoriously difficult concept to define. Somewhat ironically, this may not be because it is overly complicated. In fact, the more complicated accounts of the nature of truth are some of the least plausible, since they utilize concepts less understood than the concept of truth itself. It is our view that the nature of truth is so obvious and fundamental that, for this reason, it resists definition.

Wait—what?!

Now, you may be thinking that we are off to a bad start here. We've provided little reason to be excited about the forthcoming discussion. Hang on, though, because this is an important point, and you can get it.

In philosophy, when we define or analyze a concept, we identify more basic and presumably better understood terms that help illuminate the concept we are defining. This same sort of thing happens in everyday life. A person may not understand the concept "bachelor," but we may help him understand the concept by identifying better-understood concepts, such as (1) a person (2) who is unmarried and (3) male. The notion of an unmarried male person illuminates the concept of what it is to be a bachelor.

But think about it: how can there always be more and more basic terms? It seems that we must eventually hit limits with basic concepts that can be analyzed no further.[1] What if the concept one is intending to define is of the fundamentally basic sort? There would be no more basic terms to define it. Does this mean that we do not grasp or understand these basic concepts? No, our claim is that the notion of truth, for example, is so basic that it is well understood by virtually everyone!

The idea of truth is grasped even by young children. Suppose little Johnny is seen with crumbs on his shirt and a chocolate smear on his cheek, but he says that he did not eat the missing cookies from the cookie jar. When his mom says, with a motherly tone, "Johnny! Is that true?" it seems he understands perfectly well what he is being asked. Johnny couldn't give us a robust definition of truth, but he certainly grasps the concept.

On this view, notions like these function in thought as a kind of (unanalyzable) logical atom from which all of our other concepts are understood. That is, it is our grasp of these basic concepts that we use to understand the rest of logical thought.

None of this should suggest that we cannot describe or give a (perhaps rough) characterization of the concept of truth. Though we can't give a robust philosophical analysis of the concept of truth, we can, in our view, get a good idea of what we mean by the concept, how it is used in making claims about the world, and characterize it as such.

---

1. If we did not hit basic and fundamental terms in our analysis, then every analysis would produce what's known as a *vicious infinite regress* of analysis. That is, the analysis would never stop (it is infinite), and one never ends up with a substantive analysis (it is vicious).

A discussion of the nature of truth often begins with Aristotle's characterization of truth: "To say of what is that it is not, or of what is not that it is, is false, while to say of what is that it is, and of what is not that it is not, is true."[2]

So, what, according to Aristotle, is truth?

Truth is saying p is the case when p is the case.

Now, this is not too bad, in terms of a characterization of truth. One problem with the Aristotelian notion is that it is not just things that are *said* that are true (or false). We can *write* things that are true (or false). We can even just *think* things that are true (or false).

Let's broaden this out a bit.

One can say that "triangles have three sides," and this is true. But one can also write that "triangles have three sides," and one can even just think that "triangles have three sides." In fact, one can say that "triangles have three sides" in a variety of ways. One can say the same thing in English, Spanish, Latin, sign language, or any number of languages. One can write "triangles have three sides" in English, Spanish, hieroglyphics, braille, and so forth. One can also think that "triangles have three sides," believing or even just considering whether "triangles have three sides" is true.[3] Each of these is radically different, and yet they have something in common. They each have an identical content.

Philosophers have often referred to this content as a state's *propositional content* or, more simply, as the *proposition*. A proposition is always descriptive and, as such, is either true or false. One helpful way to understand a proposition is that a proposition can always be plugged into a that-clause. For example, when I identify a belief, I will say something like "I believe *that p.*" Whatever makes good sense to plug in for the p is the proposition believed. Or if I was going to identify a proposition that I spoke, it will take the form "I said *that p.*" Again, whatever I plug in for the p will be the proposition. So these statements all make good sense as propositional claims:

2. Aristotle, *Metaphysics* in *Aristotle: Selected Works*, 3rd ed., trans. and ed. Hippocrates Apostle (Grinnell, IA: Peripatetic Press, 1991), 1011b25.

3. I can also fear that triangles have three sides, I can hope that triangles have three sides, I can desire that triangles have three sides, and so on. All of these have the same content, though they are very different mental states.

I believe that God exists.

He said that triangles have two sides.

I believe that unicorns are real.

I wrote that New Jersey is a coastal state.

These all make sense, though some are true and some are false. What doesn't make sense is to say:

I think that God.

I said that unicorns.

The reason is that this type of phrase doesn't make any claim *about* God or unicorns. There really is no descriptive (propositional) content here. We are left wanting to know what about God do we think is the case and what did one say about unicorns. Is it that God exists? Do you think what he says in the Bible is true? Is it that unicorns are mythical creatures? Answering these claims will require us to assert propositions that will be either true or false.

I think that what God says in the Bible is true.

I said that unicorns are mythical creatures.

So it is important to understand that, strictly speaking, it is propositions that are true (or false). This makes propositions the primary *truth bearers*. The truth bearer is the thing that is either true or false. It, in this sense, bears the truth. We use language (spoken or written) to express propositions, but language itself is not, strictly speaking, the truth bearer.

Okay, so truth has to do with propositions. But when is a proposition true (or false)? In Aristotle's characterization a claim is true when there is a match with reality. He said, "To say of what is that it is . . . is true." What Aristotle seemed to have in mind is that when our claims (what we have now clarified as the propositional content of our claims) match up with reality, then our claims are true and they are false when they do not.

It is then a fact of reality that makes a claim true. This is known as the *truth maker*.

Facts Are Stubborn

A fact is an objective thing—a mind-independent reality. President John Adams was philosophically astute when he quipped: "Facts are stubborn things; and whatever may be our wishes, our inclinations, or the dictates of our passion, they cannot alter the state of facts and evidence."

What is a fact? A fact is an objective feature of the world. It is simply the way the world is, no matter what anybody thinks or believes or claims. So what makes the proposition "God exists" true? Answer: the fact of God's existing. Why is the proposition "unicorns exist" false? It is because there are no unicorns in reality that would make this proposition true.

So we have two distinct things in view: a proposition and a fact. There is one last piece to complete this characterization of the concept of truth. Not just any fact can make a specific proposition true. It is the fact of God's existence that makes the proposition that "God exists" true. But why doesn't the fact that New Jersey is a coastal state make the proposition "God exists" true? The answer is that these two things (i.e., the fact of New Jersey's being a coastal state and the proposition "God exists") do not stand in the appropriate relation. The fact of God's existing and the proposition "God exists" do stand in the appropriate relation in the sense that the proposition *corresponds* to the fact. Call this the *correspondence relation*.

What is it for a proposition to correspond to a fact? This is where saying something about the nature of truth gets very difficult. Probably the best we can do is grasp the notion of correspondence by means of analogy. Correspondence, in the relevant sense, is when the descriptive content of a propositional state "fits" or "maps onto" or "pictures" the facts of reality.

Consider, for example, a photograph of a squirrel. A photograph is nothing but paper with ink arranged in a certain way. Its every property is different compared to the actual squirrel. Squirrels are fuzzy, enjoy nuts, are three-dimensional, and weigh a few pounds. But the photograph (as in, the image) isn't itself fuzzy, it is two-dimensional, and it hardly weighs anything. And yet we do not hesitate to call it a photograph *of* a squirrel. It is not a photograph of a river or an automobile. So, what makes it a picture of a squirrel? The photograph stands in the appropriate relation, what we might call the *picturing relation*, to a squirrel.

Again, this analogy will quickly fall short. We do not have a little picture in our minds when making an assertion (e.g., what picture would you have of God or a 256-sided object?). But something analogously similar is going on when a proposition stands in the correspondence relation to a fact of reality. This is hopefully sufficient to grasp the correspondence relation. We may not be able to define it, but we can move forward knowing what it is we are talking about.

So, in summary, when we assert a claim, the claim has a propositional content. This is the truth bearer. This content is true (or false) insofar as it corresponds (or fails to correspond) to a fact. If the proposition does correspond to a fact, then this fact makes it the case that the claim is true.

Some Implications of the Correspondence Theory

Whether a claim is true depends solely upon facts. No amount of hoping some claim is true makes it any truer. One can be supremely confident that a proposition is true, but this has no effect on whether it is true. It is true when and only when there is a fact to which the proposition corresponds. This is sometimes referred to as the *objectivity of truth*, in the sense that whether or not a claim is true is an objective matter not dependent on any subjective state of a person.

We do not need to *know* whether a claim is true in order for it to be true. In fact, something can be true and we may *never know* that it is indeed true. At the precise moment you started reading this chapter, there was a specific number of cells that composed your body. Let's suppose that you suddenly came to believe "I had exactly 37 trillion living cells at the moment I began reading this chapter" and let's also suppose that it is a fact that you had exactly 37 trillion cells at that time. Do you *know* that this is true? No, and we likely will never know whether it was true, since presumably the precise number of living cells in your body changed in an instant and there is now no way to know what it was. But the belief is still true given the correspondence with a fact at that moment. Yet, despite its being true, we do not and *cannot* know that it is true.

Truth does not come in degrees. A proposition is either true or false. There either were or were not 37 trillion living cells in your body at the moment you began reading this chapter. The claim that "there are 37 trillion living cells in your body" either corresponds to this fact, or there is no corresponding fact. This is often framed as a law of logic called the *law of the excluded middle* (or, sometimes, the principle of bivalence). When it comes to truth, there is no middle option (i.e., between true and false). Again, we may not know whether some claim is true or whether it is false, but this we know: it is either true or false. This is the law of the excluded middle. This is expressed as "A or not-A."

It is also the case that a claim cannot both be true and false, at least not at the same time and in the same sense. If you claim that "the Christian God exists" and your neighbor claims "the Christian God does not exist," these cannot both be true. This is because they cannot both correspond to reality. Since your claim corresponds (or so we will claim), your neighbor's claim does not. This is called the *law of noncontradiction*. It is expressed as "It is not the case that A and not-A."

Objections to a Correspondence Theory of Truth

It is difficult to object to the correspondence theory of truth precisely because it will always seem that one is using the theory to reject the theory. To see this, suppose someone says the correspondence theory of truth is false because you have your truth and I have my truth. This view is commonly

known as *relativism*. A crude version of this theory states that if I believe that
p is true, then *p* is true (for me). The relativist will of course claim that relativism is true. But when relativists claim that relativism is true, it certainly
seems as though they are saying that relativism corresponds to the way the
world is. It sure seems as if they mean to say that relativism is true for me,
true for you, and true for everyone. But this is not relativistic! In fact, the
very assertion of the view seems obviously to contradict itself. This is called
being *self-refuting*. When a claim is self-refuting, it undercuts itself: the sentence "There are no true sentences" is self-refuting, because it is itself a sentence that would have us believe that no sentences are true. Do you see that?
If I say to you, "I cannot speak a word of English," that claim would likewise
undercut itself since it was spoken in English! If the relativist is saying that
relativism itself corresponds to reality, this would mean that relativism, as a
view about truth, is false.

We end this section with a tip for engaging with a person who says,
"That's just your truth" in response to your Christian claims. In this situation, one should press for clarification. What does someone mean when
he or she says something is true for one but not true for another? In our
experience, this is often just a way to say that people have different beliefs,
perspectives, and experiences. Though this is certainly true, it doesn't follow

that truth itself is relative and everyone's perspective is correct. Rather, this just seems to say that we have different views about the world, and we would do well to appreciate this fact. However, don't we then have to ask who has the right view about the world? Whose view is true and reasonable? This steers the conversation back to a meaningful discussion.

Knowledge

Is Christianity true? How do you *know* that Christianity is true? Can we have knowledge of Christianity's truth? So far, we've only argued that truth is objective and is a matter of correspondence to reality. What is it, then, to know truth?

Plato explored this issue in his work the *Theaetetus* and thus began the discipline known as *epistemology*, the philosophical study of knowledge and rational justification. In the dialogue, Socrates presses the young Theaetetus for a definition of *knowledge*. After a few failed attempts, Theaetetus comes on a definition of knowledge according to which "knowledge is true judgment."[4] When we have made a judgment (or a claim or belief) and that judgment is true, then we have knowledge.

Now, this might strike us as initially plausible. It seems clear that truth and belief are necessary for knowledge. It would seem exceedingly odd to think that we can have knowledge about something when we don't even believe it. It seems similarly odd to call something we believe knowledge when the belief is false. Let's suppose Smith claims that the city bus stops at precisely noon. Someone else asks, "Do you *know* that the bus stops at noon?" and Smith's response is "Yes, I know this fact." Let's suppose further that this is wrong. It stops at 11:30 a.m. What's our diagnosis? Did Smith have knowledge? The right thing to say here seems to be that, though Smith thought he had knowledge, it turns out that he did not in fact know that the bus stops at noon. In any case, it has seemed to many epistemologists that knowledge requires both truth and belief.

But is true belief sufficient for knowledge? We should recall the example we gave earlier about the cells in one's body. Let's suppose Smith guesses at

---

4. Plato, *Theaetetus*, trans. M. J. Levett, in *Plato: Complete Works*, ed. John M. Cooper (Indianapolis: Hackett, 1997), 200e.

random that he had precisely 37 trillion living cells composing his body at a specific time *t*. Let's also suppose that Smith's judgment happens to be true. (What would make this true? You've got this. See the previous "Truth" section for help.) Does Smith then *know* that he had 37 trillion cells at *t*, when he has merely guessed at this fact and happened to get it right? It seems that if Smith is only guessing, even if he guesses correctly, this does not constitute knowledge. He doesn't really *know* that he had 37 trillion cells at *t* even if it is in fact a true belief. Knowledge requires something further.

Socrates and Theaetetus landed on saying that knowledge is true judgment *with an account*. It's debated precisely what Plato had in mind here by an "account," but many philosophers have embraced the idea that in addition to true belief, one must have some good reason for thinking the belief is true. If Smith had a body cell scanner that could reliably tell the exact number of cells, and it said he had 37 trillion cells at *t*, then this would provide him with good reason—it provides an account—for believing that he had precisely 37 trillion cells at *t*. This would transform Smith's random guess into something far more secure—perhaps even knowledge. His belief is grounded in reason (and evidence) and, in many cases, this would be sufficient for knowledge. This reason or evidence need not prove or make certain the truth of the belief. On most accounts, it only needs to make it likely that the belief is true.

Thus "knowing that *p*" may be understood, for our purposes, as the satisfaction of three conditions.

1. A person must believe *p*.
2. The proposition *p* must be true.
3. The person must have good reasons for believing *p*.

Alas, this definition of knowledge has certain philosophical problems.[5] We won't go into these technical difficulties here. But despite these problems, many epistemologists think that this definition of knowledge is sufficient for most cases of knowledge, and it will do for our purposes.

This definition allows us to highlight an important point about knowledge. There is a critical relationship between conditions 2 and 3. Condition

5. Edmund Gettier, "Is Justified True Belief Knowledge?" *Analysis* 23 (1963): 121–23.

2 only requires the proposition *p* to be true. Knowing that *p* doesn't require that we *know that p* is true. The proposition simply needs to be true to satisfy this second condition. But we of course want to have true (rather than false) beliefs. So what can we do to ensure that we have true beliefs? We work on our reasons, satisfying condition 3, for believing the proposition. The nature of good reasons is such that they are *truth-conducive*, in the sense that they lead us to truth. That is, when we have good reasons for a belief (i.e., condition 3 is satisfied), we have reason to think that condition 2 is satisfied (i.e., the belief is true). We are, in a way, well positioned for believing truly.

Evidence

We take "good reasons" to be synonymous with evidence. However, it is worth noting there is considerable debate as to the role of evidence in coming to know or rationally believe that Christianity is true. There are some who think that evidence is the only or at least primary source for believing something rationally. That is, if one does not have evidence for *p*, then one thereby does not believe *p* rationally. Others think that evidence plays a minor role or is even completely unnecessary.

Unfortunately, this debate is not always carried on very carefully. Oftentimes, the term *evidence* is used to mean academic arguments, the kind that seem to require advanced degrees to understand. But this is an overly narrow understanding of evidence. We will assume here that training in higher education is not necessary for rationally believing that Christianity is true, especially since many Christian saints, including some of Jesus's own disciples, lacked such training!

We think of evidence broadly. In our use of the term, evidence for a belief should be understood as any fact that indicates the truth of *b* (including experiences, testimonies, premises of an argument, etc.). If this is one's notion of evidence, then the evidence for Christianity is plentiful with no advanced degrees necessary.

To make this point, let's imagine a little old country grandma who has faithfully served Christ her whole life, despite having a limited education. Let's say she got the basic skills provided in elementary school, but never went any further. Could her belief in Christianity possibly be rational? Sure! The country grandma, just like the rest of us, can look around and see that the world testifies of God's existence. She has also likely made specific prayer requests to God, and if God showed up in big ways (as he tends to do with the prayers of country grandmas), this would stand as a stellar evidence for her Christian belief. The country grandma can have real and powerful encounters with the risen Christ and can experience the realness and power of the gospel. She can also have a plenitude of testimonial evidence from others experiencing miraculous events, as well as the testimony of Scripture. All of these things stand as evidence for reasonably taking Christianity as true.

Now, we can sometimes get cornered by hostile objectors, and we may fail to articulate the reasons we have. However, it doesn't follow that we don't possess these reasons and that they don't inform our faith.

It seems most committed Christians have a fairly wide repertoire of evidence for their belief in Christianity. This isn't to say that we can't all work on getting more and better evidence. Indeed, this is the reason for this book! But to think that most people lack evidence in this broad sense seems to simply misunderstand the notion of evidence.

Knowing and Showing

In an influential book on Christian apologetics, William Lane Craig says that the proper basis for knowing that Christianity is true is not the evidence for Christianity. This might strike one as more than a bit odd given that Craig is one of the world's foremost Christian apologists. Craig certainly has a high view of the evidence for Christianity's truth given that he routinely takes on Christianity's most difficult critics in formal debates on the evidence for Christianity. So what's going on?

In the book, Craig makes a distinction between *knowing* that Christianity is true and *showing* that Christianity is true. He says:

> The way we know Christianity to be true is by the self-authenticating witness of God's Holy Spirit. Now what do I mean by that? I mean that the experience of the Holy Spirit is veridical and unmistakable (though not necessarily irresistible or indubitable) for him who has it; that such a person does not need supplementary arguments or evidence in order to know and to know with confidence that he is

in fact experiencing the Spirit of God; that such experience does not function in this case as a premise in any argument from religious experience to God, but rather is the immediate experiencing of God himself; that in certain contexts the experience of the Holy Spirit will imply the apprehension of certain truths of the Christian religion, such as "God exists," "I am condemned by God," "I am reconciled to God," "Christ lives in me," and so forth.[6]

Craig's idea is that the inner experience of the Spirit of God himself—where he testifies to his existence and the truths of the gospel—is the primary way people come to the knowledge of Christianity. However, he goes on to say that we cannot share our inner experience of these matters with others. This is simply a fact about our inner experiences—they cannot be literally shared with others. We might say to another, "I feel your pain," but we don't mean it literally because experiences are entirely private. We can, of course, tell people about inner experiences of God, but Craig seems to think this is too weak, in terms of evidence, to constitute knowledge. Thus, if we are to *show* others that Christianity is true, we must use arguments and evidence, which is what Craig does in his debates, his books, and his interactions with students across the globe. Thus, arguments and evidence play a ministerial or subsidiary role.

Craig's distinction is problematic. Though we certainly agree that the inner experience of the Holy Spirit is important for coming to a genuine and full knowledge of Christianity's truth, we claim that it should be understood as part (indeed a crucial part) of one's overall evidence set. That is, we deny that there is a substantive distinction between evidence on one hand and the inner testimony of the Holy Spirit on the other. The direct experience of God is evidence—indeed, great evidence—for the truth of Christianity. This is described as *testimony* and inner *experience*, after all, and these typically fall within the category of evidence broadly construed.[7]

---

6. William Lane Craig, *Reasonable Faith: Christian Truth and Apologetics*, 3rd ed. (Wheaton, IL: Crossway, 2008), 43.

7. There are some approaches to Christian apologetics that understand "evidence" as only arguments and "evidentialism" as the view that apologetic arguments are necessary for faith. There are very few Christians that have this view, and it is an overly narrow view of the term *evidence*. In the wider discussion of evidence in epistemology, evidence is understood much more broadly to include experiences of which one is directly aware.

We also think that it can't be inner experience all by itself—raw, uninter-preted experience—that provides the basis for knowing Christianity is true. Inner experiences seem crucially to need interpretation. The typical religious experience does not seem to have enough content to serve as the primary basis of our knowledge. For example, let's say one is in an evangelistic service and experiences an overwhelming sense of awe. Is this sufficient all by itself to rationally believe that the claims being made in the service are true? It seems not. Many Christians would agree that this is inadequate if it were, say, a Mormon evangelistic service. But why should this experience justify the belief in the Christian gospel?

Craig is quite aware of this objection and says that the counterfeit expe-rience of, say, the Mormon does nothing to take away from his own veridical experience.[8] But one seems to need reason for thinking that the experience is in fact veridical. If merely being veridical were sufficient, then all skepti-cal concerns could similarly be dismissed. The skeptic asks how one knows that one is not in the Matrix given a Matrix-experience would be qualita-tively indistinguishable from veridical experience. However, it simply doesn't address the skeptical concern to assert that one's experience is veridical. The skeptic is likely to ask again, "But how do you know it's veridical?" Now, Craig might not think that the Christian and Mormon experiences are qual-itatively indistinguishable, but this seems impossible to verify. But if they are qualitatively indistinguishable, then the rest of our evidences will need to play more than a subsidiary role. It will have to be this experience of God along with the Christian evidences that rationally justifies our belief.

One motivation for Craig's view is the fact that many Christians have never considered the apologetic evidence for Christianity, and yet they cer-tainly seem to believe Christianity in a rational way. Craig thinks that one need not have familiarity with apologetics (especially academic apologetics) to know that Christianity is true. And we agree! But, again, as we argued earlier, we think that the typical believer does have evidence (even if not the formal evidence of academic apologetics) to rationally believe that Christianity is true.

On the basis of this broad evidence, we claim that we not only believe rationally that Christianity is true, but that we may *know* Christianity's truth.

---

8. Craig, *Reasonable Faith*, 49.

Faith

But knowing Christianity's truth is not the full picture. As Christians, we are called to faith. But what does "faith" mean? Here there is much disagreement. Consider what many atheists have said about religious faith.

Mark Twain: "Faith is believing what you know ain't so."[9]

Peter Boghossian: Faith is "pretending to know things that you don't know" and "belief without evidence."[10]

Richard Dawkins: "Faith is the great cop-out, the great excuse to evade the need to think and evaluate evidence. Faith is belief in spite of, even perhaps because of, the lack of evidence."[11]

For many atheists, all that one has to do is get Christians to admit that they believe Christianity on the basis of faith and this is sufficient to refute the view. After all, how could you win a rational debate if you admit to pretending to know something you don't know? To concede this seems to be to surrender before the war even starts.

But are these understandings of faith correct? The answer is no, not by a long shot! At best, these are mere caricatures of faith. We will argue that faith is best understood as *ventured trust*. We will also argue that everyone has faith and that faith is not inherently contrary to reason.

What, then, is faith? As a first pass, we should understand faith as simply a state of trust. When we trust, there is always some thing or person that we trust. This is to say that faith always has an object. That is, one cannot have faith in some nebulous way. There

> **Faith as Ventured Trust**
>
> "I am not asking anyone to accept Christianity if his best reasoning tells him that the weight of the evidence is against it. That is not the point at which Faith comes in. . . . Faith, in the sense in which I am here using the word, is the art of holding on to things your reason has once accepted, in spite of your changing moods."[12] —C. S. Lewis

---

9. Mark Twain, *Following the Equator* (New York: Dover, 1989), 132.

10. Peter Boghossian, *A Manual for Creating Atheists* (Durham, NC: Pitchstone, 2013), 23–24.

11. Richard Dawkins, speech, Edinburgh International Science Festival, April 15, 1992, quoted in Alister McGrath, *Christianity: An Introduction*, 2nd ed. (Malden, MA: Blackwell, 2006), 102.

12. C. S. Lewis, *Mere Christianity* (New York: HarperOne, 2001), 140.

must be some thing or person one has faith in. So this could be a chair one is considering sitting in. Or one could trust an airplane one is waiting to board. Or one may place one's trust in a person to whom one is about to say, "I do" in a wedding ceremony. The object of one's faith would be the chair or the airplane or the soon-to-be-if-all-goes-well spouse. Now, according to this understanding of faith, faith is not, by itself, a set of beliefs, or a proposition, or even a claim. So an immediate problem with the above caricatures of faith is that they do not place faith in the right sort of category. Faith cannot be "belief without evidence" since it is not a belief to begin with. It is a state that may involve beliefs or may be caused by beliefs, although it is not itself a belief. It seems to be a state of trust.

Faith, as we will be using the term, also seems to connote the idea that we trust in action. When we place our faith in an object, we always *venture* something. If we trust the safety of the airplane, but we never get on board, then we haven't really placed our faith in the airplane. Faith requires not trust from a distance but an *entrusting of ourselves*, where we venture or risk ourselves and our well-being to some thing or person. To truly place our faith in a chair, we must sit down and risk the chair's collapsing. Or a much better illustration is the risk one takes when one gets married. A healthy marriage requires us to entrust virtually every area of our lives to our spouse, and this opens us up to the deepest hurt when there is betrayal. A toxic marriage is of course one in which there is deep distrust and suspicion. But the marriage will also suffer if one merely trusts from a distance. A healthy marriage requires us to jump in with deep and mutual ventured trust.

Everyone has faith, in this sense, insofar as they entrust themselves to someone or something. Again, when we get married, we entrust our feelings, well-being, livelihood, possessions, and so on, to our spouses. When we fly on an airplane, we entrust ourselves to the aircraft, the pilots, the mechanics who serviced the plane, and so forth. When we do science, we entrust ourselves to certain methodologies, prior theories and data, and our empirical and mental faculties. There is nothing unique about Christian faith other than the object of that faith.

What is the object of Christian faith? Christian faith is entrusting ourselves to Christ and venturing on the truth and reality of the gospel. We place our faith in Christ as Savior and Lord. It is not merely the truth of the gospel, and it is not merely the evidence and reasons constitutive of the knowledge of the gospel, but we are literally entrusting ourselves to Christ and his gospel.

Faith and Reason

What is the relationship between faith and reason? Unfortunately, there have been Christians who have conceded something like the above caricatures of faith. The notion that faith and reason stand in some degree of tension is a view called *fideism*. On the one hand, the fideist might say reason plays a role, but only carries us so far. That is, we might know some truths of Christianity by reason and evidence, but at a certain point, reason and evidence run out, and faith, in a way, takes over or fills the gap.

Or the more radical fideist might say that you have your rational pursuits on one hand (science, political platforms, automobile repair, etc.) and your faith pursuits on the other, and never the twain shall meet. Evidence literally has nothing to do with and might even be detrimental to what one believes on the basis of faith. When it comes to challenges to the faith, the fideist can always shut down a challenge by appealing to that old canard "We just got to have faith."

Though it is not uncommon for Christians to make this appeal when their Christian beliefs get pressed, fideism has always been a minority view. Most Christians think that reason and evidence are very important for faith. They don't believe things they "know ain't so," and they certainly don't merely pretend that they are true. They have faith in Christ precisely because they have become convinced by the preaching of the gospel, the testimony of the Spirit, the richness of Scripture, a work the Lord has done in their own lives, answers to prayer, the evidence seen in the world, a testimony from others, and so on. In fact, we don't know of anyone for whom reason has played no role whatsoever in coming to faith.

As long as we don't narrowly restrict the notion of reason (as discussed above), we should see that faith and reason are perfectly compatible and, indeed, are importantly related. Reason, in our view, is a tool for coming to know upon what sort of object we should venture our trust. It helps us to know what objects are trustworthy—or, what we may call *faithworthy*. We will often have competing reasons when we consider where to place our faith, and we oftentimes venture trust with less-than-ideal reasoning. This fact requires that we engage the life of the mind and carefully consider and weigh out our reasons as we grow in faith.

It is our sincere hope that through the forthcoming chapters, you are provided with more and greater reasons for placing even greater faith in Christ and the truth of the gospel. To this content, we now turn.

Assignments

Assignment 2-1: Making Gospel Connections

Ask your nonbelieving friend how he or she defines truth. Are facts about God and religion either true or false? Does he or she think there is objective truth in science and engineering? Can we have knowledge of the world? If one can present compelling reasons for thinking that Christianity is true, would this mean that we may have knowledge of it? Try to discern whether your friend is requiring a different standard for truth or knowledge when it comes to religious belief. This will help you know how to approach him or her with the evidence.

Assignment 2-2

Discuss the many ways faith is understood. What are reasons for thinking that faith and reason are compatible?

Assignment 2-3

Answer the following questions:

1. What is the correspondence theory of truth (be sure to define the terms *truth bearer* and *truth maker*)?
2. Why doesn't relativism work as a theory of truth?
3. What are the three ingredients for knowledge?
4. What role does the Holy Spirit play in someone coming to genuine knowledge of Christianity's truth? Does the Holy Spirit provide evidence, or is this non-evidential?
5. How is faith typically understood by nonreligious people?
6. Define *fideism*.
7. Discuss how reason and faith work together.

Suggested Reading

Audi, Robert. *Epistemology: A Contemporary Introduction*. 3rd ed. New York: Routledge, 2011.

Boa, Kenneth, and Robert M. Bowman. *Faith Has Its Reasons: Integrative Approaches to Defending the Faith*. 2nd ed. Downers Grove, IL: InterVarsity Press, 2006.

Conee, Earl, and Richard Feldman. *Evidentialism: Essays in Epistemology.*
    New York: Oxford University Press, 2004.
Craig, William Lane. *Reasonable Faith: Christian Truth and Apologetics.* 3rd
    ed. Wheaton, IL: Crossway, 2008. See chapter 1.
Craig, William Lane, and J. P. Moreland. *Philosophical Foundations for a
    Christian Worldview.* Downers Grove, IL: InterVarsity Press, 2003.

CHAPTER 3

God

"So far as I can see, belief in God is on a par with belief in Santa Claus," says Alex Rosenberg, professor of philosophy at Duke University.[1] "There are," he continues, "compelling reasons to deny God's existence, but those reasons don't just support a negative conclusion: no God, end of story. They provide everything we need to answer all the other questions that come along with the God question."[2] Oxford zoologist Richard Dawkins, perhaps the most well-known of the new atheists, agrees: God is "the most unpleasant character in all fiction: jealous and proud of it; a petty, unjust, unforgiving control-freak; a vindictive, bloodthirsty ethnic cleanser; a misogynistic, homophobic, racist, infanticidal, genocidal, filicidal, pestilential, megalomaniacal, sadomasochistic, capriciously malevolent bully."[3] Belief in God, he exclaims, "is a delusion" held on the basis of "local traditions of private revelation rather than evidence."[4]

These are strong claims which, if true, go a long way toward undermining belief in the existence of God (theism). We saw in the previous chapter that "faith," when properly understood, is not opposed to reason and evidence—yet we must ask whether the evidence for theism is any good. In this chapter we shall consider several arguments we believe show that theistic belief, far from being delusional, enjoys strong evidential support; it is more reasonable to believe than to deny the existence of God.

---

1. Alex Rosenberg, *The Atheist's Guide to Reality: Enjoying Life without Illusions* (New York: W. W. Norton, 2011), xii.
2. Rosenberg, 3.
3. Richard Dawkins, *The God Delusion* (New York: Houghton Mifflin, 2006), 31.
4. Dawkins, 31–32.

Natural Theology and Theism

Christian theists traditionally have pointed to a variety of types of evidence in support of their belief in God. This includes "natural" evidence, that is, evidence that does not presuppose the authority of any sacred scriptures or other special revelation. Psalm 19:1–4 says, "The heavens declare the glory of God, and the expanse proclaims the work of his hands. Day after day they pour out speech; night after night they communicate knowledge. There is no speech; there are no words; their voice is not heard. Their message has gone out to the whole earth, and their words to the ends of the world."

In the opening chapter of Romans, the apostle Paul wrote that "what can be known about God is evident among them, because God has shown it to them. For his invisible attributes, that is, his eternal power and divine nature, have been clearly seen since the creation of the world, being understood through what he has made" (vv. 19–20). Taking their cue from these passages, Christians appeal to such natural evidence in constructing arguments for God's existence (this project typically is called "natural theology").

As shall soon be clear, however, such arguments yield an incomplete conception of God. The God of these arguments, it is sometimes alleged, is not the triune God of the Bible who offers salvation to a lost world through faith in Jesus Christ and with whom sinners may gain a personal relationship. This is true, as far as it goes; the arguments of natural theology hardly quench the soul's full spiritual thirst. It is important to realize, though, that they *are not intended* for such a purpose; the arguments for God's existence are not themselves meant to satisfy the deepest longings of our souls, but rather to prompt further search for the One who does. A big part of the project of natural theology, of course, is subverting the naturalism entrenched in contemporary culture.[5]

We cannot assess the arguments for God by assuming from the outset that God exists, nor can we expect to get far without clarifying what we mean by "God." Following philosopher Richard Swinburne, by "God" we mean to refer to a being "without a body (i.e., a spirit) who necessarily is eternal, perfectly free, omnipotent, omniscient, perfectly good, and the creator of

---

5. Naturalism is the view that only natural or material facts exist. There is no such thing in this view as the supernatural. See pages 64-66 for a discussion.

all things."[6] The arguments surveyed in this chapter treat certain natural evidence as "theistic natural signs" pointing to this God, whose purposes in creating them include this function.[7] Attending to these signs (in this case via the arguments surveyed) brings, as C. Stephen Evans explains, an awareness of God which, due to humankind's natural propensity to believe in God, induces one to form some belief about God.[8] In short, such reflection points us toward the satisfaction of our souls' deepest longings. This is why Augustine confesses that "our heart is restless until it rests in you."[9] The idea is that, "not only are human beings constructed in such a way that they hunger for the love of other persons, but in fact their deepest, inbuilt hunger is for God. On the Augustinian view shared by Aquinas, unless a person takes God as her deepest heart's desire, her heart will always have at its deepest core a yearning that is both inchoate and unsatisfied."[10]

Again, though, the arguments *themselves* are not meant to satisfy this desire, nor should they be taken as assuming that God has furnished natural evidences of himself or that God has created man with a propensity to believe in himself (such assumptions in the arguments would be question-begging).

Arguments for God

The arguments we'll consider fall into two groups, according to the type of natural evidence to which they appeal: external or internal.

Figure 3.1 — Arguments for God	
External Evidence:	*Internal evidence:*
kalam cosmological argument	moral argument
teleological argument	argument from reason
ontological argument	

6. Richard Swinburne, *The Existence of God*, 2nd ed. (New York: Oxford University Press, 2004), 7.

7. C. Stephen Evans, *Natural Signs and Knowledge of God: A New Look at Theistic Arguments* (New York: Oxford University Press, 2010), 35.

8. Evans, 36–37.

9. Augustine, *Confessions*, 1.1.1 (see chap. 1, n. 21).

10. Eleonore Stump, *Wandering in Darkness: Narrative and the Problem of Suffering* (Oxford: Clarendon Press, 2012), 440.

The *kalam cosmological argument* and the *teleological argument* each point to external features of reality in support of the claim that God exists, while the *moral argument* and the *argument from reason* each appeal to evidence internal to us—moral intuitions and rational seemings—to support theism. A fifth and interestingly unique argument, the *ontological argument*, deduces the existence of God from the very concept of God ("the greatest conceivable being"). In each case we must ask whether the arguments are logically valid—where the truth of the conclusion follows necessarily from true premises—and contain premises that are either "more reasonable or plausible than their denials" or are "known to be more reasonable or plausible than their denials," which is the aim of each argument for God's existence.[11]

Kalam Cosmological Argument

Our first argument is one version of a family of arguments called "cosmological" arguments. We see that the universe exists, and that fact demands some explanation. Cosmological arguments seek to demonstrate that God exists as the cause of the existence of the cosmos (or universe). Largely the product of medieval Arabic philosophers, the kalam cosmological argument contends that the universe's having a beginning implies the existence of an ultimate Cause.[12]

Marveling at the enormity and splendor of the universe naturally evokes questions: did the universe have a beginning, or is it simply beginningless? If it began, was its beginning caused or uncaused? If caused, what was the nature of that cause? Ancient Greek philosophers held that, while God may have been needed to bring *order* to the universe, the materials composing the universe are themselves uncreated and eternal.[13] Long before the Greeks, ancient Hebrew cosmology held the sharply contrasting view that "in the beginning God created the heavens and the earth" (Gen 1:1). This view of a caused beginning of the universe was later affirmed by New Testament Christians, evidenced, for example, in John 1:1–3.

---

11. Stephen Davis, *God, Reason and Theistic Proofs* (Grand Rapids: Eerdmans 1997), 4.
12. The history of this argument is recounted and further developed in William Lane Craig's *The Kalām Cosmological Argument* (Eugene, OR: Wipf and Stock, 2000).
13. Plato, *Timaeus*, trans. Donald J. Zeyl, in Cooper, *Plato*, 37d (see chap. 2, n. 4).

William Lane Craig's formulation of the kalam argument is straightforward.

William Lane Craig

Figure 3.2

| 1. Whatever begins to exist has a cause of its existence. | 2. The universe began to exist. |

3. Therefore, the universe has a cause of its existence.

The argument is logically valid (to see this, notice that *if* the two premises are true, then the conclusion must also be true), but does it contain plausible premises?

One of the historically most well-established philosophical principles is *ex nihilo nihil fit* ("from nothing, nothing comes"). The idea is that *something* simply cannot derive from *nothing*, and this is the claim of our first premise. The concept of "nothing," after all, just means "non-being" (or "absence of existence").[14] In other words, existence does not—indeed, cannot—come from nonexistence; if some X begins to exist, then X's existence is not the result of just nothing at all.

Whereas this principle seems, to us, at least, intuitive and noncontroversial, it has nevertheless faced challenge of late. Consider the apparent absurdity of denying premise (1), that is, the possibility of things (staplers, babies, galaxies) suddenly beginning to exist from nothing. Are any of us genuinely open to this possibility? Arizona State University physicist Lawrence Krauss, for one, insists the universe did come into existence from "nothing." Tellingly, though, his claim rests on a redefinition of "nothing" as being "every bit as physical as 'something,' especially if it is to be defined as the 'absence of something.'"[15] This is probably as unclear to you as it is to us! It is not

---

14. Thomas Aquinas, *The Summa Theologiæ of Saint Thomas Aquinas*, vol. 1: *Prima Pars, Q. 1–64*, trans. Fathers of the English Dominican Province (Scotts Valley, CA: NovAntiqua, 2008), Ia.45.1, *ad* 3; cf. Aristotle, *Physics*, trans. Hippocrates G. Apostle, in *Aristotle: Selected Works*, I.8, 191b1–30 (see chap. 2, n. 2).

15. Lawrence M. Krauss, *A Universe from Nothing: Why There Is Something Rather Than Nothing* (New York: Free Press, 2012), xiv. See the discussion in William Lane Craig and James D. Sinclair, "The *Kalam* Cosmological Argument," in *The Blackwell Companion to Natural Theology*, ed. William Lane Craig and J. P. Moreland (Malden, MA: Blackwell, 2009), 182–86.

hard to detect the error: if some *X* (a quantum vacuum, say, or just empty space and energy) has any properties whatsoever, then that *X* is not nothing; if some *X* has physical properties, then that *X* is, in fact, *something*.

What about the claim that the universe began to exist? In addition to amazing discoveries in physics and cosmology, we have strong philosophical evidence that the universe must have begun at some point in the finite past. To see this consider the denial of premise (2): the claim that the universe is beginningless. If the universe had no beginning, then its past consists of an actually infinite number of temporal events (or, if you prefer, has existed through an actually infinite number of days). Obviously the collection of events comprising history did not occur all at once. Rather, it is a collection that has been formed successively, that is, by adding one event at a time, one after another, sequentially (event after event, day after day, year after year), until we arrive at the present moment. Therefore, to claim that the universe is beginningless is to claim that the collection of past events has been grow-ing this way from infinity past up to the present.

A little careful thinking, however, reveals this is problematic. Imagine you're taking a road trip. You've been driving for some time, and you begin to wonder how much farther away is your destination. You pull into a rest stop to calculate how many miles you've already driven and to deduce the remaining distance, but notice: this is only possible because there is a fixed distance between your starting point and your destination. Now imagine that your destination is an actually infinite number of miles from your start-ing point. In this case, regardless of how many miles you've driven before pulling into the rest stop, an actually infinite number of miles remain—you'll literally never arrive! What happens when we apply that reasoning to the history of the universe? If the universe's history is actually infinite, then today would never arrive because an actually infinite number of days would first have to come and go. Yet here we are at today, and so it seems the denial of premise (2) is implausible.

From the premises of the kalam argument, therefore, we conclude that the universe did have a beginning in the finite past and that begin-ning requires a cause. Not just any cause will do, however. For example, no cause that is merely physical, spatial, or temporal will do because "the universe" includes matter, space, and time; each of these stand in need of a transcendent Cause. When we consider that this Cause brought the universe into existence a finite time ago out of nothing, we realize this Cause must have chosen to do so and is therefore personal in nature.[16] In addition to being transcendent and personal, the Cause of the universe must also be breathtakingly intelligent and powerful—if not omniscient and omnipotent.

Teleological Argument

Teleological arguments look to the apparent design and order in the universe as natural signs of God. Such arguments seek to establish God's existence as the intelligent designer of the universe. The version of the teleological argument we will consider is called the "cosmic fine-tuning argument," which capitalizes on the insights of modern science into the astonishingly unlikely coincidence of the cosmic constants requisite for a life-permitting universe. These cosmic constants (i.e., the mathematical values of certain physical features of the universe) are narrowly balanced to permit not only life as we know it but any life whatsoever, but is their coinciding a case of extraordinary luck or divine design?

Although there are more than thirty such constants, focusing on only a few will suffice.[17] First, the strong nuclear force, which holds together the protons and neutrons within the nuclei of atoms, would render the universe non-life-permitting if either increased or decreased by a mere 1 percent.[18] Similarly, if the gravitational force were either increased or decreased even slightly, the effect on the existence of intelligent life would be prohibitive. Mathematical physicist Roger Penrose, addressing the requisite initial conditions of the universe, writes:

> How big was the original phase-volume . . . that the Creator had to aim for in order to provide a universe compatible with the second law of thermo-dynamics and with what we now observe? . . . The Creator's aim must have been [precise] to an accuracy of one part

16. J. P. Moreland, *Scaling the Secular City* (Grand Rapids: Baker, 1987), 42.

17. Fuller presentations of the cosmic constants are made in John D. Barrow and Frank J. Tipler, *The Anthropic Cosmological Principle* (New York: Oxford University Press, 1986); and Walter L. Bradley, "The 'Just So' Universe: The Fine-Tuning of Constants and Conditions in the Cosmos," in *Signs of Intelligence: Understanding Intelligent Design*, ed. William A. Dembski and James M. Kushiner (Grand Rapids: Brazos, 2001).

18. These examples are borrowed from Robin Collins, "The Teleological Argument," in *The Rationality of Theism*, ed. Paul Copan and Paul K. Moser (New York: Routledge, 2003), 134–35.

in $10^{10^{(123)}}$. This is an extraordinary figure. One could not possibly write the number down in full in the ordinary denary notation: it would be 1 followed by 10^{123} successive "0"s! Even if we were to write a "0" on each separate proton and on each separate neutron in the entire universe—and we could throw in all the other particles as well for good measure—we should fall far short of writing down the figure needed.[19]

What is the best explanation of such staggering evidence? Given the possibility that any one of the cosmic constants might have had a different value, we must ask whether the cosmic fine-tuning is more plausibly explained by lucky happenstance or divine design. Theism can easily explain the fine-tuning of the universe in terms of the benevolent activity of the Creator God. Naturalism, however, can only punt to chance: the existence of this universe is something akin to winning the cosmic lottery. It must be admitted that this is a logical possibility; people do win the lottery, after all. The cosmic lottery comparison, however, is disanalogous. This is because although the likelihood of *some* participant winning the lottery may be great, the likelihood of some *particular* participant winning certainly is not. Getting dealt a royal flush for several hundred consecutive hands would be a closer analogy, but would it be rational to attribute this to luck? The odds of a life-permitting universe resulting from chance are infinitesimal, verging on impossible, making it far more reasonable to conclude the universe was designed.

It seems, then, more plausible to explain the cosmic fine-tuning in terms of design rather than happenstance. Thus, there must be a Designer, transcendent of the universe, possessing the intelligence and power to realize the cosmic fine-tuning and who willfully acted on the design to create the universe.

Moral Argument

In addition to these examples of external natural evidence, there is also internal natural evidence for God, including the reality of moral values.

---

19. Roger Penrose, "Time-Asymmetry and Quantum Gravity," in *Quantum Gravity 2*, ed. C. J. Isham, Roger Penrose, and D. W. Sciama (Oxford: Clarendon Press, 1981), 249, quoted in Groothuis, *Christian Apologetics*, 250 (see chap. 1, n. 3).

When we talk about moral values, we mean such things as goodness and badness, justice and hate. The moral argument seeks to establish God's existence as the explanatory basis for such moral values.

We are accustomed to the idea of value judgments: family heirlooms are carefully preserved; culture treats various denominations of currency as having different values; and morning coffee is deeply valued (at least by Travis and Keith). These values, however, are importantly different than moral values. Each of these is an example of *subjective* value, that is, value that people either individually or collectively assign to things. In each of these cases, it is perfectly appropriate that different people assess value differently: the Smith family heirlooms are not particularly valued by the Romanov family; twenty-dollar bills are not treated as having the same value as fifty-dollar bills; Paul (inexplicably) does not like coffee.

Whereas subjective value is prone to change with opinion, *objective* value as a feature of the world is fixed and independent of anyone's preference. This is the sort of value we recognize in moral values such as "justice" or "evil." It seems, after all, that certain things are good or evil regardless of what any human being believes. The torture of innocent children for mere pleasure, for example, is objectively morally wrong. Likewise, the anti-Semitism systematically carried out by the Nazis during the Holocaust was morally evil, despite the Nazis themselves believing it to be morally acceptable. The objectivity of these values is mind-independent. As Paul Copan points out, when America's Declaration of Independence asserts as "self-evident" truth "that all men are created equal, that they are endowed by their Creator with certain unalienable rights," this is an affirmation that moral values are objective in nature.[20] The claim that human beings are equally valuable and therefore ought to be treated with dignity (regardless of anyone's opinion) seems to capture a fundamental, innate intuition that moral values are objective.

Moral relativists, one kind of subjectivists, on the other hand, claim that moral values are subjective relative to culture ("morals are social conventions," "that may be right for you, but not for me"), but there are good reasons to deny this. One reason is called the "reformer's dilemma." We

---

20. Paul Copan, "The Moral Argument," in Copan and Moser, *The Rationality of Theism*, 152.

(rightly) celebrate those who bravely have challenged unethical standards such as slavery or women's suffrage. Yet if moral values are subjective—that is, if they are decided upon by society—then attempting to reform a society's moral code is *ipso facto* immoral. The idea is that, since moral reformers belong to the society against whose moral code they stand, and (according to relativists) it is society that defines what is "good" or "evil," then the reformer is by definition behaving *immorally* in standing against society's moral code. But it seems absurd to think that all moral reformers are immoral!

Moreover, the view that moral values are subjective implies that moral codes cannot be improved; they can only be changed. If a moral code changes from viewing the oppression of women, for example, as morally acceptable to viewing such behavior as wrong, on what grounds could a moral subjectivist deem this an improvement? At best he could say that *from the new code's perspective* the old moral code was wrong (but the same could be said vice versa). In fact, to declare some new moral code a genuine improvement requires a vantage point—a standard—outside and above society's code from which to make that judgment, but this is just the thing moral subjectivism denies. Thus, we have good reason to reject the subjectivist view. Moral values are not invented, but discovered.

What can be the foundation, the explanation, of the objectivity of moral values? According to theism the explanation of objective moral values is the existence of a personal and omni-benevolent God. On this view moral values are reflections of God's perfect and eternal character, and humans possess dignity and worth precisely because we are created in the image of this God (Gen 1:26–27). The customary subjectivist explanation of morals as the result of Darwinian evolution cannot give us *objective* moral values. Why not? For the simple reason that, as atheist philosopher Michael Ruse puts it: "we could as easily have evolved a completely different moral system from that which we have."[21] Therefore, if God does not exist, then objective moral values do not exist. As we have seen, we have good reasons to believe objective moral values do exist, so this implies that God exists.

What about people who do not believe in God who can nevertheless recognize the difference between good and evil and who live morally? Here

<hr>

21. Michael Ruse, "Naturalist Moral Nonrealism," in *God & Morality: Four Views*, ed. R. Keith Loftin (Downers Grove, IL: InterVarsity Press, 2012), 65.

it's important to note the difference between a person's ability to *recognize* moral principles, on the one hand, and the explanatory *basis* for why those moral principles exist, on the other hand (philosophers call this the distinction between moral epistemology and moral ontology). A person does not have to believe in God to be a good person. Christians believe that nontheists can behave morally precisely because all humans, atheists and theists alike, are created in the image of God. To be clear: the issue is not *belief* in God, but whether objective moral values themselves can *exist* without God. One can be completely mistaken about the foundation of morality and yet still benefit from being created in the image of God, specifically in having a conscience that allows one to recognize right from wrong (or, per Rom 2:15, in having the work of the law written on their hearts).[22]

Argument from Reason

When attending to the kinds of arguments summarized in this chapter, one must think carefully about those arguments. It's at just such times, though, that one is most likely to overlook the subtle fact that one is *thinking*. As C. S. Lewis observes, such "instances show that the fact which is in one respect the most obvious and primary fact, and through which alone you have access to all the other facts, may be

C. S. Lewis

precisely the one that is most easily forgotten—forgotten not because it is so remote or abstruse but because it is so near and so obvious."[23]

Our capacity to reason—that is, to draw rational inferences—is another example of internal evidence for God. The version of this argument from reason we shall consider points to God as a more plausible explanation of this capacity than is naturalism.[24]

---

22. Copan, "The Moral Argument," 152.

23. C. S. Lewis, *Miracles*, 2nd ed. (New York: HarperCollins, 1947), 64.

24. There are numerous versions of the argument from reason, a number of which are developed in J. P. Moreland, *Consciousness and the Existence of God: A Theistic Argument* (New York: Routledge, 2008); Victor Reppert, *C. S. Lewis's Dangerous Idea* (Downers Grove, IL: InterVarsity Press, 2003); and Angus Menuge, *Agents Under Fire* (Lanham, MD: Rowman & Littlefield, 2004).

According to naturalism our capacity to reason is the result not of the purposive creation of an essentially good and rational God, but rather of the purely naturalist process of Darwinian evolution. On this view our capacity to "reason" evolved over a long period of time. As Richard Dawkins explains:

> Natural Selection, the blind, unconscious, automatic process which Darwin discovered, and which we now know is the explanation for the existence and apparent purposeful form of all life, has no purpose in mind. It has no mind and no mind's eye. It does not plan for the future. It has no vision, no foresight, no sight at all. If [Natural Selection] can be said to play the role of watchmaker in nature, it is the *blind* watchmaker.[25]

In other words, our cognitive faculties gradually developed pursuant to the dictates of the laws of physics, implying that instances of "thinking" are occurrences that ultimately are likewise expressions of the laws of physics.

Much could be said about this account of the origin of our capacity to reason, but let us focus on just one subtle challenge: if human reason is the result of a blind (i.e., purposeless) and nonrational process, then the deliverances of human reason—our thoughts—cannot be the results of rational inference and are therefore not trustworthy.[26] Interestingly, Charles Darwin himself shared this concern. He confided in a letter: "With me the horrid doubt always arises whether the convictions of man's mind, which has been developed from the mind of the lower animals, are of any value or at all trustworthy. Would any one trust the convictions of a monkey's mind, if there are any convictions in such a mind?"[27] This is a formidable problem for naturalism, because the door seems opened to our common experience of "thinking" (regarded as a rationally valid process) turning out to be an illusion. If this is so, then the naturalist faces the untenable situation of affirming a view that undercuts the trustworthiness of the reasoning process. In light of this realization, Alex Rosenberg's claim that "the 'thoughts' in the

---

25. Richard Dawkins, *The Blind Watchmaker* (New York: W. W. Norton, 1986), 5.

26. Lewis, *Miracles*, 21.

27. Charles Darwin, letter to William Graham Down, July 3, 1881, in *The Life and Letters of Charles Darwin*, vol. 1, ed. Francis Darwin (London: John Murray, 1887), 285.

brain can't be about anything at all" so that our experience of thinking is an "illusion" is striking, to put it mildly.[28]

The Christian theist's explanation of humans as created in the image of a good and rational God, however, has no trouble explaining the reliability of human reason. In this purposive account we find a plausible explanation of the human capacity for valid reasoning. This is not to say, of course, that human beings are perfect reasoners; humans' ability to draw valid inferences, rather, is a finite reflection of God, who is supremely rational.

Ontological Argument

Thus far we have found in theism a more plausible explanation of the universe's coming into existence a finite time ago, the cosmic fine-tuning for life, the reality of objective moral values, and our capacity to reason than is offered by naturalism. Taken collectively, these arguments point to the existence of a personal, morally perfect being of incalculable knowledge and power who transcends matter, space, and time. The final argument we will consider, the ontological argument, adds to this by arguing that God, defined as "the greatest possible being," must exist. In other words, as the greatest possible being, God is maximally perfect, fully omniscient, omnipotent, maximally loving, and so forth.

Originally conceived by Anselm of Canterbury, an eleventh-century monk, the ontological argument builds on the conviction that God is "something than which nothing greater can be thought."[29] As Thomas Morris notes, the conception of God as the greatest possible being is not meant as an exhaustive definition but rather as "a single focus for all our reflections about divinity, one point of light to guide all our thinking about the nature of God."[30] The idea is that, whatever else we believe about God, God cannot fail to be maximally perfect.

Before stating the argument itself, it will prove helpful to have a familiar distinction before our minds: the difference between *necessity* and *contingency*. As we write this, it's 86 degrees Fahrenheit in Fort Worth, Texas; Barack Obama is president of the United States; and the Golden State

28. Rosenberg, *Atheist's Guide to Reality*, 195. Rosenberg's claim is especially curious as it is found in a book apparently meant to *convince* readers of the validity of various claims!

29. Anselm, *Proslogion*, trans. Thomas Williams (Indianapolis: Hackett, 1995), 3.

30. Thomas Morris, *Our Idea of God* (Notre Dame, IN: University of Notre Dame, 1991), 35.

Warriors and the Oklahoma City Thunder meet tonight for game 7 of the NBA's Western Conference finals. Each of these is true, but obviously each of them could have been false had circumstances been different; their truth is contingent upon various circumstances. Similarly, your very existence is dependent upon that of your parents, and so your existing to read this book is contingent. Some things, by contrast, cannot fail to be; these are said to be necessary. That "2+2=4" and that "all bachelors are unmarried," for example, is true—and would be true even if the world were somehow different (or, as philosophers put it, even if a different possible world were actualized[31]).

According to the ontological argument, a maximally great being cannot fail to exist. This is because if the nonexistence of some being is possible, then (regardless of how impressive that being may otherwise be) that being could fail to exist. In other words, as philosophers put it, there are possible worlds in which such a being exists and possible worlds in which such a being does not exist. In short, a being who could fail to exist is not *maximally* great—after all, we could easily imagine a greater being.

All this has been said to make the following point: understood as the maximally great being, God's existence cannot be contingent but must be either necessary or absolutely impossible. This is because if it is possible for God to exist (viz., if God exists in any possible world), then since God is maximally great it follows that a necessary being exists. In other words, since a necessary being cannot fail to exist, then it follows from the mere possibility of God's existence that God exists.[32] The argument therefore comes down to the question of whether it is impossible for God to exist, and there's neither any incoherence in the concept of God nor does God's existence seem logically impossible. Therefore, the ontological argument proves the necessary existence of a single maximally perfect being—a view of God uniquely

31. William Lane Craig and J. P. Moreland, *Philosophical Foundations for a Christian Worldview* (Downers Grove, IL: InterVarsity Press, 2003), 50.

32. Alvin Plantinga discusses this argument in his *God, Freedom, and Evil* (Grand Rapids: Eerdmans 1977), 85–112. See also E. J. Lowe, "A Modal Version of the Ontological Argument," in *Debating Christian Theism*, ed. J. P. Moreland, Chad Meister, and Khaldoun A. Sweis (New York: Oxford University Press, 2013), 61–71.

congruous with Christianity; not only is polytheism ruled out, any view of
God as capricious or less than maximally loving is precluded, as well.[33]

Reflecting on the Case for God

As this survey of arguments for God bears out, God has indeed made himself
known to us, including via natural evidence. Each of these arguments can
stand on its own, but their cumulative weight adds up to an extremely plausible case for God's existence. That case only gets stronger when additional
arguments are taken into consideration.

Yet despite the apparent strength of this case, many people remain
unconvinced of God's existence. Is this a shortcoming in the arguments we
have surveyed? If the evidence is really as strong as we have suggested, should
we expect all who consider it to be convinced? We don't think so, for these
arguments should not be regarded as *commanding* belief. There are many
who consider these arguments yet reject them, after all. However, as Peter
van Inwagen notes, to expect theistic arguments—but not arguments about
other subjects—to command belief is to hold a double standard: "this double
standard consists in setting religious belief a test it could not possibly pass,
and in studiously ignoring the fact that almost none of our beliefs on any
subject could possibly pass this test."[34] Besides, theistic natural signs may be
resisted or denied for various reasons.[35] An important (and too often over-
looked) factor in how one approaches the evidence for God is one's expectations regarding God. "These expectations may prevent us," Paul Moser
correctly observes, "from having the needed eyes to see and ears to hear
genuine revelation from God."[36] What, though, is the basis for these expectations? Ought we to expect God to conform to our expectations? As Moser
suggests, "perhaps our expectations clash with God's own aim to bring us
freely to acknowledge and gratefully to trust God (rather than false gods) as

33. Further, as Richard Swinburne (echoing Augustine) argues, since love is a supreme good, God
must be triune. Richard Swinburne, *The Christian God* (New York: Oxford University Press, 1994),
177–81; cf. Augustine, *The Trinity*, trans. Edmund Hill (New York: New City Press, 2012), bk. 9.

34. Peter van Inwagen, "Quam Dilecta," in *God and the Philosophers*, ed. Thomas V. Morris (New
York: Oxford University Press, 1994), 46.

35. Evans, *Natural Signs and Knowledge of God*, 37.

36. Paul K. Moser, "Cognitive Idolatry and Divine Hiding," in *Divine Hiddenness: New Essays*, ed.
Daniel Howard-Snyder and Paul K. Moser (New York: Cambridge University Press, 2002), 121.

the ultimate source of our flourishing."[37] In other words, might God want to be known in a certain manner—a manner incompatible with the subtle idolatry our expectations often belie? Given the kind of God our arguments point to, it seems "the kind of knowledge of God valued by the true God would be volitionally transformative rather than merely intellectual," that is, it would "concern a change of will."[38]

In making a plausible case for theism, not only have the arguments of this chapter subverted naturalism, but they have also displayed theism's ability to answer abiding questions about reality. Contrary to Rosenberg's claim that naturalism provides all the answers, questions of tremendous import remain—and only theism promises answers. Beyond subverting naturalism, the arguments for God prompt us to expect more: the argument from reason and the moral argument, for example, suggest (as Christianity teaches) that having created us in his own image, God intends us "to sustain properly loving relationships with God and with each other."[39] As the morally perfect being, God would provide the means for achieving this; that is, God "would be a *redeemer*."[40] These arguments point well beyond a merely abstract being. The evidence, in fact, points to a far more beautiful God than we could ever have expected—a God who pursues us! As C. S. Lewis writes, in Christianity "the human soul is not the seeker but the sought: it is God who seeks . . . to find and heal Man."[41] In short, we are pointed toward the God who is the author of the gospel.

---

37. Moser, 121.
38. Moser, 124.
39. Moser, 124.
40. Moser, 124.
41. C. S. Lewis, *Studies in Medieval and Renaissance Literature*, ed. Walter Hooper (New York: Cambridge University Press, 2013), 144.

Assignments

Assignment 3-1: Making Gospel Connections

Seeing that naturalism cannot answer all of life's important questions, after all, ask your non-believing friend, "Do you agree that if God does exist, life's biggest questions are answerable—and we're primed to expect *more*?"

Assignment 3-2

Discuss the definition of God as "the greatest possible being." Why must God be the greatest? What is the connection between worship worthiness and greatness?

Assignment 3-3

Answer the following questions:

1. How does the proper use of arguments for God presented in this chapter differ from the "gunslinger" approach to using arguments for God?
2. Which of the five arguments seems most compelling to you? Why?
3. Do you agree with Moser that the morally perfect God these arguments point to must be a *redeemer*? Why?

Suggested Reading

Copan, Paul, and Paul K. Moser, eds. *The Rationality of Theism*. New York: Routledge, 2003.

Craig, William Lane, and J. P. Moreland, eds. *The Blackwell Companion to Natural Theology*. Malden, MA: Blackwell, 2009.

Davis, Stephen. *God, Reason and Theistic Proofs*. Grand Rapids: Eerdmans, 1997.

Groothuis, Douglas. *Christian Apologetics: A Comprehensive Case for Biblical Faith*. Downers Grove, IL: InterVarsity Press, 2011.

CHAPTER 4

Miracles

In February 1980, as the final decade of the Cold War dawned, the American and Soviet Union men's hockey teams met on Lake Placid in the gold medal game of the Winter Olympics. Having taken the gold in each Olympics since 1964, the Soviet team was heavily favored over the younger, untested Americans. Yet against all expectations, the American team defeated the Soviets 4–3—an outcome that prompted one announcer to exclaim, "Do you believe in miracles? Yes!" The game has since been known as the "miracle on ice."

An American victory was doubtlessly unexpected, perhaps even unlikely. But is great improbability enough to qualify such an event as a miracle? Contemporary culture seems to think so, labeling events from unlikely sports victories, to winning the lottery, to finding a good parking place at the mall the week of Christmas as "miracles." This culturally accepted, colloquial sense of miracles, however, differs significantly from Christianity's understanding of miracles as supernatural.

Miracles such as the creation of the cosmos, the virgin birth of Jesus, and the resurrection of Jesus are touchstones of the Christian faith. The Gospels repeatedly give us to believe that performing miracles was a prominent element of the earthly ministry of Jesus, including raising Lazarus from the dead (John 11:38–44)! In fact, the role of miracles in Christianity is one of its distinctive features. As Winfried Corduan notes, "In most other religions miracles are merely an added attraction because only the teaching of the religion is what is centrally important about the religion, but Christianity is founded on the miraculous event of Christ's resurrection . . . Christianity is based not just on the teachings of Christ but also on what he did."[1] Indeed, the apostle Paul was willing to hang the entire credibility of Christianity on the truth of the miracle of Christ's resurrection. He said in 1 Cor 15:14, "If Christ has not been raised, then our proclamation is in vain, and so is your faith."

It is plain to see that the Christian understanding of miracles goes further than the widely accepted cultural sense, but have Christians gone too far? Post-Enlightenment culture has largely rejected any supernatural sense of miracles, but why? Can a rational person believe in supernatural miracles, especially in light of the modern increase in scientific knowledge? This chapter will address these and related questions, beginning with the question, what is a miracle?

What Is a Miracle?

As with all discussions of any consequence, clarifying terms is key to clear thinking. Unfortunately, discussions of miracles frequently become bogged down on the issue of defining just what is a miracle. Since the Enlightenment of the seventeenth and eighteenth centuries, with its conception of the universe as a grand machine that functions according to fixed laws of nature, miracles typically have been thought of as violations of these natural laws. The French philosopher Voltaire (1694–1778), reflecting this Enlightenment mindset, defines a miracle as "the violation of mathematical, divine, immutable, eternal laws," which is, he observes, "a contradiction in terms."[2] Indeed this is a contradiction, because immutable—that is, inviolable—laws obviously cannot be violated.

We shall say more about this problematic view of miracles when we consider the arguments of Enlightenment philosopher David Hume later in the chapter. The biblical understanding of miracles knows nothing of violating the laws of nature. Yet surely the miracles of the Bible lie *somehow* beyond the laws of nature. After all, virgins do not normally become pregnant and dead people do not normally return to life! This is true, but perhaps it would

---

1. Winfried Corduan, "Miracles," in *To Everyone an Answer*, ed. Francis Beckwith, J. P. Moreland, and William Lane Craig (Downers Grove, IL: InterVarsity Press, 2004), 162.
2. Voltaire, *The Works of Voltaire: A Philosophical Dictionary*, trans. William F. Fleming, 42 vols. (New York: E. R. DuMont, 1901), 11:272.

be helpful to ask, what is a law of nature? There is a discernible normality to the behaviors of the natural world. Careful observation of these behaviors—for example, the constancy of the speed of light or the tendency of entropy to decrease within closed thermodynamic systems—yields generalized descriptions of how things normally happen in the world.[3] These descriptions, which are themselves the "laws of nature," however, each contain a tacit *ceteris paribus* (meaning "all else being equal") clause. This means that each law of nature describes the way things normally happen in the world, *assuming no outside factor interferes*. C. S. Lewis illustrates this nicely:

> It is with them [the laws of nature] as with the laws of arithmetic. If I put six pennies into a drawer on Monday and six more on Tuesday, the laws decree that—*other things being equal*—I shall find twelve pennies there on Wednesday. But if the drawer has been robbed I may in fact find only two. Something will have been broken (the lock of the drawer or the laws of England) but the laws of arithmetic will not have been broken.[4]

The claim that the biblical portrayal of miracles knows nothing of violating the laws of nature, therefore, should be understood simply as an invocation of a given law's *ceteris paribus* clause.

To say that a miracle has occurred is to say a factor outside the ordinary, natural order has "interfered." That is, a *supernatural* cause has been introduced into the natural order. The laws of nature tell us that, assuming no outside factor interferes, dead people do not return to

Miracle:

An event that is performed supernaturally, beyond the ability of the natural order.

life. To say that after his death Jesus returned to life is not a refutation or denial of the laws of nature, but rather an acknowledgment that in this particular instance a supernatural cause has been added to the equation. It remains the case that given n natural conditions, then, assuming no outside factor interferes, y will occur. Rather than being a violation of the laws of nature, a miracle may be defined as an event performed by God, beyond the ability of the natural order (i.e., supernaturally).

---

3. Robert A. Larmer, *The Legitimacy of Miracle* (New York: Lexington Books, 2014), 37ff.
4. C. S. Lewis, *Miracles*, rev. ed. (New York: Macmillan, 1960), 58.

Culture's Disbelief in Miracles

The question of miracles is important to Christians; indeed, miracles are essential to the
gospel. But in contemporary culture we are
confronted with widespread *disbelief* in miracles. The attacks of Scottish philosopher David
Hume (1711–1776) on the believability of miracle claims largely set the table for contemporary culture's disbelief in the miraculous. Hume
has been called the most important philosopher
ever to write in English. Whether that's true or

David Hume

not, we leave to others to decide—but such remarks do, at least, indicate
Hume's perceived importance as a philosopher. Antony Flew, arguably the
preeminent atheist of the twentieth century, whose own thought bears the
influence of Hume, was convinced "that Hume was right in his main contention, that 'a miracle can never be proved so as to be the foundation of a
system of religion.'"[5] After assessing Hume's arguments, we shall turn our
attention to the widespread sentiment that miracles are, in some fashion, at
odds with science and therefore should be rejected.

Hume's Argument against (Belief in) Miracles

Although not an atheist, Hume objects "to everything we commonly
call Religion, *except* the Practice of Morality & the Assent of the Understanding to the Proposition *that God exists*."[6] While willing to affirm God's
existence (in a deistic sense), Hume regards the belief that God would supernaturally act to perform a miracle as "superstitious delusion."[7] In his famous
essay titled "Of Miracles," Hume presents an argument that, at least among

---

5. Antony Flew, *God and Philosophy* (New York: Prometheus Books, 2005), 156. Flew has written
extensively against miracles, although toward the end of his career he actually changed his mind in favor
of the miraculous. See "My Pilgrimage from Atheism to Theism: A Discussion between Antony Flew and
Gary Habermas," *Philosophia Christi* 6, no. 2 (2004): 197–211, although he remained unconvinced of
particular miracle accounts.

6. David Hume, *New Letters of David Hume*, ed. R. Klibansky and E. C. Mossner (Oxford: Oxford
University Press, 1954), 10f.

7. David Hume, *An Enquiry Concerning Human Understanding*, ed. Eric Steinberg, 2nd ed. (1777;
Indianapolis: Hackett, 1993), 73. Oxford zoologist Richard Dawkins amplifies Hume's sentiment, labeling belief in a supernatural God a "pernicious delusion." Dawkins, *The God Delusion*, 31 (see chap. 3,
n. 3).

the "wise and learned," is intended to stand as "an everlasting check to all kinds of superstitious delusion."[8] Interestingly, Hume does not argue that miracles are impossible, plainly admitting "there may possibly be miracles, or violations of the usual course of nature."[9] His strategy, rather, is subtler: Hume cleverly argues we can never have sufficient grounds for *believing* a miracle has occurred. Before he presents his argument, Hume provides several clues about how his argument is to be understood. It soon becomes clear, though, that by framing the discussion as he does, Hume unwittingly subverts his own case.

"A wise man," Hume begins, "proportions his belief to the evidence." What kind of evidence? According to Hume, "experience [can] be our only guide in reasoning concerning matters of fact."[10] Although our experience is normally a reliable guide, Hume acknowledges it is sometimes "apt to lead us into errors." For example, based on experience, we would expect a typical November day in north Texas to have much nicer weather than a typical February day in north Texas—but in comparing some particular day from November and some particular day from February, we may well be mistaken. So, in relying on our experience, we must proceed cautiously.

In considering evidence garnered via experience, Hume says, we shall arrive at a conclusion that qualifies as either a "full proof" or merely a "probability." If our experiential evidence renders some conclusion virtually certain, we have a proof. For example, all humans will agree, based on our "infallible experience," that the sun will rise tomorrow—after all, we've never had any experience to the contrary. Because this evidence based on experience constitutes a "proof," Hume says the wise man will believe wholeheartedly (that is, with utmost confidence) that the sun will rise tomorrow. The idea is that, the more and better evidence available, the more confidence a wise person has in believing some conclusion.

If, on the other hand, our experiential evidence is weaker (perhaps due to conflicting experiences), our conclusion can only be a "probability." If the evidence makes some conclusion *more likely than not*, then, Hume advises,

8. Hume, *An Enquiry Concerning Human Understanding*, 73.
9. Hume, 88.
10. Hume, 73.

the wise man will still believe the conclusion—but not with complete confidence; in this case his belief will be tinged with "doubt and hesitation."[11]

In evaluating evidence based on experience, Hume says we must measure and weigh that evidence to determine whether it constitutes a full proof or merely a probability. But how does one go about collecting evidence based on experience? There seem to be two ways: (1) consider one's own memory to recall what one's experience has been, and (2) consider the testimony of others about what their experience has been. Regarding the testimony of others, Hume reserves the status of "proof" for testimony that is "found to be constant," relegating any "variable" testimony to the status of "probability."[12] In other words, we investigate, inasmuch as we are able, the human testimony surrounding some event: is the person testifying a known liar? Is he or she frequently drunk? Does the testimony of various witnesses agree, or do they contradict one another? Or—and this is a big one for Hume—does the testimony come directly from an eyewitness, or does it rely on, say, some ancient text or hearsay? According to Hume, such factors render some testimony less reliable as evidence.

To understand Hume so far, it might be helpful to imagine a sort of mental scale in which you measure the evidence for and against some question of fact. You place on one side of the scale all the evidence in favor of some miracle, including any testimony in support of its occurrence, and any opposing evidence on the other side.

Hume's *In Principle* Argument

With these clues in mind, let's turn to Hume's case against miracles, which actually consists of two distinct arguments: the *in principle* argument and the *in fact* argument. In the former it is argued that we cannot, even in principle, ever have good enough evidence to believe a miracle has occurred. Remember: Hume does not claim that miracles are impossible. Rather, he attacks the grounds for *believing* a miracle has occurred.

His overall strategy goes as follows: consider some miracle claim. Let's take the Christian belief in the resurrection of Jesus, for example. The experiential evidence for the resurrection available to us comes exclusively from

---

11. Hume, 73–74.
12. Hume, 74.

ancient texts; no eyewitnesses to the event are alive today. Regarding this ancient testimony, Hume says, "Let us suppose, that the fact, which they affirm, instead of being only marvelous, is really miraculous; and suppose also, that the testimony . . . amounts to an entire proof; in that case, there is proof against proof, of which the strongest must prevail, but still with a dim-inution of its force, in proportion to that of its antagonist."[13] In other words, Hume is claiming that even if the evidence for the resurrection amounts to a full proof, a wise person nevertheless should not believe a miracle has occurred. Why? Because, Hume says, it is impossible *in principle* to have sufficient experiential evidence to believe a miracle, such as the resurrection, has occurred.

Hume thinks this because, as we just saw, he defines a miracle as a vio-lation of the laws of nature. In Hume's thinking the laws of nature enjoy the testimony of "a firm and unalterable experience," which means "the proof against a miracle . . . is as entire as any argument from experience can possibly be imagined."[14] In considering whether Jesus's resurrection really happened, then, Hume weighs the evidence in the scales of his mind: On one side is the testimony in favor of the miracle (which, for the sake of argument, he regards as the strongest possible evidence—a "full proof"!). On the other side, however, goes evidence *against* the miracle: the "firm and unal-terable experience" of the laws of nature. How strong is that evidence? Well, it is supported, he says, by "a uniform experience," and "as a uniform expe-rience amounts to a proof, there is

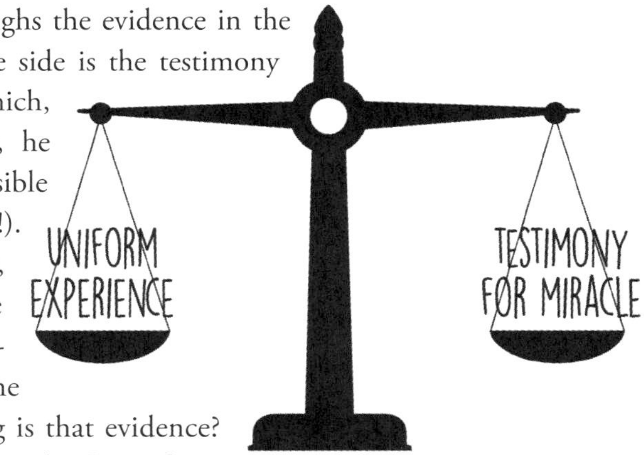

FIGURE 4.1 Experience vs. Testimony

here a direct and full *proof* . . . against the existence of any miracle."[15] Hume thinks that this uniform experience, this evidence from all people at

13. Hume, 76.
14. Hume, 76.
15. Hume, 77.

all times that the laws of nature don't fail, is as powerful as any evidence in favor of miracles could ever be. Thus, we are faced with the highest caliber evidence on both sides of the scale, and so no evidence—even *in principle*—could overturn our "uniform experience" of the laws of nature; in other words, there can never be sufficient evidence to establish a miracle.

So what is the wise man to do? According to Hume, he's faced with "proof against proof." Even if there is a full *proof* for Jesus's resurrection on one side of the scales, there is nevertheless a full *proof* against it on the other side. The scales remain evenly balanced. Therefore, in the absence of sufficient evidence, the wise man must refrain from believing any miracle has occurred.

Hume's *In Fact* Argument

The second argument in Hume's case against miracles is much simpler. Remember that in his *in principle* argument, Hume was merely granting for the sake of argument that the evidence for miracles was good enough to be considered a proof. Now, in his second argument, Hume tells us that *in fact* the evidence for miracles is not that great—not even rising to the level of a probability. Why does Hume think the evidence for miracles so poor? He offers four reasons, which may be summarized: (1) no miracle has ever been vouched for by enough honest and educated people who would be unlikely to lie; (2) people naturally want to believe in the miraculous and so allow themselves to believe almost anything; (3) alleged miracles only occur among primitive peoples, who lack credibility; and (4) all religions have miracle claims which conflict with one another and so cancel each other out (since they support contradictory doctrines).

Hume concludes, then, Christianity "not only was at first attended with miracles, but even at this day cannot be believed by any reasonable person without one . . . And whoever is moved by *Faith* to assent to it, is conscious of a continued miracle in his own person"![16] In other words, the only miracle is that anyone would actually believe in miracles, which no wise or reasonable person would ever do.

---

16. Hume, 90. See also David Hume, *The History of England*, ed. W. B. Todd (Indianapolis: Liberty Classics, 1983), 2:398.

Evaluating Hume's Case against Miracles

Although quite a lot could be said in response to Hume's arguments, we shall focus on three important points. First, Hume is correct that we should be hesitant to believe a person who claims to have seen a miracle. No one wants to be gullible and believe every purported miracle story they hear (such as Jesus appearing to someone in a tortilla chip)! Yet, notice that Hume says nothing about whether we can know via direct observation that a miracle has occurred. In other words, all Hume's argument establishes is that if I personally observe or experience a miracle, then I should expect other people to be skeptical when I tell them about it. But just because others are skeptical of something I claim to have experienced, does it follow that I should doubt myself? Of course not! If a crime has been committed and there is evidence that suggests I am guilty, should I therefore doubt my own innocence—especially if I *know* I'm innocent? Of course not! Similarly, Hume gives no reason for people to doubt their own direct observations.

A second and greater problem for Hume is that his argument commits the logical fallacy known as "begging the question." Recall Hume's definition of a miracle as "a violation of the laws of nature." Now, remember that according to Hume, the laws of nature are established by "firm and unalterable experience." Indeed, Hume claims we have "uniform experience" against miracles. But as C. S. Lewis explains:

> We must agree with Hume that if there is absolutely "uniform experience" against miracles, if in other words [miracles] have never happened, why then they never have. Unfortunately we know the experience against [miracles] to be uniform only if we know that all the reports of them are false. And we can know all the reports to be false only if we know already that miracles have never occurred.[17]

In other words, Hume must *assume* that no miracle has ever occurred in order to "prove" that no miracle has ever occurred!

The third and final difficulty we'll mention regards Hume's *in fact* argument. None of Hume's four accusations call into question the occurrence of any particular miracle. Even if they were each true, it may still be the case

---

17. Lewis, *Miracles*, 162.

that some miracle—such as the resurrection of Jesus—actually occurred. Again, even if these four accusations should urge us to be cautious in believing any given miracle account, they do not yield the conclusion that some miracle account is automatically bogus. As for Hume's fourth charge in particular—that the religious claims of competing religions cancel each other out simply because they support conflicting religious claims—this is plainly false. Significantly, Christianity is not only the sole religion founded upon the supernatural miracle of a dying *and rising* Savior; it is also the only religion that hinges its entire credibility on the truth of a single miracle claim. Recall the apostle Paul's claim in 1 Corinthians 15 that "if Christ has not been raised, then our preaching is futile and your faith is empty" and "if Christ has not been raised, your faith is useless" (vv. 14, 17 NET).

Although clever, Hume's case against miracles is not persuasive. Despite its flaws, however, his arguments are instructive in how they prompt careful thinking about the miraculous.[18] After the wave of the Enlightenment washed over popular thinking about miracles, another objection emerged in its wake: the claim that a rational person cannot believe in supernatural miracles in light of the modern increase in scientific knowledge.

Science and Miracles

In 1961 theologian Rudolf Bultmann famously claimed that modern science undermines belief in the miraculous:

> It is impossible to use the electric light and the wireless and to avail ourselves of modern medical and surgical discoveries and at the same time to believe in the New Testament world of spirits and miracles. We may think we can manage it in our own lives, but to expect others to do so is to make the Christian faith unintelligible and unacceptable to the modern world.[19]

Chances are that at some point you've encountered this sort of assumption—that miracles should be rejected because they are somehow in opposition to

---

18. Further discussion of Hume's case against miracles may be found in Craig, *Reasonable Faith*, 250ff (see chap. 2, n. 6); and Douglas Geivett and Gary R. Habermas, eds., *In Defense of Miracles: A Comprehensive Case for God's Action in History* (Downers Grove, IL: InterVarsity Press, 1997).

19. Rudolf Bultmann, "New Testament and Mythology," in *Kerygma and Myth*, ed. Hans Werner Bartsch (New York: Harper & Row, 1961), 5.

science. But why is this assumption so prevalent in contemporary culture? Is there any good reason to think that science is in conflict with miracles, or that miracles should be rejected because of science?

Scientism

Oxford professor Richard Dawkins, perhaps the most famous atheist of our day, in his book *River out of Eden*, writes, "Scientific beliefs are supported by evidence, and they get results. Myths and faiths are not and do not."[20] Here notice the division Dawkins invents: on the one hand he places science, which operates according to evidence, and on the other hand he places myths (such as Peter Pan or the Easter Bunny) as well as faiths (such as Christianity), which are said to be divorced from evidence. Alex Rosenberg, who is chair of the philosophy department at Duke University, similarly writes: "We trust science as the only way to acquire knowledge. That is why we are so confident about atheism."[21] Here Rosenberg draws the same division: science alone yields knowledge; other sources of inquiry, such as ethics or theology, are not genuine sources of knowledge.

Such pronouncements—which could be multiplied countless times over—are expressions of the view called "scientism." Scientism is a claim about knowledge. Specifically, it's the claim that science is the only way we can come to know reality. In other words, it's the idea that science, in particular the so-called hard sciences, such as physics and biology, are our only sources of *knowledge* about the world, while other, nonscientific disciplines (such as philosophy or history or literature or theology) can at best give us *opinions* about reality—but not knowledge. What this means, then, is that if you have a question that cannot be answered or resolved scientifically, then you have a question that is either meaningless or simply a matter of opinion. On this view, we simply cannot know things such as whether embryonic stem cell research is right or wrong, because that isn't a properly *scientific* question. That's scientism.

Needless to say, this idea—scientism—is widely held in contemporary culture. "I'll only believe it if it can be scientifically proven," we hear people say. Culture regards science as the "gold standard" of knowledge; when seeking

---

20. Richard Dawkins, *River out of Eden* (New York: Perseus Books, 1995), 33.
21. Rosenberg, *The Atheist's Guide to Reality*, 20 (see chap. 3, n. 1).

truth, culture looks to *scientists*, because people tend to regard science as the arbiter of truth. The presumption of scientism explains the widespread assumption that miracles are at odds with science and should therefore be rejected.

Before explaining why scientism is inadequate as a theory of knowledge, we need to make a clarification: scientism is not *science*; the two are not identical and should not be confused. Science is, generally speaking, the endeavor to explain natural phenomena. Christians need not and ought not think that science, in and of itself, is in conflict with Christianity; in fact, contrary to the modern myth of their antipathy, Christianity and science have a long and fruitful friendship.[22] Indeed, the celebrated astronomer of the seventeenth-century scientific revolution, Johannes Kepler, considered scientific discovery to be "thinking God's thoughts after him."[23]

With this clarification in mind, we see that contemporary culture confuses science with scientism. Whereas science investigates natural phenomena, miracles are by definition supernatural occurrences and are thus beyond the domain of science. This clarification, however, implies no conflict whatsoever between miracles and science, nor does it diminish science. Conflict with miracles arises not from science, but from scientism.

Scientism and Naturalism

As a theory about knowledge, scientism claims that we can only know that which is discoverable or testable or provable scientifically, and we know that science restricts its focus to the natural world. It's not surprising, therefore, that commitment to scientism often leads to the claim that the natural world is all that exists. In other words, scientism seems to suggest that the only things in existence are those things studied by the sciences, and this is called *naturalism*.

In the early 1980s PBS broadcasted an enormously popular series titled *Cosmos*, featuring Cornell University astronomer Carl Sagan. If you missed the original series, perhaps you noticed the somewhat less popular reboot by the same name starring astrophysicist Neil deGrasse Tyson, which aired on Fox early in 2014. Both Sagan and Tyson raise fascinating questions, prompting

22. See Ronald L. Numbers, ed., *Galileo Goes to Jail and Other Myths about Science and Religion* (Cambridge, MA: Harvard University Press, 2009).
23. John Lennox, *God's Undertaker* (Oxford: Lion Book, 2009), 21. Alvin Plantinga capably makes a similar argument in his *Where the Conflict Really Lies* (New York: Oxford University Press, 2011).

their viewers to reflect on the dazzling magnificence of the universe—but in both cases there is an undertow of bias against supernaturalism. We detect it, for example, in what has proved to be Sagan's most famous quote from the series: "The universe is all that is, or ever was, or ever will be." In other words, the vast collection of molecules and energy we know as the universe comprises *all* of reality; there is simply *nothing* beyond the natural universe.

This is an expression of what we mean by "naturalism," that is, the belief that the natural or the material world is all there is, or ever was, or ever will be; nothing supernatural is real. The implication is that if naturalism is true, then all that *exists* are those things studied by the hard sciences (so there's no God, no angels, no souls, no heaven), and all that *occurs* in reality are natural events; there are no supernatural events.

It's easy to see, then, why naturalism has no place for miracles: such events don't exist, and besides, there are no supernatural beings to perform them! Coupled with scientism, naturalism dismisses the miraculous as superstitious and outdated, and this mentality is prevalent in contemporary culture.

Naturalism and Supernaturalism

What can we say about this mentality? Scientism is inadequate as a theory of knowledge, and here are a few reasons why. First, far from supporting science, scientism (ironically) undercuts the scientific enterprise. This is because science, in order to get started and operate, depends on a number of assumptions or presuppositions. These include, for example, that there's such a thing as truth: scientists perform experiments, arrive at conclusions, and claim their findings are "true." But that claim must assume an understanding of what truth is, and that understanding is not itself the result of any physics or biology or chemistry experiment; it must be known independently of science.[24]

Here's another example: when doing their work, scientists recognize the importance of fairness and integrity in practicing science and honesty in reporting results. In other words, whether they pause to think about it or not, scientists recognize that there are genuine moral values—but such values cannot themselves be known via science.

---

24. See J. P. Moreland's excellent discussion in *Christianity and the Nature of Science* (Grand Rapids: Baker, 1989), chap. 3.

Additionally, there are things we know to be true for which scientism cannot account. Consider, for example, truths regarding goodness and beauty (aesthetics): "this painting is beautiful." Or again: truths such as "I'm thinking about Frodo's ring," which is something one can know to be true but which cannot be known scientifically. Given that we know these kinds of truths and scientism cannot account for them, then so much the worse for scientism.

The most crippling difficulty with scientism, however, is that it is self-refuting. Recall from our discussion in chapter two that a claim is self-refuting when it undercuts itself. The sentence "there are no true sentences" is self-refuting, because it is itself a sentence that would have us believe that no sentences are true. Now, think about the claim that "all true knowledge comes via science; that only those things discoverable or testable or provable scientifically count as knowledge." Culture generally regards this as a true claim. But notice, as well, that this claim itself is not discoverable or testable or provable scientifically. The claim of scientism is not itself a scientific claim. It is rather a philosophical claim *about* science (made from outside of science), but the claim of scientism itself asserts that we cannot know anything outside of science! In short, if scientism is true, then we know that scientism is not true—and that is self-defeating.

We have seen that scientism is inadequate and unacceptable as a theory of knowledge, but a moment's reflection reveals that with the failure of scientism goes the objection that "miracles are in conflict with science and should therefore be rejected."

Does naturalism fare any better than scientism? No, it does not. This is not the place for a fully developed discussion of naturalism's many problems, but let us briefly note two points: first, with the collapse of scientism, naturalism loses its greatest support. Second, as we saw in chapter three, there is strong evidence for God's existence, and any evidence that supports God's existence is therefore evidence against naturalism.[25]

---

25. Two thoughtful critiques of naturalism are Stewart Goetz and Charles Taliaferro's *Naturalism* (Grand Rapids: Eerdmans, 2008); and William Lane Craig and J. P. Moreland, eds., *Naturalism: A Critical Analysis* (New York: Routledge, 2000).

Conclusion

What all of this amounts to is that there's no good reason to think science is in conflict with miracles, much less to think that miracles should be rejected because of science. This much is clear once we carefully distinguish between science and scientism. But Christians face one final difficulty when it comes to thinking correctly about miracles, and that is themselves. Whether because they have absorbed the scientism of culture or because they have simply never given it much thought, many Christians simply don't know how to think about miracles. We tend to overuse the word "miracle" to include trivialities such as finding an open parking spot at the mall the week before Christmas or an unlikely sports victory, but such usages serve to dilute the biblical concept of miracles.

Many Christians unmindfully adopt the typical naturalist definition of miracles as "violations of the laws of nature," but as we have seen this is not a good definition. A better definition of "miracle," rather, is an event that is performed supernaturally, beyond the ability of the natural order, which is just what we see at the center of the gospel. When God acts within the spatiotemporal world to perform a miracle (such as the incarnation of Christ), he has not thereby "broken" the laws of nature any more than catching a falling object means that you "break" the law of gravity. These so-called "laws" are simply our best descriptions of how the natural world behaves in the absence of interference, but of course a miracle just is an interference by God: God acts and, as C. S. Lewis explains, "nature digests or assimilates this event with perfect ease and harmonises it in a twinkling with all other events. It is one more bit of raw material for the laws to apply to, and they apply."[26] This insight not only sidesteps confusion regarding the laws of nature; it also prompts Christians to adopt a worshipful posture when considering miracles.

---

26. Lewis, *Miracles*, 94.

Assignments

Assignment 4-1: Making Gospel Connections

Strike up a conversation with a skeptic about the definition of *miracle*, paying careful attention to how presuppositions shape one's understanding. Ask how, if she or he were to accept the possibility of miracles, would this impact her or his openness to the possibility of Jesus's resurrection?

Assignment 4-2

Could Christianity be true in any sense if miracles were impossible?

Assignment 4-3

Answer the following questions:

1. In your estimation, how significant is the distinction between "science" and "scientism"?
2. Can you think of any additional reasons why contemporary culture rejects the miraculous?
3. Explain Hume's *in principle* argument against belief in miracles, and then explain why it is unsound.
4. Do you agree that the failure of scientism jeopardizes naturalism? Why?

Suggested Reading

Geivett, R. Douglas, and Gary R. Habermas, eds. *In Defense of Miracles*. Downers Grove, IL: InterVarsity Press, 1997.

Goetz, Stewart, and Charles Taliaferro. *Naturalism*. Grand Rapids: Eerdmans, 2008.

Larmer, Robert A. *The Legitimacy of Miracle*. New York: Lexington Books, 2014.

Lewis, C. S. *Miracles*. Rev. ed. New York: Macmillan, 1960.

CHAPTER 5

The Reliability
of the New Testament

Without a trustworthy Bible, the case for Christianity would suffer considerably. The Bible is many things, but when seen as a historical work, it serves as our access to the events and earliest teaching that constitute our faith. If there is no good case for the reliability and trustworthiness of the Bible, then the case for Christianity is all but impossible.

Happily, the case for the reliability and trustworthiness of the Bible is very good!

In this chapter, we will not be arguing for the inerrancy of Scripture. We will not even be arguing for the general inspiration of the Bible or that it is divine revelation. Though we believe these things and think they are crucial for an orthodox Christianity, inerrancy and inspiration are not the focus of this chapter. We will argue that the Bible is a reliable source of historical truth. If we can provide reason to think that the Bible is a reliable source of historical truth, especially for its central claims, then one is on reasonable grounds for believing the claims it makes and perhaps coming to believe these further theological claims. The point is that seeing it as reliable is an important first step, as it forces one to take seriously the outrageous, virtually scandalous claims made by and about Jesus of Nazareth. One is thereby confronted with the Christian gospel even if one does not (yet) think Scripture is inspired or inerrant.

To further our modesty, we will not attempt to establish the reliability of the entire Bible. There are far too many issues, even if this were a volume exclusively on the reliability of Scripture rather than a single chapter. We will focus on the reliability of the New Testament (hereinafter NT in this chapter) as a historical account. Our basic contention is that there are good reasons to take the NT as a trustworthy historical record, especially in its central claims.

The Standard Objection

The standard objection to the reliability of the NT is that though it may have a historical core, what we have today is full of embellishments, deletions, and additions. Most scholars believe that a man from Nazareth named Jesus existed early in the first century, and did some of what is described in the NT.[1] He likely preached, had a following, and got himself killed. However, critical scholars think this historical core is marred by changes and nonhistorical (i.e., false) accounts being added alongside the historical ones. The objection is we don't really know which claims and accounts are historical and which are fabricated, and thus we do not have a reliable and trustworthy account.

There are two periods or gaps in the history of the NT that are easily the most challenging for thinking about its trustworthiness. The first is the gap between the events (especially Jesus's life) and the accounts that describe the events (the original writing of the NT documents). We'll need to ask whether the accounts accurately reflect the events they describe. The second is the gap between the original autographs (i.e., the writings of the authors) and the extant or surviving copies, called manuscripts, of these originals. Here, we'll ask whether there is reason to believe that our existing manuscripts are accurate representations of the originals.

We'll address these two "trouble spots" in turn. However, before doing so, there's a very important point that needs to be kept in mind throughout this discussion. These two periods are "trouble spots" precisely because there are gaps in the evidence during these two periods. That is, we must conjecture on the basis of the evidence we have about what was going on during these times. But in order for there to be genuine problems for believing that the NT is a reliable historical account, there would have to be *large-scale* and

---

1. See the discussion of the so-called Christ mythicists, those who deny the existence of Jesus, in chapter 6.

consequential problems. For a critic to allege minor errors in the peripheral details, for example, is *not* a problem for the overall reliability and trust-worthiness of the documents.[2] So, our task is to show that it is reasonable to believe there were no large-scale and consequential additions, deletions, or embellishments made in either the original reporting of facts and in the preservation of these originals.

Trouble Spot #1: The Gap between the Events and the Accounts That Describe These Events

Jesus and the Eyewitnesses

Let's say you go fishing. You are with some friends out in the deep sea and you catch a fish. As you reel it in, you realize it is a scrawny little six incher unworthy of the bait it just consumed! Your fishing buddies see your prize and give you the appropriate amount of ribbing fishing buddies are obligated to give. Imagine later that day you start telling people that you caught a six-foot marlin. This is never going to fly (or swim!) with your buddies, since as eyewitnesses, they would instantly disconfirm your claim.

Suppose, however, you keep quiet about the fish. You let a few years go by. You begin talking about your six incher as a seven incher. If the fish in the story slowly gets bigger and bigger, could it then become a six-foot marlin? The answer to this seems crucially to depend on whether the eye-witnesses are still in the picture. Some legendary development of the story can happen (a few inches may be tolerated), but it cannot turn into some-thing radically different (such as a six-foot prize fish) if the eyewitnesses are still in the picture. Even if many decades have passed, one will still not get away with one's myth in the presence of eyewitnesses given the radical nature of the claim.

Well, there are eyewitnesses involved with Jesus—lots of them. A central reason to think that there were no large-scale and consequential embellish-ments from the time of the events surrounding Jesus's life to the accounts that record those events is the presence and authority of the eyewitnesses.

---

2. Even minor errors in peripheral details is a problem for inerrancy, and so these must ultimately be addressed. However, our focus is only on the general reliability of the NT, and reliability tolerates minor errors.

There is a gap here. However, this gap is regulated and overseen, so to speak, by the presence of the eyewitnesses to these events.

Let's look at reasons why this is very plausible historically.

The NT Claims to Be Eyewitness Testimony

The first reason to think that the eyewitnesses are presiding over the development of the text is that many of the NT writers claim authoritatively to be eyewitnesses or to have involved the eyewitnesses.

Luke began his Gospel by saying:

> Inasmuch as many have undertaken to compile an account of the things accomplished among us, just as they were handed down to us by those who from the beginning were eyewitnesses and servants of the word, it seemed fitting for me as well, having investigated everything carefully from the beginning, to write it out for you in consecutive order, most excellent Theophilus; so that you may know the exact truth about the things you have been taught. (Luke 1:1–4 NASB)

This phrase "from the beginning," which appears twice in this passage, conveys an important notion for connecting with eyewitnesses who didn't just experience part of Jesus's ministry but experienced it in its entirety. Richard Bauckham argues that this makes the "eyewitnesses" Luke is referring to the original and earliest followers of Jesus. He says, "Luke can tell the story 'from the beginning' because he is familiar with the traditions of those who were eyewitnesses 'from the beginning.'"[3]

Peter said, "For we did not follow cleverly contrived myths when we made known to you the power and coming of our Lord Jesus Christ; instead, we were eyewitnesses of his majesty" (2 Pet 1:16). Peter went on to recount his experience (which is described in greater detail in Matthew 17) of being on the mountain with Jesus and hearing God's voice. Peter recalled, "For he received honor and glory from God the Father when a voice came to him from the Majestic Glory: 'This is my beloved Son, with whom I am well-pleased!' We ourselves heard this voice when it came from heaven while we were with him on the holy mountain" (vv. 17–18).

---

3. Richard Bauckham, *Jesus and the Eyewitnesses: The Gospels as Eyewitness Testimony* (Grand Rapids: Eerdmans, 2006), 124.

In a similar vein, 1 John 1:1–3 says:

What was from the beginning, what we have heard, what we have seen with our eyes, what we have observed and have touched with our hands, concerning the word of life—that life was revealed, and we have seen it and we testify and declare to you the eternal life that was with the Father and was revealed to us—what we have seen and heard we also declare to you, so that you may have fellowship with us; and indeed our fellowship is with the Father and with his Son Jesus Christ.

In 1 Corinthians 15, Paul presented the gospel (vv. 3–4). He then proceeded to list eyewitnesses of the resurrection who testified to the fact that they had witnessed the risen Christ (vv. 5–8). Paul was confronting those who would say there is no resurrection of the dead (v. 12). He countered this claim by actually listing the eyewitnesses!

Now, to claim the NT is best seen as eyewitness testimony (or something near enough) only because it claims to be eyewitness testimony would be a bit circular. However, it's at least noteworthy that they made this claim, and this allows us to evaluate these accounts in those terms. If some account does not claim to be eyewitness testimony (or it is claimed to be figurative or fictional), then we would not evaluate it in those terms.

Perhaps more importantly, these claims suggest that eyewitness testimony is both valuable and important to early Christians. Even if the authors are straightforwardly lying about being eyewitnesses, the claim suggests that the accounts would be better received if they were. That is, there was a desire for eyewitness testimony; it was valued by the early church. If this is right, then to claim to be an eyewitness, especially if the claim is early, is a bold claim indeed. If the actual eyewitnesses were still around during the composition of these accounts, then it would be exceedingly difficult to pull off the eyewitness claim if one was only making it up. But this turns on whether the eyewitnesses were still around. Spoiler alert: they were still around!

It's Early, REALLY Early

The primary reason for thinking that eyewitnesses were present during the composition of the NT documents is that these documents all date *very* early. The accounts date quite closely to the events they describe, and, without doubt, this puts them within the lifetimes of many of the eyewitnesses. Of course, in our day of social media and a twenty-four-hour news cycle, these dates are not going to seem all that early. Today, something could occur on the other side of the planet and the report could reach us within minutes! However, by the standards of ancient history, ten years or twenty or even fifty years of separation between the events and the records is extraordinarily good by comparison.

To be sure, a lot can happen in that amount of time. As time passes, we all forget details of the events we experience. Sometimes we can barely remember the details of what happened a week ago—much less ten to twenty years ago! However, we forget *insignificant and periphery* details. If we experience something life changing—and even world changing—we can often remember at least the important details with crystal clear detail. Many people can vividly remember the moment they heard that President John F. Kennedy was shot on November 22, 1963. That's now more than fifty years ago! There were many eyewitnesses to the assassination and surrounding events. Can these eyewitnesses reliably recount the significant details of that fateful day even fifty years later? Yes, they are asked to do it all the time on the many documentaries, TV specials, and books on the life of JFK.[4] So it's eminently possible for a testimony to be considered reliable even when decades separate the event and the testimony.

Dating the New Testament

We can get an accurate picture of when to date the NT both by what the specific documents mention and what they fail to mention.

The world changed forever for Jews living in and around the Mediterranean in AD 70. It is well attested that that year Roman forces completely crushed Jerusalem and, as a result, the Jewish temple was destroyed. This siege was both brutal and extreme. With the temple destroyed, Judaism, as a culture and a religion, was forever changed.[5] This would have been a definitive and watershed moment for Jews everywhere, especially in the vicinity of Jerusalem.

---

4. We have video evidence of many aspects of JFK's assassination. However, there are details for which we do not have video evidence. For these details, we trust the accounts of the eyewitnesses.

5. In fact, within a few decades all Jews were expelled from Jerusalem under the threat of death and did not have an official presence until Israel regained statehood in 1948.

Here's a striking reality. The book of Acts, which details the history of the early church, is silent on the destruction of the temple. Even if the temple had lost some significance for the Christian church, Jerusalem was still its center of gravity. However, Acts abruptly ends with Paul in Rome, awaiting his trial. This is odd, to say the least. The best explanation is that the book of Acts was authored and disseminated before AD 70.[6]

The book of Acts also doesn't detail or even mention Paul's death, which happened in the mid to late 60s. It also doesn't mention the persecution under Nero in the mid-60s or the death of James, the brother of Jesus, which, due to a reference in Josephus, we can date precisely to AD 62.[7] Events involving James and especially Paul are featured in the book of Acts. A perfect ending would have been to describe the martyrdom of these two apostles, unless, of course, these events hadn't happened at the time of publication. This pushes the date of Acts to sometime before the early 60s.

Now, if this is right, this puts other portions of the NT even earlier. There is ample evidence to conclude that the author of the book of Acts is also the author of the Gospel of Luke and that the Gospel was written before Acts.[8] This means that Luke was completed sometime before the early 60s.

This is early, but it gets earlier still.

Luke, in his prologue, quoted earlier, made reference to other accounts of Jesus's life. A majority of scholars think these other accounts would have included the Gospel of Mark since it appears that Luke used Mark's material in a variety of places. This places Mark even earlier than Luke, which means that there is a plausible case that Mark was written sometime in the 50s.[9]

---

6. Craig L. Blomberg, *The Historical Reliability of the New Testament: Countering the Challenges to Evangelical Christian Beliefs* (Nashville: B&H Academic, 2016), 13–16.

7. Josephus, *The Life and Works of Flavius Josephus*, trans. and ed. William Whiston (Peabody, MA: Hendrickson, 1987), 537–38.

8. We think that the author is Luke (a companion of Paul), but the argument for the early date does not turn on who wrote it as long as it was written by the same author. See Joel B. Green, "Luke-Acts, or Luke and Acts? A Reaffirmation of Narrative Unity," in *Reading Acts Today*, ed. Steve Walton et al. (New York: T&T Clark, 2011), 101–19.

9. Critical scholars often date Mark sometime after AD 70, but this is often because in Mark, Jesus predicts the destruction of the temple. The thought is that he couldn't have known that the temple was going to be destroyed, and so it must be that the author made up this prediction to make it look as though Jesus knew the future. But this obviously presupposes that Jesus wasn't actually predicting the future. If we approach this neutrally (i.e., leaving it an open question as to whether he accurately predicted the future), the overall evidence favors the earlier date.

Okay, where does this put us in terms of the events these books describe? Jesus was crucified in AD 30.[10] Given the preceding argument, we have reason to believe there is Gospel material written down and circulated by the 50s, just twenty years later. Now, this early date is contested by some (but certainly not all) scholars. However, even with somewhat later dates, we have a completed Gospel plausibly within about twenty to thirty years after the events it describes.

This places the material easily within the lifetimes of the eyewitnesses. But what were the eyewitnesses doing? They were leading the church, which would have certainly included presiding over the development of these accounts. Stephen T. Davis makes the point:

> There is no denying that stories about Jesus were translated, edited, paraphrased, and recontextualized. But many NT critics ignore the effect of the continuing presence of eyewitnesses. It is almost as if they assume that the witnesses simply disappeared during the oral period, so that the stories were told and passed on only by anonymous communities.[11]

Perhaps minor details could be changed or added, but eyewitnesses would have prevented large-scale changes and additions. Given the value placed on eyewitness accounts by the early church, a large-scale fabrication would have been very difficult to pass off as historical.

Can we get earlier than this? Yes, we can!

Paul

Paul's letters date even earlier than the four canonical Gospels. Interestingly, there is today considerable scholarly consensus that Paul was indeed the author of many of the Pauline epistles and that they date very early.[12] The so-called undisputed epistles include 1 Thessalonians, Galatians, 1 and 2 Corinthians, Philippians, and Romans. These all date to the early to mid-50s.

---

10. There is some debate about the exact year Jesus was crucified. However, on virtually all accounts, it is between AD 29 and at the latest AD 33. For ease of reference, we're using AD 30 as an approximate date.

11. Stephen T. Davis, "The Gospels Are Reliable as Historically Factual Accounts," in Moreland, Meister, and Sweis, *Debating Christian Theism*, 418 (see chap. 3, n. 32).

12. See, for example, Bart D. Ehrman, *The New Testament: A Historical Introduction to the Early Christian Writings*, 2nd ed. (New York: Oxford University Press, 2000), 43–44; Helmut Koester, *Introduction to the New Testament*, vol. 2, *History and Literature of Early Christianity* (Philadelphia: Fortress, 1982), 103–4.

What's interesting is that Paul provides a great number of details about the life and teaching of Jesus, all being proclaimed within about twenty years of the life of Jesus—easily within the lifetimes of the eyewitnesses. For a sampling of these claims, see chapter 6.

But, amazingly, we can take this one step further.

Creeds

There are parts of Paul's letters that date even earlier than the letters themselves. Paul quoted a number of early Christian creeds. These are short, memorable passages that summarize Christian doctrine. The most important of these, for our purposes, is 1 Cor 15:3–7:

> For I passed on to you as most important what I also received:
> that Christ died for our sins according to the Scriptures,
> that he was buried,
> that he was raised on the third day
> according to the Scriptures,
> and that he appeared to Cephas,
> then to the Twelve.
> Then he appeared to over 500 brothers at one time;
> most of them are still alive,
> but some have fallen asleep.
> Then he appeared to James,
> then to all the apostles.

Most scholars, critical and conservative, date this creed within just a few years after Jesus's crucifixion.[13] Even Gerd Lüdemann, himself no friend of the resurrection theory, grants "that all the elements in the tradition are to be dated to the first two years after the crucifixion of Jesus . . . not later than three years after the death of Jesus."[14] Compare this to the sources about another major historical figure: do you remember your lessons about Alexander the Great? Our earliest accounts of his life (those of Arrian and Plutarch) are from more than 400 years after Alexander's death in 323 BC.

---

13. Gary Habermas, "The Case for the Resurrection," in Beckwith, Craig, and Moreland, *To Everyone an Answer*, 184 (see chap. 4, n. 1). See also our further discussion in chap. 7.

14. Gerd Lüdemann, *The Resurrection of Jesus: History, Experience, Theology*, trans. John Bowden (Minneapolis: Fortress Press, 1994), 38.

Despite such a sizable time gap, historians are confident we can have a reliable picture of Alexander.[15]

Scholars date this so very early because they think Paul received this creed from Peter and James themselves. This would explain why Cephas (i.e., Peter) and James were the two specific names mentioned. Even more compelling is the fact that in Gal 1:18–19, Paul reported, "After three years [following his conversion] I did go up to Jerusalem to get to know Cephas, and I stayed with him fifteen days. But I didn't see any of the other apostles except James, the Lord's brother." Given the name-dropping in the creed, this strongly suggests that Paul's visit to Jerusalem shortly after his conversion was the exact time Paul received the creed.

This implies two things. First, as we've said, this passage dates astonishingly early—almost certainly within five years of the crucifixion. Second, this not only puts it easily within the lives of the eyewitnesses, but this just is eyewitness testimony. This is as good as a deposition given in a legal trial shortly after the crime. It is practically signed by Peter, a primary disciple, and James, Jesus's own brother, who, incidentally, did not follow Jesus during the ministry of Jesus.[16]

The reports of the central claim of the Christian gospel, namely Jesus's resurrection, date to a time in which memories are still vivid and emotions are still raw. The dust has barely settled and we already have an account that Paul then defended, as we mentioned earlier, by listing eyewitnesses! There is nothing in all of ancient writing with this sort of pedigree.

This doesn't prove that every claim in the Gospels and the rest of the NT are therefore true. However, we are on strong grounds in believing that the major contours of the life of Jesus could not have been made up out of whole cloth. That is, no large-scale changes or additions could have been made given the presence of the eyewitnesses during the composition of the accounts.

Marks of Authenticity

The final reason to think that the NT is comprised of eyewitness accounts is that they bear the marks of authenticity. The claims of the NT

15. A. N. Sherwin-White, *Roman Society and Roman Law in the New Testament* (Oxford: Clarendon Press, 1963), 188–91.

16. It is said that James was an early skeptic. This is an inference that is made from the fact that John tells us, "For not even His brothers were believing in Him" (John 7:5 NASB; cf. Mark 6:3–4).

are continually tied to real places, real people, and real events that eyewitnesses would be best positioned to know. Let's look at a few examples.

Luke 3:1–3 says:

> In the fifteenth year of the reign of Tiberius Caesar, while Pon-
> tius Pilate was governor of Judea, Herod was tetrarch of Galilee, his
> brother Philip tetrarch of the region of Iturea and Trachonitis, and
> Lysanias tetrarch of Abilene, during the high priesthood of Annas
> and Caiaphas, God's word came to John the son of Zechariah in the
> wilderness. He went into all the vicinity of the Jordan, proclaiming
> a baptism of repentance for the forgiveness of sins.

Notice that the event of John the Baptist's preaching is located to a precise
historical moment. This would be difficult for someone who was not present
or in contact with eyewitnesses. All of these eight names mentioned in the
Lukan passage are real people, known to history, whose lives overlapped precisely at the point Luke references. This grounding in history is a consistent
theme for Luke's writings. Eddy and Boyd have said, "it cannot be denied
that in both the Gospel of Luke and in Acts the author does exhibit a profound historical interest."[17] Why ground the events surrounding Jesus's life
in history if the central events are mere fabrications? If these are fabricated
accounts, this seems profoundly counterproductive. Savvy fabricators would
avoid testable claims. However, if this is historical narrative, then this is just
good historiographical practice.

Even more compelling is the existence of so-called undesigned coincidences all throughout the Gospels and other parts of the NT. What is an
undesigned coincidence? According to Lydia McGrew, "An undesigned
coincidence is a notable connection between two or more accounts or texts
that doesn't seem to have been planned by the person or people giving the
accounts. Despite their apparent independence, the items fit together like
pieces of a puzzle."[18] Undesigned coincidences suggest historical accuracy
because it is extremely unlikely they would occur unless they were the result

---

17. Paul Rhodes Eddy and Gregory A. Boyd, *The Jesus Legend* (Grand Rapids: Baker Academic, 2007),
329.

18. Lydia McGrew, *Hidden in Plain View: Undesigned Coincidences in the Gospels and Acts* (Chillicothe,
OH: DeWard Publishing, 2017), 12.

of actual witnesses describing the same real event. They are far too subtle to be fabricated or planned. And given the way they illuminate what's going on in different accounts, they are independently tied to the event.

In her recent book, *Hidden in Plain View: Undesigned Coincidences in the Gospels and Acts*, McGrew outlines dozens of these interesting intersections in the New Testament. One such example occurs in John 6, when Jesus miraculously feeds five thousand people. In the account Jesus asks Philip where they can buy bread to feed the crowd of people. What's not clear is why Jesus asks Philip this question, as opposed to one of the other disciples. There's nothing in John 6 that suggests a reason to ask Philip. However, in Luke 9:10 we find out that the feeding of the five thousand occurred near Bethsaida. Does Philip know something about Bethsaida? He sure does. From John 1:44, we see that Philip was from the area.

Again, this does not prove the whole account is historically accurate. But it does provide evidence that the event is rooted in history. If it were completely fabricated, there would be no reason for John to record Jesus asking Philip in particular this question. These two passages connect in a way that suggests this question for Philip actually happened this way, and this lends credibility to the overall account.

These historical claims are in the course of talking about extraordinary events such as healings and miracles. However, these events themselves are not dressed up. They are typically merely reported in the context of real places and real people. Jesus, for example, walked on water. This is extraordinary. But the description of this event is completely straightforward. Matthew 14:25 says, "And in the fourth watch of the night He came to them, walking on the sea" (NASB). This won't do for good mythmaking, but it works well for mere fact reporting.

There are many more examples of this sort all across the Gospels and Acts. Important and extraordinary events tend to have named witnesses, be located to real places, and have these marks of authenticity. And this provides evidential backing to the claims that are made.

The Value of Eyewitnesses

Given that the accounts claim to be eyewitness testimony or derived from eyewitness testimony, the fact that many of the accounts clearly date well within the lifetimes of the eyewitnesses, and the fact that the reporting of facts are tied to real people, real locations, at real times provides good evidence to believe that these accounts are indeed genuine eyewitness testimony.

Now, it's possible that the eyewitnesses were lying. Eyewitnesses do in fact lie from time to time. But people do not tend to lie unless they stand to gain something from lying. More important, people almost never lie if they stand to lose something, and especially if they stand to lose their lives. We know from history that the early eyewitnesses gained little in terms of wealth or other material goods. Moreover, most of them went to their deaths precisely for the claims of the gospel.[19]

But should we trust these testimonies? Richard Bauckham has argued, "An irreducible feature of testimony as a form of human utterance is that it asks to be trusted."[20] Bauckham makes the point that testimony is, all by itself, evidence for the claims that it makes. If we can independently confirm the testimony, then this is better, but the point is that independent confirmation is not necessary for testimony to have significant evidential value. Again, there may be further evidence to suggest that the testimony is untrustworthy. But when there isn't, then testimony is just good evidence. Bauckham says, "Trusting testimony is not an irrational act of faith that leaves critical rationality aside; it is, on the contrary, the rationally appropriate way of responding to authentic testimony."[21]

So though it is possible that they were lying, it is not *plausible* in light of the evidence. Thus, it seems that we are on good grounds for believing the original accounts of the NT are historically trustworthy.

Trouble Spot #2: The Gap between Original Autographs and Earliest Manuscripts

The Preservation of the New Testament

We now look at the second gap, the gap that stands between the original autographs and the earliest extant manuscript copies. We no longer possess the autographic documents. These, as NT textual critic Daniel Wallace puts

---

19. For a historical discussion of the deaths of each the apostles, see Sean McDowell, *The Fate of the Apostles: Examining the Martyrdom Accounts of the Closest Followers of Jesus* (New York: Ashgate, 2015).
20. Bauckham, *Jesus and the Eyewitnesses*, 5.
21. Bauckham, 5.

it, "turned to dust long ago." But do we have the original material from those works accurately preserved in our manuscript copies? Or has it been hopelessly corrupted by the many iterations of scribes who copied the text and, either inadvertently or on purpose, changed the text? Even if eyewitnesses are behind the NT accounts, if what we have today has large-scale and consequential changes from what they wrote, then we do not have a reliable and trustworthy text.

Bart Ehrman has said:

> Not only do we not have the originals, we don't have the first copies of the originals. We don't even have copies of the copies of the originals, or copies of the copies of the copies of the originals. What we have are copies made later—much later . . . And these copies all differ from one another, in many thousands of places . . . These copies differ from one another in so many places that we don't even know how many differences there are. Possibly it is easiest to put it in comparative terms: there are more differences among our manuscripts than there are words in the New Testament.[22]

The problem that Ehrman raises is that the manuscripts that survive are late and all differ from one another. This leads him and other critical scholars to doubt that we have in our manuscripts the autographic material.

The New Testament Manuscript Tradition

As it stands right now, there are around 5,600 Greek manuscripts of the NT.[23] The documents of the NT were almost immediately translated into other languages. So, we also have an astonishing 20,000 surviving manuscripts of the NT in other languages.[24] In addition to this, we have many writings from the early Christians where they quote passages from the NT. According to Metzger and Ehrman, "so extensive are these citations that if all other

---

22. Bart D. Ehrman, *Misquoting Jesus: The Story Behind Who Changed the Bible and Why* (New York: HarperCollins, 2005), 10.

23. Daniel B. Wallace, "Has the New Testament Text Been Hopelessly Corrupted?" in *In Defense of the Bible: A Comprehensive Apologetic for the Authority of Scripture*, ed. Steven B. Cowan and Terry L. Wilder (Nashville: B&H Academic, 2013), 146.

24. Wallace, 146.

sources for our knowledge of the text of the NT were destroyed, they would be sufficient alone for the reconstruction of practically the entire NT."[25]

It is often pointed out in defense of the NT that no other work of antiquity even comes close to the manuscript evidence of the NT. It is always just a bit shocking to learn that for Tacitus, an extremely important Roman historian from the early second century, the text of his *Histories* and *Annals* "depends entirely on two [manuscripts], one of the ninth century and one of the eleventh."[26] No other copy exists until the fifteenth century, and then we have only a few dozen. That's more than 700 years between the original document and the earliest surviving manuscript!

Figure 5.1	Date of composition	# of manuscripts	Time span
New Testament	1st century	26,000	50 years
Tacitus	2nd century	2	700 years

There is a powerful case to be made for the superiority of the NT vis-à-vis Greco-Roman works of antiquity. However, a critic like Ehrman is well aware of this fact and concedes that the sheer number of NT manuscripts is terrifically unique. In his coauthored work with Bruce Metzger, Ehrman says:

> In contrast with these figures, the textual critic of the New Testament is embarrassed by a wealth of material. Furthermore, the work of many ancient authors has been preserved only in manuscripts that date from the Middle Ages (sometimes the late Middle Ages), far removed from the time at which they lived and wrote. On the contrary, the time between the composition of the books of the New Testament and the earliest extant copies is relatively brief. Instead of a lapse of a millennium or more, as is the case of not a few classical authors, several papyrus manuscripts of portions of the New Testament are extant that were copied within a century or so after the composition of the original documents.[27]

25. Bruce M. Metzger and Bart D. Ehrman, *The Text of the New Testament: Its Transmission, Corruption, and Restoration*, 4th ed. (New York: Oxford University Press, 2005), 126.
26. Metzger and Ehrman, 51.
27. Metzger and Ehrman, 51.

This is an important point, but it is not going to solve the problem as stated. Though we have a superior number of manuscripts, and these date earlier than anything in antiquity, the problem is still that no two manuscripts are identical and they don't, for Ehrman, date early enough.

How Early?

Let's take a closer look. How early do our earliest manuscripts date?

At this point, our earliest manuscript is a small fragment of the Gospel of John that dates to around AD 125–150. Depending on when the Gospel of John was authored, this puts this fragment within about 50 years of the original autograph.[28] Though this is extraordinary, the fragment is very small, containing only seven lines from five verses of the Gospel of John. We have a handful of other fragments from the second century. From the third century, we have quite a number of manuscripts that, when put together, give us most of the NT. From the fourth century, we get complete copies of the NT in single works.

Another way to present this is that within about 50 years we have fragments. Within about 150 years we have fragments that comprise most of the NT. And within 250 years we have complete NT manuscripts.

Manuscript Variants

Let's look at the variation.

It's true that there are many variations among the manuscripts. The latest estimate is that there are around 500,000 variations across the Greek manuscripts.[29] So when Ehrman says that there are more differences among our manuscripts than there are words in the NT (the NT has around 140,000 words), he's not kidding!

But let's put this into perspective. The reason we have such a staggering number of variants in the manuscripts is that we have a staggering number of manuscripts. These are all hand-copied manuscripts. It is virtually impossible for a hand-copied manuscript to not have a few variants from its exemplar, the manuscript from which it is being copied. We should also keep in mind that this staggering number includes every single variant, big and small. If there

---

28. There is much debate about when the Gospel of John was written. Many scholars date it late in the first century. The irony is that this makes the gap between the original and this fragment much smaller.

29. Peter Gurry, "The Number of Variants in the Greek New Testament," *New Testament Studies* 62, no. 1 (2016): 97–121.

is a difference of word order ("Christ Jesus" versus "Jesus Christ"), then this counts as a variant.

We actually have very few variants that are what Daniel Wallace calls both *meaningful* and *viable*.[30] Viability has to do with the likelihood of a variant reading representing the original wording. If a single late-dating manuscript has a variant reading different from numerous early manuscripts, then this is not a viable variant. That is, the single late-dating manuscript has an extremely low probability of representing the original texts. Meaningfulness of course has to do with the meaning of the text. Many variants do not change the meaning of the text in any significant way. These include easy-to-spot spelling errors, slight word order variation, and the like. There may also be a variant reading that does change the meaning, and yet the meaning is completely absurd given the context. These do not constitute genuinely meaningful variants because they are so easy to spot and are typically easily solved by the context of the passage.

Daniel Wallace:

"In comparison with the average ancient Greek author, the New Testament copies are well over a thousand times more plentiful. If the average-sized manuscript were two and one-half inches thick, all the copies of the works of an average Greek author would stack up four feet high, while the copies of the New Testament would stack up to over a mile high! This is indeed an embarrassment of riches."[31]

How many variants are both meaningful and viable? According to Wallace, less than 1 percent of variants fall in this category.[32] A vast majority of variants are just simple spelling errors, making a majority of our variants perhaps viable but not meaningful. Also, a majority of our manuscripts were made after AD 1000. As the church grows, the number of manuscripts being copied and preserved grows exponentially. Again, with many manuscripts come many variants. But these are, by definition, not viable (even if meaningful), since we have much earlier manuscripts that trump these late-dating manuscripts.

Still, 1 percent of 500,000 is not an insignificant number of variants. But just because a variant is both meaningful and viable, this does not mean that

30. Daniel B. Wallace, "How Badly Did the Scribes Corrupt the New Testament Text?" in *Revisiting the Corruption of the New Testament: Manuscript, Patristic, and Apocryphal Evidence*, ed. Daniel B. Wallace (Grand Rapids: Kregel, 2011), 40.

31. J. Ed Komoszewski, M. James Sawyer, and Daniel B. Wallace, *Reinventing Jesus: How Contemporary Skeptics Miss the Real Jesus and Mislead Popular Culture* (Grand Rapids: Kregel, 2006), 82.

32. Wallace, "Has the New Testament Text Been Hopelessly Corrupted?," 156.

the original meaning is unknown. It is often quite possible to determine what the original text likely said. In fact, a very specialized discipline has developed, called *textual criticism*, which develops methodologies to determine what an original text said on the basis of manuscript evidence. Many of the meaningful and viable variants can be figured out with these methodologies.

There are a handful of meaningful and viable variants about which there is significant debate. What is interesting is that no core Christian doctrine depends on solving these disputes. An example of this sort of disputed variant is Mark 3:32. It says, "Someone said to Him, 'Behold, Your mother and Your brothers are standing outside seeking to speak to You'" (NASB). However, a number of early manuscripts add, "Your mother and your brothers *and your sisters.*" This is a meaningful and viable variant, and we really don't know whether the original text included the phrase about Jesus's sisters. But nothing hangs in the balance. Other passages attest to the fact that Jesus had sisters (e.g., Matt 13:56), and so maybe Mark 3 originally mentioned them or maybe it did not. Köstenberger and Kruger have said of these disputed readings, "Not only are they very rare, but most of the time they affect the meaning of the text very little (and thus are relatively boring)."[33] They conclude, "All the teaching of the New Testament—whether regarding the person of Jesus (divinity and humanity), the work of Jesus (his life, death, and resurrection), the application of his work to the believer (justification, sanctification, glorification) or other doctrines—are left unaffected by the remaining unresolved textual variations."[34]

So we cannot prove our NT text is, for every "jot" and "tittle" (see Matt 5:18 KJV), exactly what was dispatched by the original authors of those texts. However, it seems very reasonable to believe that what we have today is virtually the same, especially in general content if not exact wording, as what was originally penned.

So What?

But have a few changes crept in to the NT manuscript tradition? The answer is almost certainly yes.[35] What should we say about this situation? It

---

33. Andreas J. Köstenberger and Michael J. Kruger, *The Heresy of Orthodoxy: How Contemporary Culture's Fascination with Diversity Has Reshaped Our Understanding of Early Christianity* (Wheaton, IL: Crossway, 2010), 226.

34. Köstenberger and Kruger, 228

35. Most inerrantists believe that it is the original autographs that are without error.

seems that as evidence surfaces for the existence of a meaningful and viable variant, we should take an honest look at how it affects our Christian claims.

This can be illustrated with a story that is much beloved by Christians. In John 7:53–8:11, in the middle of Jesus's teaching, the Jewish leaders bring out a woman caught in adultery and set her in front of the crowds to challenge Jesus. They ask, "Teacher . . . this woman was caught in the act of committing adultery. In the law Moses commanded us to stone such women. So what do you say?" (8:4–5). Jesus responded with his famous line, "The one without sin among you should be the first to throw a stone at her" (v. 7).

This is a powerful moment. Here's the problem: it's likely not in the original of John's Gospel. Virtually none of the earliest and most reliable manuscripts include this story. Now, this is not to say that the event described definitely didn't happen. The passage certainly sounds like something Jesus would have done, as his ministry was often characterized by grace for sinners (e.g., "Neither do I condemn you," v. 11a) and seriousness about sin (i.e., "Go, and sin no more," v. 11b KJV). But the best evidence that we currently have strongly suggests that this story was not in the original autograph of John. If one is in doubt about this, then all one needs to do is read the footnotes in one's personal Bible. Most Bibles bracket this passage and note that it is not in the earliest and best manuscripts.

Okay, so what? This is a lovely passage, but if it is not in the original, does this hurt the case for Christianity? No, not at all. It does not affect any doctrine. It takes away a good passage for illustrating Jesus's compassion for sinners, but there are a variety of other passages that do this. All the same, we can lose this passage as original and all of the core claims of Christianity remain completely untouched.

Did Jesus walk on the water, or was this an embellishment from an overzealous scribe? Did Jesus turn water into wine? Did Jesus miraculously feed 5,000 folks on a beach? Did Jesus heal the blind, the lame, and the leper? Did Jesus raise people from the dead? All evidence that we have suggests that these are authentic to the original text. Is it possible that one or two of these are early embellishments that slipped into the manuscript tradition? Yes, it is. But until we have evidence that they are, then we are on good grounds to consider them as original.

The point is that even if the evidence begins to suggest that one or two of these stories are not original, Christianity would still be in good shape. These would simply be earmarked in our personal copies of the Bible as probably unoriginal, and Christianity would go on alive and well. This is again the point: not just any embellishment or addition would bring the edifice of Christianity to its knees. It would have to be large-scale embellishment that affects core Christian doctrines. This is of course possible too, but when we consider the evidence, it's simply not plausible to believe there has been large-scale embellishment that would affect core doctrines.

In sum, it seems reasonable to believe, on the basis of this evidence, that the Bible is an accurate eyewitness representation of the events surrounding Jesus's life and the early church. It also seems reasonable to believe, on the basis of the foregoing evidence, that the Bible has suffered no large-scale and consequential change from the time of its writing to the earliest extant copies.

Conclusion

We close this chapter noting the extraordinary nature of the Bible. There is seemingly no end to its beauty and depth. Though it makes astonishing claims, these accounts are grounded in historical evidence to a degree that nothing else from history approaches. In fact, no other religious work comes close either. Many religious accounts have no historical grounds and don't attempt to talk in terms of evidence. The category of evidence is simply not relevant to its claims. Others do but leave the historical details conspicuously vague. A revelation is claimed to have happened in a cave with no witnesses or to involve mysterious golden tablets that were found in a field and taken back up to heaven a short time later. The Bible, and the NT in particular, is not like this. Jesus validated he was who he claimed to be with the evidence of miraculous power. This beautiful and brilliant message was grounded in the evidence of his miracles and ultimately his resurrection. He and his early followers turned the world on its ear as they preached this incredible message claiming the evidential value of eyewitness testimony. We too stand in this great tradition, showing the terrific case from history of a beautiful and brilliant gospel.

Assignments

Assignment 5-1: Making Gospel Connections

Ask an unbeliever what he or she thinks of the Bible. Ask what keeps him or her from thinking that Scripture is historically reliable. Ask what it would mean if one could show that the Bible is historically reliable (i.e., not necessarily inspired or inerrant).

Assignment 5-2

Discuss why textual problems must affect core doctrines to be a genuine problem for historical reliability.

Assignment 5-3

Answer the following questions:

1. What does it mean for a textual variant to be both meaningful and viable? Does a meaningful and viable textual variant mean that the text is unreliable?
2. Discuss the significance of the earliness of writings of the New Testament. What would it mean if the text was many generations removed from the eyewitnesses of the events described in the text?
3. What are reasons to think that the New Testament is largely eyewitness accounts or based on eyewitness accounts?
4. How does the fact that there are so many manuscripts explain the fact that there are so many textual variants?
5. Compare the New Testament manuscript record with that of other works of antiquity.

Suggested Reading

Bauckham, Richard. *Jesus and the Eyewitnesses: The Gospels as Eyewitness Testimony.* Grand Rapids: Eerdmans, 2008.

Blomberg, Craig. *The Historical Reliability of the New Testament: Countering the Challenges to Evangelical Christian Beliefs.* Nashville: B&H Academic, 2016.

Cowan, Steven, and Terry Wilder, eds. *In Defense of the Bible: A Comprehensive Apologetic for the Authority of Scripture.* Nashville: B&H Academic, 2013.

Köstenberger, Andreas J., and Michael J. Kruger. *The Heresy of Orthodoxy: How Contemporary Culture's Fascination with Diversity Has Reshaped Our Understanding of Early Christianity.* Wheaton, IL: Crossway, 2010.

Metzger, Bruce, and Bart Ehrman. *The Text of the New Testament: Its Transmission, Corruption, and Restoration.* 4th ed. New York: Oxford University Press, 2005.

Wallace, Daniel B., ed. *Revisiting the Corruption of the New Testament: Manuscript, Patristic, and Apocryphal Evidence.* Grand Rapids: Kregel, 2011.

CHAPTER 6

Jesus

The question "Who is Jesus?" has perplexed and fascinated since he arrived on the scene more than 2,000 years ago. In our own day we seem to have a Jesus for everyone: Superhero Jesus, Common Guy Jesus, Homosexual Jesus, Straight Jesus, Transgender Jesus, Democrat Jesus, Republican Jesus, Independent Jesus, Warrior Jesus, Pacifist Jesus, Socialist Jesus, Capitalist Jesus, Polygamist Jesus, Celibate Jesus, Teetotaling Jesus, Alcohol-Loving Jesus, White Jesus, Black Jesus, Oriental Jesus, Jewish Jesus(!), Mormon Jesus, Alien Jesus, and so on. Pick a cause or an agenda, and there is a Jesus waiting in the wings, ready to be the figurehead of the cause. As Boston University professor of religion Stephen Prothero puts it when speaking of the many conceptions of Jesus in modern America, "In the book of Genesis, God creates humans in His own image; in the United States, Americans have created Jesus, over and over, in theirs."[1] Why does everyone want a piece of Jesus yet so often not the whole? Why do we hesitate to call him Lord yet so often employ him in support of our personal and political agendas?

Surely part of the answer is that, as a culture, we are simply confused about Jesus. With the panoply of images of Jesus, it is only natural that each of us would latch onto the Jesus we find most attractive,

Will the real Jesus stand up?

---

1. Stephen Prothero, *American Jesus: How the Son of God Became a National Icon* (New York: Farrar, Straus & Giroux, 2004), 298.

convenient, or helpful in our own quest to find meaning and purpose in life. The question of truth has been set aside at the altar of personal desire. The main questions to be explored in this chapter are these: Who is Jesus? Given the many portraits of Jesus, is it possible to rediscover the real Jesus? Moreover, is the real Jesus capable of satisfying our desires for (along with truth) goodness and beauty? We think the answer to these questions is yes, and we will begin to explore them by considering an expanded version of an argument made famous by C. S. Lewis.

Aut Deus Aut Malus Homo

As C. S. Lewis famously pointed out, most notably in his book *Mere Christianity*, an honest look at the life of Jesus reveals that Jesus was (is) either God or a bad man.[2] As he put it in a little essay titled "What are we to make of Jesus?":

> On the one side clear, definite moral teaching. On the other, claims which, if not true, are those of a megalomaniac, compared with whom Hitler was the most sane and humble of men. There is no half-way house and there is no parallel in other religions. . . . The idea of a great moral teacher saying what Christ said is out of the question. In my opinion, the only person who can say that sort of thing is either God or a complete lunatic suffering from that form of delusion which undermines the whole mind of man. . . . It is either lunacy or lies . . . [or] one turns to the Christian theory.[3]

Jesus is either a liar, lunatic, or Lord. This is Lewis's famous trilemma argument. In this chapter, we've expanded the list of options to five instead of three: legend, lama (holy man), liar, lunatic, or Lord.[4] We think the question of Jesus's identity can be established, following Lewis, by asking three key questions, in the following order: (1) Did Jesus exist? (2) Did Jesus

---

2. See especially "The Shocking Alternative," in Lewis, *Mere Christianity*, 47–52 (see chap. 2, n. 12).

3. Lewis, "What Are We to Make of Jesus Christ?" in Hooper, *God in the Dock*, 157–160 (see chap. 1, n. 20).

4. Peter Kreeft and Ronald Tacelli develop the argument for the divinity of Christ in a similar way in their *Handbook of Christian Apologetics* (Downers Grove, IL: InterVarsity Press, 1994), chap. 7. While they consider the same five options, the logic of their argument is not as simple and easy to follow as our three-step argument offered in this chapter.

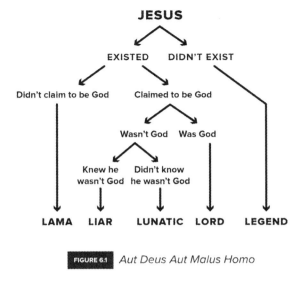

FIGURE 6.1 *Aut Deus Aut Malus Homo*

claim to be God? (3) Was Jesus God? We think there are good reasons to answer yes to each, and as we walk through the argument, those reasons will become clear.

Did Jesus Exist?

While the vast majority of New Testament and early Christian studies scholars, whether historical or contemporary, liberal or conservative, affirm the existence of Jesus, there is of late a growing number of skeptics who claim that Jesus is a myth.[5] These so-called mythicists, or "Christ-mythers"—folks such as Robert Price, Richard Carrier, Michael Paulkovich, and a slew of internet atheists—deny Jesus existed and argue that Christianity was a fabrication of the early church, modeled on the myths of dying-and-rising gods.[6] Even staunch New Testament critic and atheist-leaning agnostic Bart Ehrman thinks the mythicists are "almost certainly wrong," driven more by

5. Consider: "Every single source that mentions Jesus up until the eighteenth century assumes that he actually existed. . . . The idea that Jesus did not exist is a modern notion. It has no ancient precedents. It was made up in the eighteenth century. One might well call it a modern myth, the myth of the mythical Jesus." Bart Ehrman, *Did Jesus Exist?* (New York: HarperOne, 2013), 96.

6. See Robert Price, *The Christ-Myth Theory and Its Problems* (Cranford, NJ: American Atheists Press, 2011); Richard Carrier, *On the Historicity of Jesus* (Sheffield, UK: Sheffield Phoenix Press, 2014); and Michael Paulkovich, *No Meek Messiah* (Annapolis, MD: Spillix, 2012).

agenda than by a dispassionate search for truth. Yet, "[the mythicists'] claims are seeping into the popular consciousness at an alarming rate."[7] It would be wise to consider them in detail.

The mythicist's case typically begins by noting that there are no reliable references to the existence of Jesus in any non-Christian writings of the first and early second centuries. Michael Paulkovich, for example, claims to have researched 126 writers from the first few centuries who should have written about Jesus but didn't, concluding that "Jesus is a phantom of a wisp of a personage."[8] Upon examination, Paulkovich's claim is problematic. There

The Mythicist Argument

1. No credible external sources

2. No evidence of a historical Jesus in Paul's writings

3. Stories of Jesus are paralleled in the many myths of dying-and-rising gods

are, in fact, as we shall shortly see, a number of credible external sources that mention Jesus. Moreover, the fact that Jesus was mentioned at all in these sources is noteworthy, given that in his own day, Jesus just wasn't considered that important. He was an itinerant miracle worker and preacher from a backwater town (Nazareth) in an unimportant region (Israel) of the Roman Empire who claimed to be the Messiah (not uncommon). As historian John Meier notes, "Jesus was a marginal Jew leading a marginal movement in a marginal province of a vast Roman Empire."[9] Thus, that there is relatively little mention of Jesus from non-Christian sources is not surprising. Still, there are a number of credible sources that, contrary to the claims made by Paulkovich and other mythicists, provide convincing evidence that Jesus existed. We shall consider two such sources, statements made by the early second-century Roman historian Tacitus and the late first-century Jewish historian Josephus.

---

7. Ehrman, *Did Jesus Exist?*, 6–7.

8. Michael Paulkovich, "The Fable of the Christ," *Free Inquiry* 34, no. 5 (July 10, 2014), reprinted on the website of the Council for Secular Humanism, https://www.secularhumanism.org/index.php/articles/5656. Paulkovich notes that we do find one mention of Jesus in Josephus's *Jewish Wars* and argues that it was a forgery. Unfortunately for Paulkovich, he got the book wrong. Jesus is not mentioned at all in *Jewish Wars*. Rather, it is in *The Antiquities of the Jews*, as we shall see later, that Josephus mentions Jesus, and he mentions Jesus twice.

9. John Meier, *Marginal Jew: Rethinking the Historical Jesus: The Roots of the Problem and the Person* (New York: Doubleday, 1991), 1:56, quoted in Eddy and Boyd, *The Jesus Legend*, 168 (see chap. 5, n. 17).

Cornelius Tacitus, orator, historian, and proconsul of Asia, is the author of the *Annals*, an unfinished work describing the Roman Empire from Augustus through Nero (AD 14–68). The relevant portion of the *Annals* (15.44) was most likely written around AD 115 and concerns the emperor Nero and the great fire of Rome under his reign. To quell the charge that Nero himself was responsible for the burning of Rome, Tacitus reported:

> Nero substituted as culprits, and punished in the utmost refinements of cruelty, a class of men, loathed for their vices, whom the crowd styled Christians. Christus, the founder of the name, had undergone the death penalty in the reign of Tiberius, by sentence of the procurator Pontius Pilatus, and the pernicious superstition was checked for a moment, only to break out once more, not merely in Judea, the home of the disease, but in the capital itself, where all things horrible or shameful in the world collect and find a vogue.[10]

From this account, we learn some basic facts about Jesus. As Ehrman summarizes, "He was called Christ, he was executed at the order of Pontius Pilate, and this was during the reign of Tiberius."[11] Moreover, Tacitus claimed that a movement—based on a "pernicious superstition" of a crucified and risen Messiah—broke out again even in Rome, after temporary suppression.[12] Renowned historian Edwin Yamauchi thinks this passage is "probably the most important reference to Jesus outside the New Testament" reporting, by an unsympathetic witness, to the success and spread of Christianity, based on the historical figure Jesus.[13]

The earliest corroboration for Jesus outside the Gospels is found in the works of the Jewish historian Josephus, whose *The Antiquities of the Jews*, completed around AD 93, traces Jewish history from the time of Adam down to his own day. The shorter and less significant passage is often referred

---

10. Tacitus, *Annals*, trans. C. H. Moore and J. Jackson (Cambridge, MA: Harvard University Press, 1962), 283, quoted in Eddy and Boyd, *The Jesus Legend*, 179.

11. Ehrman, *Did Jesus Exist?*, 55.

12. See also Eddy and Boyd, *The Jesus Legend*, 179–84, for a discussion of challenges to the authenticity of this passage. After considering objections to the authenticity of the passage, Eddy and Boyd conclude: "Tacitus's report provides solid, independent, non-Christian evidence for the life and death of Jesus, the remarkable resolve of his earliest followers, and the astounding early growth of the movement he founded." *The Jesus Legend*, 184.

13. Quoted in Lee Strobel, *The Case for Christ* (Grand Rapids: Zondervan, 1998), 82.

to as "the James passage" (*Antiquities* 20.9.1) since it passingly refers to Jesus as the brother of James.[14] The short passage says, "When, therefore, Ananus was of this disposition, he thought he had now a proper opportunity. Festus was now dead, and Albinus was but upon the road. So he assembled the Sanhedrin of judges, and brought before them the brother of Jesus, who was called Christ, whose name was James."[15] This portion of text confirms the existence of Jesus and the New Testament's claim that James was the brother of Jesus (see Gal 1:19).[16]

The second passage from Josephus is known to scholars as the *Testimonium Flavianum* and has been the focus of intense scholarly attention. The passage reads as follows:

> About this time there lived Jesus, a wise man, if indeed one ought to call him a man. For he was one who wrought surprising feats and was a teacher of such people as accept the truth gladly. He won over many Jews and many of the Greeks. He was the Messiah. When Pilate, upon hearing him accused by men of the highest standing among us, had condemned him to be crucified, those who had in the first place come to love him did not give up their affection for him. On the third day he appeared to them restored to life, for the prophets of God had prophesied these and countless other marvelous things about him. And the tribe of the Christians, so called after him, has still to this day not disappeared. (*Antiquities* 18.3.3.)[17]

If authentic, we have here the most important Jewish historian of the first century attesting that Jesus not only existed, but that he was more than a man—he was the Messiah—and that he even rose from the dead![18] This may turn out to be too good to be true. The question of central importance is whether or not this passage is authentic.

---

14. Eddy and Boyd, *The Jesus Legend*, 185.

15. Josephus, *The Life and Works of Flavius Josephus*, 537–38 (see chap. 5, n. 7), quoted in Eddy and Boyd, 185–86.

16. For a discussion of the challenges to the authenticity of this passage, see Eddy and Boyd, *The Jesus Legend*, 186–90.

17. Josephus, *Antiquities*, trans. L. H. Feldman, LCL (Cambridge, MA: Harvard University Press, 1965), 48, 50, quoted in Eddy and Boyd, 190.

18. Eddy and Boyd, *The Jesus Legend*, 190.

The trouble with this passage is that it was written by a Jew who, as far as we know, never became a follower of Christ. But this passage affirms things only a Christian would uphold. This conundrum begins to unravel when we consider that Josephus was not a beloved author read by his own people.[19] He was viewed as a traitor for his actions in the Jewish wars when he surrendered to Vespasian instead of committing suicide like his fellow soldiers. Thus, in the Middle Ages, Christians, not Jews, transmitted his writings. It is generally accepted today that the *Testimonium Flavianum* contains a historical core as well as later Christian interpolations. When these interpolations are removed (these are thought to include the allusion to Jesus's divinity, the confession that Jesus was the Messiah, and the acknowledgment that Jesus rose from the dead), we arrive at the following:

> About this time there lived Jesus, a wise man. For he was one who wrought surprising feats and was a teacher of such people as accept the truth gladly. He won over many Jews and many of the Greeks. When Pilate, upon hearing him accused by men of the highest standing among us, had condemned him to be crucified, those who had in the first place come to love him did not give up their affection for him. And the tribe of the Christians, so called after him, has still to this day not disappeared.

There is nothing in this reconstruction that a Jewish historian could not have said about Jesus. Moreover, the probable authenticity of the James passage, which comes after the *Testimonium Flavianum*, seems to presuppose that Josephus had informed his readers previously in the text about Jesus, further supporting the earlier passage's authenticity. Thus, most scholars today agree that something like the above reconstructed version of the *Testimonium* was authored by Josephus.[20]

John Dominic Crossan summarizes the broad agreement between Tacitus and Josephus: "First, there was a *movement* started by Jesus or Christ. Second, there was an *execution* by Pilate. Third, there was a *continuation*

---

19. Ehrman, *Did Jesus Exist?*, 60. This paragraph as well as the possible reconstruction of the *Testimonium Flavianum* summarizes Ehrman's discussion in 59–66.

20. For a discussion of the challenges to the authenticity of this passage, see F. F. Bruce, *Jesus and Christian Origins Outside the New Testament* (Grand Rapids: Eerdmans, 1974), 36–41.

despite that attempt to end it. Fourth, there is still an ongoing movement of 'Christians.'" [21] If we add to this external evidence the historical biographies of Jesus found in the Gospels and the important independent sources among Christian writers from the turn of the second century—such as Papias, Ignatius of Antioch, and Clement of Rome[22]—we have ample historical evidence for thinking Jesus existed.

The second pillar in the mythicist case is to argue that there is little to no evidence in the writings of the apostle Paul, the earliest Christian writer, of a historical Jesus. Paul's silence regarding the Jesus of history is evidence, according to the mythicist, that he did not believe in Jesus as a recent historical figure. In support of this claim, the mythicist argues that Paul never quoted from the earthly Jesus even when it would have been to his advantage to do so, nor would we suspect by reading Paul that Jesus died in any significant historical context, performed miracles, or was a teacher.[23]

An examination of Paul's writings shows the mythicist's claim to be false. Paul knew Jesus was born and raised as a Jew (Gal 4:4), a descendant of David (Rom 1:3), and that his ministry was to and for the Jews (Rom 15:8). He knew that Jesus was the brother of James (Gal 1:19) and perhaps had other brothers (1 Cor 9:5). Paul was aware that Jesus instituted a memorial meal the night before his death (1 Cor 11:23–26), and after his death by crucifixion, was buried and resurrected three days later (Rom 4:24–25; 1 Cor 15:4–8). Moreover, Paul knew that Jesus was a teacher because he quoted several of his sayings, including Jesus's teachings on the Last Supper (1 Cor 11:23–26; cf. Luke 22:17–20), on marriage and divorce (1 Cor 7:10–11; cf. Matt 19:3–12; Mark 10:2–12), and on whether apostles should be financially supported for their missionary efforts (1 Cor 9:14; cf. Luke 10:7). While assessments by New Testament scholars vary, there are up to twenty-five instances where Paul certainly or probably made reference to the sayings of Jesus and more than forty possible "echoes" or allusions to the sayings of Jesus in the writings of

---

21. John Dominic Crossan, "Response to Robert M. Price," in *The Historical Jesus: Five Views*, ed. James K. Beilby and Paul Rhodes Eddy (Downers Grove, IL: InterVarsity Press, 2009), 86.

22. For a good discussion of these early Christian writers and their belief in a historical Jesus, see Ehrman, *Did Jesus Exist?*, 98–105.

23. This line of argument is advanced, for example, by Robert Price, "Jesus at the Vanishing Point," in Beilby and Eddy, *The Historical Jesus*, 63–67.

Paul.[24] Contrary to the mythicist's claim, Paul did believe in and write about the historical Jesus, acknowledging key events in the life of Jesus, and quoting or alluding to the sayings of Jesus dozens of times.

Still, an important question remains. It must be acknowledged that Paul could have said more about the historical Jesus. In short, why did Paul not quote Jesus more often, especially when it would have been to his advantage to do so? In response, we offer two points. First, it is important to remember that at the time of Paul's writings, "the Jesus tradition was not yet set in fixed and unyielding forms."[25] Thus, as with the Old Testament, the Jesus tradition is best understood as shaping Paul's thought and not as an external source "whose authority can be called on only by formal dictation."[26] Second, Paul wasn't writing in the genre of gospel/biography. His writings were letters directed to churches or individuals to deal with problems that had arisen.[27] His letters were written primarily to exhort believers and not as theological tomes detailing all he knew about God, Jesus, the Holy Spirit, the nature of man, or the nature of the world.[28]

In summary, given Paul's aim and literary genre, the number of historical references to Jesus is not all that unusual or unexpected. What Paul did tell us about Jesus makes it perfectly clear that he believed Jesus to be a historical person.

The third pillar in the mythicist case is to offer a positive reconstruction of how belief in a historical Jesus arose. One of the most widely asserted claims is that Jesus was an invention of the early Christians based on the prevalent notion of a dying-and-rising god.[29] The idea is that many ancient religions worshipped gods who died and rose again, and Jesus was just a Jewish version of these pagan deities, later historicized by his followers.

There are two major problems with this claim. First, there is scarcely any evidence that there were in fact dying-and-rising gods in the ancient

---

24. Eddy and Boyd, *The Jesus Legend*, 217–18. For a detailed discussion of the above passages as well as some of the "echoes" of Jesus's sayings found in Paul, see Eddy and Boyd, 216–28.

25. James Dunn, "Prophetic 'I'-Sayings and the Jesus-Tradition: The Importance of Testing Prophetic Utterances within Early Christianity," *New Testament Studies* 24 (1977–78): 175, as quoted in Eddy and Boyd, 229.

26. Dunn, 176, as quoted in Eddy and Boyd, 230.

27. Ehrman, *Did Jesus Exist?*, 129–30.

28. Eddy and Boyd, *The Jesus Legend*, 232.

29. See, for example, Price, "Jesus at the Vanishing Point," 75–77.

world. As Eddy and Boyd summarize, when carefully studied, each case of a supposed dying-and-rising-god reveals "that either there was no death, no resurrection, and/or no 'god' to begin with."[30] For example, there is nothing in the original myth of Adonis—the typical example of a dying-and-rising god—to suggest either death or resurrection. Rather, Adonis undergoes *bilocation*, spending part of the year in the realm of the living and part in the realm of the dead.[31] In another form of the myth of Adonis, coming from the Roman author Ovid, we do have a definite death. It is only, as Bart Ehrman points out, in later texts, long after Ovid and after the rise of Christianity, that we find the suggestion that Adonis also resurrected, suggesting the influence goes from Christianity to the Adonis myth and not the other way around.[32] Attempts to identify other dying-and-rising gods—Osiris, Attis, Tammuz, Heracles, Baal, and so on—have not fared any better. As the eminent historian of religion at the University of Chicago Jonathan Z. Smith summarizes, "The category of dying and rising gods, once a major topic of scholarly investigation, must now be understood to have been largely a misnomer based on imaginative reconstructions and exceedingly late or highly ambiguous texts."[33]

Second, even if there were dying-and-rising gods in the pagan world, they did not influence early Christian thought about Jesus. The differences are far too significant.[34] For example, the pagan gods were connected with the seasonal cycles, whereas Jesus's death and resurrection were each known to be a onetime event. Moreover, Jesus's death was understood as an atonement for the sins of man, whereas there is nothing comparable in the pagan myths. Most important, the background for the early Christian understanding of resurrection is Jewish apocalypticism and not a pagan dying-and-rising god myth. The Jewish apocalyptic view anticipated a soon-to-come judgment by God of the world and a general resurrection of the dead. That is why the apostle Paul talked about Jesus as the "firstfruits" (1 Cor 15:20) of the resurrection. For Paul, if there was no resurrection of Jesus, there will be

---

30. Eddy and Boyd, *The Jesus Legend*, 143. See also N. T. Wright, *The Resurrection of the Son of God* (Minneapolis: Fortress Press, 2003), 80–81.

31. Eddy and Boyd, 143.

32. Ehrman, *Did Jesus Exist?*, 227–28.

33. J. Z. Smith, "Dying and Rising Gods," *Encyclopedia of Religion*, 2nd ed., ed. Lindsay Jones (Detroit: Macmillan, 2005), 4:2535, quoted in Eddy and Boyd, *The Jesus Legend*, 143.

34. For detailed discussion of these differences, see Ehrman, *Did Jesus Exist?*, 224–26.

no general resurrection. The point is that the idea of Jesus's resurrection did not derive from a pagan context of dying-and-rising gods. The background was thoroughly Jewish.

We conclude that the mythicist case against the historical Jesus fails. There are good reasons to think Jesus existed, most notably the Gospel records and the extrabiblical accounts, and no good reasons to think he did not. Thus, we join with the nearly unanimous voice of scholars who think Jesus existed. He is not a legend.[35]

Did Jesus Claim to Be God?

Once his existence is established, our second question is, did Jesus claim to be God? Either he did or did not. If Jesus did not claim to be God, then he is best understood as a "lama"—a holy man, or a great moral teacher, on the same level as Siddhartha Gautama, Lao-Tze, Confucius, Socrates, the Hindu avatars, or the prophet Moses.[36] Alternatively, if Jesus did claim to be God, then the options narrow: he is either a lunatic, a liar, or Lord. Some, such as Bart Ehrman, think that the question, "Did Jesus claim to be God?" lacks nuance and is therefore susceptible to misunderstanding. For example, Ehrman argues Jesus "thought he was a prophet predicting the end of the current evil age and the future king of Israel in the age to come."[37] We hope to show, following the New Testament scholar Michael Bird, that Jesus clearly "identified himself as a divine agent with a unique authority and

---

35. A related question not dealt with here is the issue of whether or not we find legendary development of the Jesus tradition in the Gospels. We touch on this topic in chapters 5 and 7.

36. Regarding the idea of Jesus as a great moral teacher, C. S. Lewis states, "I am trying here to prevent anyone saying the really foolish thing that people often say about Him: 'I'm ready to accept Jesus as a great moral teacher, but I don't accept His claim to be God.' That is the one thing we must not say. A man who was merely a man and said the sort of things Jesus said would not be a great moral teacher." Lewis, *Mere Christianity*, 52. For an excellent discussion of this claim of Lewis's, see David Horner, "*Aut Deus Aut Malus Homo*: A Defense of C. S. Lewis's 'Shocking Alternative,'" in David Baggett, Gary R. Habermas, and Jerry L. Walls, eds., *C. S. Lewis as Philosopher* (Downers Grove, IL: InterVarsity Press, 2008), chap. 4.

37. Bart Ehrman, *How Jesus Became God* (New York: HarperOne, 2014), 124, quoted in Michael F. Bird, "Did Jesus Think He Was God?," in *How God Became Jesus*, ed. Michael Bird et al. (Grand Rapids: Zondervan, 2014), 46. N. T. Wright, an unlikely bedfellow, agrees with Ehrman. However, Wright's conclusion on the matter is that Jesus understood his vocation "to do and be, for Israel and the world, that which according to Scripture only YHWH himself could do or be." N. T. Wright, *The Challenge of Jesus*, 2nd ed. (Downers Grove, IL: InterVarsity Press, 2015), 122. This is essentially our point: Jesus both implicitly understood himself to be divine and explicitly claimed to be so. Thanks to David Horner for the reference to Wright, as discussed in Horner, "*Aut Deus Aut Malus Homo*," 71 n.10.

a unique relationship with Israel's God."[38] In short, in both action and word, Jesus claimed to be on the same level as YHWH himself. This is what we mean when we say that Jesus claimed to be God.

Consider a few examples.[39] First, Jesus claimed to have existed before Abraham; in fact, he claimed to have been given God's very name: "Jesus said to them, 'Truly I tell you: before Abraham was, I am'" (John 8:58). Jesus was using the same phrase God used in declaring to Moses the divine name "I AM" (Exod 3:14). Second, Jesus claimed equality with God by stating, for example, "I and the Father are one" (John 10:30). His listeners understood the implications of this proclamation and immediately picked up stones to stone him, giving as a reason "blasphemy, because you—being a man—make yourself God" (John 10:33). Third, Jesus understood and proclaimed himself to be the coming King, the Messiah of Israel, with

> ### The Claims of Jesus
>
> 1. *Equates himself with God* (John 5:17–18; 8:58–59; 10:30)
>
> 2. *Claimed to be the Messiah with unprecedented authority as a divine agent* (John 4:25–26; Mark 8:27–30; 14:61–62)
>
> 3. *Accepted worship as God* (Matt 2:11; 14:33; 28:17; John 20:28)
>
> 4. *Proclaimed himself the judge of the world* (Matt 7:23; John 5:24)
>
> 5. *Claimed equal authority with God* (Matt 28:18)
>
> 6. *Claimed to forgive sins* (Mark 2:2–12)

unprecedented authority as a divine agent. Jesus forgave sins (Mark 2:1–12), a prerogative belonging only to God; he accepted worship as God (Matt 2:11; 14:33; 28:17; John 20:28); and announced himself to be the judge of the world (Matt 7:23; John 5:24). Upon being questioned in Mark 14:61–62, Jesus's identification of himself as the Messiah, the Son of the Blessed One, is significant and telling. Jesus further elaborated about himself, in response to the high priest's question, by saying: "and you will see the Son of Man seated at the right hand of Power and coming with the clouds of heaven" (v. 62). Jesus was quoting from Psalm 110 and Dan 7:13–14, clearly identifying

---

38. Bird, "Did Jesus Think He Was God?," 46.

39. Some, such as Bart Ehrman, admit that there are clear cases of Jesus claiming to be God found in the Gospel of John but reject them as inauthentic by rejecting the historical reliability of John's Gospel. Here we assume the historicity of John's Gospel, indeed of all the Gospels and the Bible in general. See our discussion of the historical reliability of the Bible in chapter 5. For more on the historicity of the Gospel of John specifically, see Bird, "Did Jesus Think He Was God?," 67–69.

himself with the enthroned messianic figure of Daniel 7, who is presented to "the Ancient of Days" and shares his throne. This is significant because, as Michael Bird explains, Jesus "is placing himself within the orbit of divine sovereignty and claiming a place within the divine regency of God Almighty. If he's wrong it isn't just bad theology; it is blasphemy and an affront to Jewish monotheism."[40]

If Ehrman is right that Jesus never claimed in any meaningful sense to be God and if Christians believe things about Jesus that Jesus didn't believe about himself, then the central creeds of Christianity are called into question.[41] Fortunately, as we have seen, there is ample evidence for thinking that Jesus understood himself to be divine and claimed as much through his words and actions. As William Lane Craig summarizes, "Today there is virtually a consensus that Jesus came on the scene with an unheard-of authority, namely with the authority of God, with the claim of the authority to stand in God's place."[42] Jesus, then, is not lama.

Was Jesus God?

We are now in position to ask our final question: Was Jesus God? We've established his historical existence and claim to be divine. With respect to our final question, there are three options. First, either he claimed to be God and knew the claim was false, in which case he was a liar, or he claimed to be God and did not know the claim was false, in which case he was a lunatic, or he claimed to be God and the claim is true, in which case he is Lord. Let's consider each of these options in turn.

If Jesus was a liar, he was deliberately misleading others regarding his identity and mission. The lie was particularly egregious and callous because he was calling his followers to give up their livelihood, entrusting matters of supreme importance—their earthly and eternal destinies—to him. If Jesus was a liar, he is a colossal moral failure; he is the "Devil of Hell."[43] We offer three reasons, in response, for rejecting the claim that Jesus was a liar. First,

40. Bird, 66.
41. Bird, 69.
42. Craig, *On Guard*, 215 (see chap. 1, n. 6).
43. Lewis, *Mere Christianity*, 52. The label "moral failure" is from Horner, *"Aut Deus Aut Malus Homo,"* 73.

people die all the time for things they believe to be true, but rarely will they die for something they know to be a lie. Jesus went willingly to his death, an action at odds with the claim that Jesus was lying about his identity and mission. Second, Jesus had nothing to gain from dying for a lie. In his earthly life he enjoyed no fame, fortune, or hedonistic pleasures.[44] Dying a martyr's death for a lie would certainly not benefit him in any way. Even if his death would secure some kind of future fame, it would not benefit him, only his memory. Finally, Jesus's whole life and teaching are at odds with the claim that he lied. With great insight and intelligence, Jesus emphasized in his ethical teachings (e.g., the Sermon on the Mount) truth-telling, honesty, and humility. It is not plausible to claim that Jesus was a liar, given the evidence of his life and especially his death and resurrection, which serves as evidence that he was right all along.[45]

If Jesus was a lunatic, he was a psychological failure, a "madman"; he was "on a level with the man who says he is a poached egg."[46] He was someone with a seriously overinflated ego, wrongly believing himself to be the creator and sustainer of the world and the one within the world who stands for and acts on behalf of God. The problem with this option is that it does not fit well with the things we know about Jesus's character and actions. Those who suffer from the kinds of delusions Jesus would have suffered from tend to exhibit unhealthy character traits. A look at Jesus, however, reveals someone who was incredibly well-balanced.

Consider Jesus's emotions. Disturbed people frequently show inappropriate emotions—bouts of severe depression, volatile mood swings, constant anxiety, inappropriate anger, and so on. Jesus never demonstrated inappropriate emotions. Rather, what we find in Jesus is the full panoply of emotions—joy, love, desire, anger, sorrow, grief, compassion, love—all manifest within the appropriate context. When his friend Lazarus died, Jesus appropriately wept (John 11:35). When he witnessed the abuse of the money changers in the temple, Jesus appropriately was full of zealous anger (Matt 21:12–13; Mark 11:15–18; John 2:13–22). When confronted with those in

---

44. Groothuis, *Christian Apologetics*, 512.

45. See, for example, N. T. Wright, where he says, "The resurrection of Jesus, and all that followed from it, would be evidence that Jesus was right all along." Wright, *The Challenge of Jesus*, 119.

46. Lewis, *Mere Christianity*, 52. The label "psychological failure" is from Horner, "*Aut Deus Aut Malus Homo*," 74.

need, Jesus felt compassion: a leper (Mark 1:40–41), a widow mourning the death of her son (Luke 7:13), two blind men seeking mercy (Matt 20:34), and the crowd who was like a sheep without a shepherd (Matt 9:36). Jesus experienced all the natural emotions of a healthy individual, not the sporadic and meteoric emotions of a madman.[47]

Consider Jesus's intellect. People who are psychologically defective often exhibit thinking disorders: difficulty maintaining conversation, hasty conclusions, or irrationality. Jesus, however, spoke with clarity, power, and eloquence. He had insight into human nature and a keen sense of awareness, revealing a pristine and clear mind. Blaise Pascal summarizes the genius of his teaching: "Jesus said great things so simply that he seems not to have thought about them, and yet so clearly that it is obvious what he thought about them. Such clarity together with such simplicity is wonderful."[48]

Finally, consider Jesus's behavior. Psychologically disturbed people often exhibit unsuitable behavior. Jesus's behavior, however, was quite in line with what you would expect of a healthy individual. He had deep and abiding relationships with a wide variety of people from different parts of society, a clear sense of purpose and calling, and his actions and words were consistent with that calling. We conclude that Jesus was a well-balanced individual, much more so than anyone we know, including ourselves! As the famed historian W. E. H. Lecky, himself an unbeliever, states when considering the life of Jesus, "The character of Jesus has not only been the highest pattern of virtue, but the strongest incentive in its practice, and has exerted so deep an influence, that it may be truly said that the simple record of three years of active life has done more to regenerate and to soften mankind than all the disquisitions of philosophers and all the exhortations of moralists."[49] The unparalleled life and impact of Jesus points us toward our final option: Jesus is Lord.

We've ruled out all options but one. Jesus was not legend, lama, liar, or lunatic. Jesus existed, claimed to be God, and is God. Jesus is Lord! The logic of our argument naturally leads to this conclusion. Jesus's life—his teaching, resolve, miracles, fulfilled prophecies, and the resurrection—shows

---

47. See also G. Walter Hanson, "The Emotions of Jesus," *Christianity Today*, February 1997, 43–46.
48. Blaise Pascal, *Pensées*, trans. A. J. Krailsheimer, rev. ed. (New York: Penguin, 1995), 97, sec. 309.
49. W. E. H. Lecky, *History of European Morals* II (London: Longmans Green, 1986), quoted in F. F. Bruce, *The New Testament Documents: Are They Reliable?* (Downers Grove, IL: InterVarsity Press, 1981), 3.

that Jesus was right. His claims are vindicated. There are good reasons to think that the Jesus of history is one and the same with the Christ of faith worshipped by believers worldwide.[50]

Two Questions

There are two chief questions humans ask. First, each of us must ask what to make of Jesus Christ. This was Jesus's question to his disciples: "'But you,' he asked them, 'who do you say that I am?'" To this Peter boldly and correctly replied, "You are the Messiah, the Son of the living God" (Matt 16:15–16). Many today are not as clear on this as Peter was. Many wrongly grasp for part of Jesus rather than the whole. The result is often a Jesus made in the image of modern sensibilities, a smorgasbord of contradictions, false images, misdirected desires, stalled hopes, and wishful thinking. These modern portraits of Jesus are a far cry from the Jesus of Christianity.

Every human being must answer this question. To answer it well, we must understand who Jesus is and what he has done on our behalf. Our eternal destinies depend on it. Our wholeness and happiness in this life depend on it. Eventually, this is the question we must get to in our evangelism. So often today, to get there we must cut through the noise. We want the gospel to get a fair hearing. We want Jesus to be seen for who he is: a brilliant and beautiful Creator, Sustainer, and Redeemer. Lord and King. The Alpha and the Omega. Our suggestion in this chapter is that the series of ordered questions discussed will help others see Jesus as he is.

But there is another question, a second question, a question that gives our first question meaning. It is the question, as C. S. Lewis aptly puts it, "What [does Jesus Christ] make of us?"[51] The answer, of course, makes all the difference. He has given all of himself. He has pursued each of us, in love, all the way to the cross. It is there that we must find him. He has given all of himself so that we might find life and happiness and forgiveness of sins. May it be so in our lives and in the lives of those we seek to introduce to Jesus.

---

50. Space prohibits discussion of the resultant philosophical puzzles of affirming Jesus as Lord. The classic statement of orthodoxy concerning the nature of Christ, formulated in AD 451 at the Council of Chalcedon, is that Jesus is fully God and fully human in one person having two natures.

51. Lewis, "What Are We to Make of Jesus Christ?," 156.

Assignments

Assignment 6-1: Making Gospel Connections

Ask your nonbelieving friend what he or she thinks about Jesus. Is his or her view of Jesus consistent with the biblical picture of who Jesus is? In what ways is the portrait similar? In what ways is it different? Try to discern the source of your friend's views on Jesus. Respond accordingly, using the three questions suggested in this chapter.

Assignment 6-2

Discuss why it is difficult to believe that Jesus is Lord. How might you respond to some of these difficulties when sharing with others?

Assignment 6-3

Answer the following questions:

1. Why do you think there is so much confusion today about the person of Jesus?
2. Why does the question of Jesus's identity matter?
3. Discuss the mythicist case. What do you find most plausible about their case? What do you find most implausible?
4. What do you think of C. S. Lewis's claim that Jesus is either God or a bad man?
5. Why is the claim that Jesus was just a great moral teacher implausible? Could Jesus have said some of the things he said and still be a great moral teacher?
6. What claims or actions of Jesus are most striking to you? What do they reveal about his own self-understanding?
7. Do you think it is plausible, given the kinds of things Jesus said and did, that he was a liar or a lunatic? Explain.
8. Why is this question important: what does Jesus Christ make of us?

Suggested Reading

Bird, Michael et al., ed. *How God Became Jesus.* Grand Rapids: Zondervan, 2014.

Eddy, Paul Rhodes, and Gregory A. Boyd. *The Jesus Legend.* Grand Rapids: Baker Academic, 2007.

Reeves, Michael. *Rejoicing in Christ.* Downers Grove, IL: InterVarsity Press, 2015.

Swinburne, Richard. *Was Jesus God?* New York: Oxford University Press, 2008.

Wright, N. T. *Simply Jesus.* New York: HarperCollins, 2011.

———. *The Challenge of Jesus.* Downers Grove, IL: InterVarsity Press, 2015.

Yancey, Philip. *The Jesus I Never Knew.* Grand Rapids: Zondervan, 1995.

CHAPTER 7

Jesus's Resurrection

In 458 BC the Greek poet Aeschylus's *Eumenides*, which portrays the legendary trial of Orestes for the murder of his mother, was first performed. In a pivotal scene before the Areopagus, an ancient court on the outskirts of Athens, Apollo asserts:

> Once the dust drinks down a man's blood,
> he is gone, once for all. No rising back,
> no spell sung over the grave can sing him back—
> not even Father [Zeus] can.[1]

Just over 500 years later, an equally compelling scene unfolded before the Areopagus: the apostle Paul there proclaimed that Jesus of Nazareth had, in fact, been raised from the dead (Acts 17:31). Is Jesus's resurrection fact or fiction?

If true, the resurrection of Jesus is *the* central event of human history. The truth and meaningfulness of the Christian faith rests on this event. As Paul says in 1 Cor 15:14, "If Christ has not been raised, then our preaching is futile and your faith is empty" (NET). For their part, opponents of Christianity for

---

1. Aeschylus, *The Oresteia*, trans. Robert Fagles (New York: Penguin Books, 1979), 259.

centuries have rejected the resurrection, dismissing it as a fabrication of the early church. Our task in this chapter, therefore, is to consider the historical evidence—this is a *historical* inquiry, after all—for the resurrection of Jesus. As we will see, Jesus's resurrection is a well-attested historical event.

Curiously, many people dismiss Jesus's resurrection out of hand, without even considering the evidence. Why? Because it is a miracle, and, they assume, miracles are impossible. As we saw in chapter 4, though, miracles are impossible only if God does not exist. But we established in chapter 3 that there are convincing reasons to think God does exist, which means miracles are possible and we cannot rationally write them off. And if God exists, and God chooses to intervene in history by performing some miracle, then there is no reason why that miracle cannot be the object of historical and scientific study—that is, there is no reason why a genuine miracle cannot be known from the standpoint of history.

Before turning to the historical evidence, it is interesting to realize that Jesus actually predicted his resurrection on several occasions (Matt 12:40; 16:21; Mark 8:31; John 2:19–22), thus casting the event in a theological frame. If Jesus claimed to have divine authority, and if he predicted that he would rise from the dead, and if he in fact did rise from the dead, then it seems we have genuine evidence of a miracle and historical verification of Jesus's claims about himself.

Three Established Facts

What evidence is there that Jesus rose from the dead? There are three "minimal facts," agreed upon by almost all biblical scholars (including many who deny the resurrection), which must be explained.[2] Like a detective whose theory of a crime must account for all the relevant clues, we must insist on an explanation that adequately accommodates all three facts. These are the empty tomb, the postmortem appearances of Jesus, and the disciples' coming to believe in the resurrection. Each of these enjoys the support of several evidences which must be taken seriously. In light of the evidence that Jesus's tomb was indeed empty, that Jesus did make multiple appearances

---

2. There are, in fact, far more than these three facts. For a full-scale defense of Jesus's resurrection, see Wright, *The Resurrection of the Son of God* (see chap. 6, n. 30).

following his death, and that the disciples' faith cannot be accounted for apart from their coming to believe in the resurrection, these facts point to one explanation: God raised Jesus from the dead.

Since we cannot travel back in time, though, how can we possibly establish any historical facts? To begin with we can agree that the past is fixed—what has happened has happened, and nothing can change that. We may sometimes wish we could change the past, but because it is "mind-independent" we cannot. We may, of course, refuse to believe something has happened (e.g., that the San Antonio Spurs lost the 2013 NBA finals), but alas, we cannot thereby change history. As responsible historians, rather, we must consider the *evidence* left behind by history. Like detectives seeking to understand certain clues, we examine the historical evidence available to us, draw inferences from what this evidence suggests must have happened, and accept the explanation that best accounts for the evidence.[3]

> **Three Minimal Facts:**
>
> 1. The empty tomb
> 2. Jesus's postmortem appearances
> 3. Disciples' belief in the resurrection

The Empty Tomb

According to the canonical Gospels—Matthew, Mark, Luke, and John—Jesus was killed on a Roman cross and buried in a sealed and guarded tomb, and yet on Easter morning his tomb was found empty by several of his followers. *That* the tomb was found empty is scarcely in dispute—the question, rather, is *why* it was found empty. By itself an empty tomb, after all, does not immediately prove Jesus was raised from the dead—although an empty tomb is essential to the resurrection theory. Let us unpack the evidence for the empty tomb.

All four Gospels explicitly affirm that Jesus's tomb was found empty (Matt 28:5–7; Mark 16:4–6; Luke 24:3–6; John 20:1–8). The first supporting evidence for the empty tomb account is that it is found in *multiple, independent sources*. Why does that matter? For a couple of reasons. First, historians consider an account more reliable if it is found in independent sources because this provides corroboration of the account. As the ancient

---

3. This method, called "inference to the best explanation," is explained in detail in Michael R. Licona, *The Resurrection of Jesus: A New Historiographical Approach* (Downers Grove, IL: InterVarsity Press, 2010), 108–14.

historian Paul Maier explains, "Many facts from antiquity rest on just one ancient source, while two or three sources in agreement generally render the fact unimpeachable."[4] In addition to the four Gospels, the empty tomb is assumed in 1 Cor 15:3–8, Peter's sermon in Acts 2:29–32, and Paul's sermon in Acts 13:36–37. Even if Matthew and Luke used Mark's earlier Gospel as a common source (as seems possible, given their frequently identical wording), it's likely both also drew from independent sources, as well.[5]

Not only is our first fact widely corroborated, the earliest account that the tomb was found empty dates to within five years of Jesus's death—again, astonishingly early! The claim of an empty tomb is contained in the pre-Pauline creed found in 1 Cor 15:3–7. As we emphasized in chapter 5, this creed dates to within five years of Jesus's crucifixion.

The second supporting evidence for the fact of the empty tomb is that the Gospels tell us it was several of Jesus's *women* followers who made the initial discovery (Matt 28:1; Mark 16:9; Luke 24:1; John 20:11). In today's culture this seems inconsequential, but in first-century Jewish society the testimony of women was not well-regarded. The Talmud (a collection of traditional rabbinic teachings), for example, says, "Sooner let the words of the Law be burnt than delivered to women" (Sotah 19a). Or again: "Any evidence which a woman [gives] is not valid (to offer). . . . This is equivalent to saying that one who is Rabbinically accounted a robber is qualified to give the same evidence as a woman" (Rosh Hashanah 1.8). The ancient Jewish historian Josephus likewise records, "But let not the testimony of women be admitted, on account of the levity and boldness of their sex, nor let servants be admitted to give testimony on account of the ignobility of their soul; since it is probable that they may not speak truth, either out of hope of gain, or fear of punishment."[6]

Given their low social status, why would the Gospel writers portray women as the first discoverers of a fact as momentous as the empty tomb? If the testimony of women was of no more account than that of criminals, then this portrayal threatens to undermine the credibility of that fact. If the early church had been attempting to save face by inventing a legend

---

4. Paul L. Maier, *In the Fullness of Time: A Historian Looks at Christmas, Easter, and the Early Church* (Grand Rapids: Kregel, 1991), 197.

5. For fuller discussion of this, see Steven B. Cowan, "Is the Bible the Word of God?" in *In Defense of the Bible*, 439 (see chap. 5, n. 23).

6. Josephus, *Antiquities of the Jews*, in *The Life and Works of Flavius Josephus*, 4.8.15 (see chap. 5, n. 7).

about Jesus, selecting *women* as the first to encounter the empty tomb would have been foolish given the availability of far more credible witnesses (e.g., Peter, Nicodemus, or perhaps one of the priests mentioned in Acts 6:7). Selecting women would seem calculated to convince no one! As if the testimony of women were not "embarrassing" enough, disciples are portrayed as not even believing the testimony of his resurrection (Mark 16:11; Luke 24:11). The presence of such "embarrassing facts" (i.e., claims or details that may be perceived as awkward or discomfiting to an author or, in this case, the church, because they "embarrass" one's position) indicates truthfulness because they are unlikely to have been invented and included by the early church.

The third supporting evidence for the fact of the empty tomb is, ironically, the earliest Jewish polemic against the resurrection itself. In Matt 28:11–15 we read:

> As they were on their way, some of the guards came into the city and reported to the chief priests everything that had happened. After the priests had assembled with the elders and agreed on a plan, they gave the soldiers a large sum of money and told them, "Say this, 'His disciples came during the night and stole him while we were sleeping.' If this reaches the governor's ears, we will deal with him and keep you out of trouble." They took the money and did as they were instructed, and this story has been spread among Jewish people to this day.

No doubt Matthew responded to this story because it was being spread around Jerusalem (for if there were no empty tomb, it's difficult to imagine a body-stealing story arising). Indeed, his response is pointless unless it was common knowledge in Jerusalem that Jesus's tomb had been found empty. But focus on the Jewish leadership's allegation: that the disciples stole Jesus's

Empty Tomb— Supporting Evidence

1. Found in multiple, independent sources

2. Initially discovered by *women* followers

3. Presupposed in earliest Jewish polemic

body. If Jesus's corpse had remained in the tomb, wouldn't the authorities simply have produced the body, thereby squashing any resurrection rumors? Of all the imaginable charges (e.g., that the disciples were crazy or simply had gone to the wrong tomb), the priests tellingly chose one that presupposes the fact of the empty tomb.[7] In light of these three supporting evidences, we regard the fact that Jesus's tomb was found empty as well established. By itself, does this fact prove the resurrection theory? No, it does not—but it does mean that whatever theory we arrive at must be able to explain why the tomb was found empty.

Jesus's Postmortem Appearances

It is unlikely, as we have seen, that the early church fabricated the empty-tomb reports. To suggest they lied about our second fact—namely, that following his death, Jesus made numerous appearances—would give a whole new meaning to the expression "go big or go home." The fact is that on multiple occasions after his death and burial, Jesus appeared alive to different people. Imagine it! "Well," you're perhaps thinking, "Jesus was dead—they *must have* imagined it." But does not such thinking reveal a biased assumption of naturalism? There are at least three telltale features of the appearance accounts that prompt scholars to regard the fact of Jesus's postmortem appearances as authentic.

Paul reports in 1 Cor 15:5–8 not only that Jesus made numerous post-mortem appearances to others, but that he personally saw the Lord Jesus alive after his death (cf. Acts 9:1–9). This is no less than a list of eyewitnesses to the risen Jesus.[8] This "most important" report, Paul says, was entrusted to him—and in light of its extremely early date, he must have received it shortly after his conversion to Christianity.[9] The contents of the report are compelling: in addition to appearing separately to Cephas (Peter), then the twelve disciples, then to James, then to all the apostles, and then to Paul, Jesus is said to have appeared to more than 500 people at one time. If this is a lie, its audacity is breathtaking! Yet in his next breath Paul notes that "most of them are still alive, but some have fallen asleep" (v. 6). Why include this detail? Surely because this group was *available to corroborate his claim*, which

---

7. William Lane Craig, *The Son Rises* (Eugene, OR: Wipf & Stock, 1981), 83–84. Cf. Wright, *Resurrection of the Son of God*, 637–38.

8. For more on the reliability of eyewitness testimony, see chapter 5.

9. As eminent New Testament scholar C. H. Dodd shows, it's likely Paul received this creed from Peter and James during his stay (Gal 1:2–18) in Jerusalem. Dodd, *The Apostolic Preaching and Its Developments* (London: Hodder & Stoughton, 1936), 13. Dodd shows that Paul must have received this creed no more than seven years after Jesus's crucifixion (Dodd, 16).

is our first supporting evidence of this fact. In short, Paul invited those skeptical of his claim to go and question the witnesses themselves. Paul could never have said this if his report were a fabrication, for in that case there would be no witnesses to interview.

In addition to Paul's claims in 1 Corinthians 15, the Gospels report postmortem appearances of Jesus to several of his followers, thereby providing multiple, independent sources for this fact. We have already seen that historians consider an account more reliable if it is found in independent sources because this provides corroboration of the account. Interestingly, the Gospels include appearances that Paul did not mention—for example, to the two men on the road to Emmaus (Luke 24:13–15), to the women at the empty tomb (independently attested in Matt 28:9–10 and John 20:11–17)—and vice versa (e.g., to the group of 500 people). However, we do find that some of the same appearances Paul listed are referred to in the Gospels: to Peter (Luke 24:34) and to the twelve disciples (Luke 24:36–43; John 20:19–20).[10] Such independent corroboration provides strong evidence that many of Jesus's followers did in fact experience appearances of Jesus alive after his death. Notice that these appearances were not vague, ghostlike apparitions (such as the wispy phantom of Creusa's appearance to Aeneas, who tried in vain three times "to encircle her neck with my arms").[11] Jesus's postmortem appearances, rather, were markedly *physical* in nature: in addition to being visible, Jesus walked and talked with people, touched people, and even ate meals with them.

A third piece of evidence that supports this fact is that Jesus appeared to *unbelievers* as well as to believers. Most of the people to whom Jesus appeared alive after his death were among his followers. James (the half brother of Jesus) and Paul (known then as Saul of Tarsus), however, were not followers of Jesus before his death. We know from John's Gospel (7:1–5; cf. Mark 3:21, 31–32) that Jesus's half-brothers did not believe him to be the Messiah, and by his own admission Paul ardently persecuted those who followed Jesus (1 Cor 15:9; Gal 1:13; Phil 3:5–6).[12] That James and Paul were not

10. Jesus appeared multiple times to his disciples (cf. Matt 28:16–17; Mark 16:7; John 21). As William Lane Craig notes, "Taken sequentially, the appearances follow the pattern of Jerusalem—Galilee—Jerusalem, matching the festival pilgrimages of the disciples as they returned to Galilee following the Passover/Feast of the Unleavened Bread and travelled again to Jerusalem two months later for Pentecost." Craig, *Reasonable Faith*, 381 (see chap. 2, n. 6).

11. Virgil, *Aeneid*, trans. Frederick Ahl (New York: Oxford University Press, 2007), 2.771–94.

12. Cf. the accounts in Acts 7:58; 8:1–3; 9:1–2; 22:3–5; 26:4–11.

believers when Jesus appeared to them is important for at least two reasons. First, it means neither of them, at the time of their respective experiences, was predisposed to believe Jesus to be the risen Christ. Quite the contrary, in fact. Yet incredibly James became a leader in the Jerusalem church (Acts 15:13–21; Gal 2:9), and Paul became a Christian missionary. This means, secondly, that we must ask what precipitated their changes of heart? This question becomes especially poignant when we recall that both men eventually were put to death for their faith in Jesus as the Christ.[13] Surely their having seen the risen Lord is the only explanation for such dramatic conversions, and—not coincidentally—this is precisely the reason we find at the center of Paul's own testimony.

Before turning to our third fact, perhaps it would be helpful to contrast the postmortem appearance accounts with legendary accounts. In its popular usage today, the word "legendary" means "awesome" or "impressive," and is frequently used as a superlative. When historians use the word, however, it is to contrast a fictional, mythical, or otherwise distorted account from a historically reliable account. Recall our earlier example of the ever-growing fish from chapter 5. Is it possible that the postmortem appearance accounts found in the New Testament are similarly nonhistorical, being based on legend that (at some point) crept into the Christian tradition?

It seems not.[14] As we have seen, the appearance accounts are not based on hearsay transmissions. Paul personally spoke with James, Peter, and John about their experiences. Paul recounted his own experience firsthand, and given his knowledge that many of the 500 witnesses were still alive, it seems reasonable to assume he had firsthand accounts from at least some of them, as well. Not only are these accounts based on firsthand experience; they date to within a few short years of Jesus's crucifixion—remember: Paul received the creed of 1 Cor 15:3–7 and met with James and Peter in Jerusalem within five years of Jesus's death. Why does that matter? It matters because, as William Lane Craig explains, *"even the span of two generations is too short to allow legendary tendencies to wipe out*

---

13. James's martyrdom is described in Josephus, *Antiquities of the Jews*, 20.197–203. Cf. Eusebius, *The Church History*, trans. Paul L. Maier (Grand Rapids: Kregel, 2007), 2.23. Paul's martyrdom is described in Bryan Litfin, *After Acts: Exploring the Lives and Legends of the Apostles* (Chicago: Moody, 2015), 174–81.

14. For more on this question, see Gary R. Habermas and Michael R. Licona, *The Case for the Resurrection of Jesus* (Grand Rapids: Kregel, 2004), 84–92.

the hard core of historical fact.[15] In short, five years is nowhere near sufficient time for the growth of enough legend to obscure the fact(s) of Jesus's postmortem appearances. Add to this the presence of living witnesses—people who knew what did and did not actually happen—who would have prevented the spread of false legend, and we see there is no reason whatsoever to confuse the postmortem appearance accounts with legend.

> **Jesus's Postmortem Appearances— Supporting Evidence**
>
> 1. Many of the 500 were available to corroborate
>
> 2. Found in multiple, independent sources
>
> 3. Jesus appeared to unbelievers as well

The Disciples' Belief in the Resurrection

For several years Jesus's disciples faithfully followed him, believing, as Peter exclaimed to Jesus, that "You are the Messiah" (Mark 8:29; cf. John 1:41). They traveled extensively with Jesus, believed his teaching, and observed him performing miracles. They were his friends. Our third fact—that Jesus's disciples came to believe that God raised Jesus from the dead—may therefore seem odd. These men were, after all, Jesus's *disciples*—of course they of all people would believe in his resurrection—big surprise!

When we consider the full story of the disciples, however, we find it is something of a surprise, actually. Immediately following Judas's betrayal and the arrest of Jesus, the disciples all "deserted him and ran away" (Matt 26:56; Mark 14:50). Peter, at least, followed furtively behind the arresting party (Mark 14:54), but when confronted altogether disowned Jesus (Mark 14:66–72; John 18:15–27). Following Jesus's death, the fearful disciples hid out in a locked room (John 20:19). Although we must be careful not to read too much into this, it is somewhat surprising to find that seven of the disciples are off fishing in Galilee—*after* having seen the risen Lord (John 21)![16] No doubt the two disciples on the road to Emmaus vocalized the shared sentiment of Jesus's followers when they lamented: "We were hoping that he was the one who was about to redeem Israel" (Luke 24:21). In the disciples' minds, though, these hopes had been dashed on the rocks of Jesus's death. And yet each of the disciples soon after came boldly to preach (e.g., Acts 2:32–36) that Jesus is indeed the Messiah. Tellingly,

---

15. Craig, *The Son Rises*, 101 (Craig's emphasis).

16. It is significant that this occurs in the interim before the arrival of the Holy Spirit (cf. Acts 2:1–4).

they came to preach this despite tremendous risk to their own well-being, including threats, imprisonment, beatings, murder attempts, and in most cases, violent death.[17] Their momentous change of mind is our first supporting evidence that the disciples did indeed come to believe in Jesus's resurrection—for apart from believing in Jesus's resurrection, the disciples' belief in Jesus as the Messiah cannot be explained.

It is worth asking, though, *why* Jesus's death on the cross was such a defeating event in the minds of the disciples. The death of an intimate friend is, of course, crippling—but something deeper is going on here: the disciples understood Jesus to be "the Messiah." The concept of the Messiah is rich with meaning in Judeo-Christian thought, but in short the Messiah is the person specifically chosen by God to save his people.[18] By the time of Jesus, the Jewish people long had anticipated the arrival of the Messiah—and over time their anticipation came to include certain moral, political, and religious expectations. Significant, though, is what we do *not* find amidst their expectations. As N. T. Wright explains: "Jewish beliefs about a coming Messiah, and about the deeds such a figure would be expected to accomplish, came in various shapes and sizes, but they did not include a shameful death which left the Roman empire celebrating its usual victory."[19] It was simply unthinkable that the Messiah would die (much less that he would die a shameful death on a Roman cross[20]). This is why when Jesus foretold his impending suffering and death, Peter "took him aside and began to rebuke him, 'Oh no, Lord! This will never happen to you!'" (Matt 16:22). Yet against all expectations Peter and the other disciples, after Jesus's death, came once again to regard Jesus as the Messiah. That

Disciples' Belief in Resurrection— Supporting Evidence

1. Disciples' momentous change of mind: willing to preach resurrection

2. Disciples' momentous change of mind: once again regard Jesus as Messiah

---

17. See, for example, Acts 4:1–31; 5:17–42; 7:57–60; 12:1–5; 14:19; 21:13; 25:11, 2 Cor 4:7–14; 11:23–32. See also McDowell, *The Fate of the Apostles*.

18. For more, see N. T. Wright, *The New Testament and the People of God* (Minneapolis: Fortress Press, 1992), 307–20; and Herbert W. Bateman IV, Darrell L. Bock, and Gordon H. Johnston, *Jesus the Messiah: Tracing the Promises, Expectations, and Coming of Israel's King* (Grand Rapids: Kregel, 2012).

19. Wright, *Resurrection of the Son of God*, 559.

20. Martin Hengel explains the particular shamefulness of public execution by crucifixion in Hengel, *Crucifixion in the Ancient World and the Folly of the Message of the Cross* (Philadelphia: Fortress Press, 1977).

their change of heart simply cannot be explained apart from their believing they had seen the risen Jesus is strong supporting evidence that they firmly believed in the resurrection of Jesus.

Explaining the Facts

These three facts—the empty tomb, the postmortem appearances of Jesus, and the disciples' belief in Jesus's resurrection—each enjoy strong support and are therefore historically well-established. Our task, like that of a detective, is to identify which theory best explains these facts. The best theory, of course, must explain all the facts, not just one or two of them. A detective who theorizes that I am the thief because (1) a witness spotted me in the vicinity and (2) footprints matching my shoes were found in the vault does have a theory of the crime, but not a *good* theory of the crime because he has ignored (3) the surveillance video of you running out of the bank, carrying sacks of cash. Like detectives, we must insist on a theory that can explain all three of our facts. Further, it must not only explain them; the best theory must make sense of the facts in a way that no competing theory can match. The theory that God miraculously raised Jesus from the dead obviously explains all three facts, but what about alternative explanations of the facts?

Naturalist Explanations

Over the course of history, alternative explanations for each of these three minimal facts have been offered. Space does not permit a full-scale appraisal of each, but a brief consideration of the most common naturalistic explanations of our three facts will prove instructive.[21]

When it comes to the three minimal facts canvassed here, skeptics of the resurrection theory have typically appealed to five alternative explanations:

1. Jesus's Disciples Stole the Body

This is, in fact, the explanation we encountered in the earliest Jewish polemic in Matt 28:11–15. If true, this would explain why Jesus's tomb was found empty. For a handful of reasons, though, this suggestion is implausible: not only does it envision the disciples—most of whom were fishermen

---

21. Fuller treatments of these alternative explanations may be found in Habermas and Licona, *Case for the Resurrection of Jesus*, 93–119; Licona, *Resurrection of Jesus*, 470–610; and Craig, *Reasonable Faith*, 361–99 (see chap. 2, n. 6).

or tax collectors—subduing the Roman guards at the tomb, this explanation would also require that the disciples knowingly perpetuated a lie. Not only is there no positive reason to think this, there is every reason to doubt it: while someone may be willing to die for something he wholeheartedly believes, as we noted in the last chapter, no one willingly dies for something he knows to be a lie. In short, if the disciples had stolen the body of Jesus, they never would have come to believe in Jesus's resurrection.

2. The Jewish Leaders Stole the Body

Whereas the previous suggestion stumbles on the disciples' sincere belief in Jesus's resurrection, if the Jewish leadership stole the body, then the tomb would, of course, be found empty by Jesus's followers, which would explain their coming to believe in and preach the resurrection, leading to the growth of Christianity. But this is precisely what the Jewish leaders wished to avoid! Even if the Jewish leadership simply did not foresee that stealing Jesus's body would spark such a response among Jesus's followers, they could have easily squashed such preaching by producing Jesus's body. Such a move would have stopped the early spread of Christianity in its tracks, so why did the Jewish leadership not do so (instead accusing the disciples of stealing the body)? Their inaction undermines the suggestion that they had stolen the body.

3. Jesus Was Not Actually Dead

Although somewhat popular in the nineteenth century, the claim that Jesus physically survived his crucifixion (traditionally called the "swoon" theory) is almost universally rejected today. Beyond the virtual impossibility of surviving a scourging of such severity followed by crucifixion, this suggestion would require that the Roman executioners were mistaken in declaring Jesus dead. Not only this, but Jesus—severely wounded and on the verge of death—somehow unwrapped his own burial shroud, made his way to the tomb entrance, rolled away the stone, and crawled out without attracting the guards' attention. From a merely physical standpoint, this stretches the imagination, yet nineteenth-century theologian David Strauss (who himself rejected the resurrection theory) shows that an insuperable difficulty remains:

It is impossible that a being who had stolen half-dead out of the sepulchre, who crept about weak and ill, wanting medical treatment, who required bandaging, strengthening, and indulgence, and who still at last yielded to his sufferings, could have given the disciples the impression that he was a Conqueror over death and the grave, the Prince of Life, an impression which lay at the bottom of their future ministry. Such a resuscitation could only have weakened the impression he had made upon them in life and in death, at the most could only have given it an elegiac voice, but could by no possibility have changed their sorrow into enthusiasm, have elevated their reverence into worship.[22]

4. The Women Went to the Wrong Tomb

One final alternative explanation for the empty tomb is that on the first day of the week, Mary and company mistakenly went to a tomb other than that of Jesus. Although this would explain why the women followers initially found an empty tomb, it introduces further questions: even if Jesus's women followers so quickly forgot the location of his tomb, are we to believe that *all* of Jesus's disciples went to the wrong tomb? Even if so, it is highly unlikely none of them would have realized—or, what is even more probable, the Jewish leadership would have all too happily corrected—their mistake and discovered Jesus's body where it was buried in the correct tomb.

None of these alternative explanations for why Jesus's tomb was found empty is plausible. Not only do they raise more questions than they purport to answer, none of them addresses the postmortem appearances of Jesus to both followers and non-followers alike or the disciples' belief in the resurrection. Saul, for example, did not come to believe in the resurrection on the basis of anyone's (correct or mistaken) testimony of an empty tomb. His belief, rather, was due to Jesus's postmortem appearance to him. This leads to our fifth naturalistic hypothesis.

5. The Appearances of Jesus Were Hallucinations

Those who deny the resurrection account almost universally attribute both the fact of Jesus's postmortem appearances and the disciples' coming to

---

22. David F. Strauss, *A New Life of Jesus* (London: Williams and Norgate, 1879), 1:412.

believe in the resurrection to hallucination. In the absence of any principled reason for doing so, it is virtually impossible to deny that the disciples (and James and Paul) had experiences that they took to be the risen Jesus appearing to them. These experiences, according to this suggestion, were actually misapprehensions. If true, this would explain the disciples' testimony that Jesus appeared to them alive after his death, as well as the disciples' coming to believe and preach the resurrection account. As with the attempted naturalistic explanations of the empty tomb, however, the hallucination theory is deeply problematic.

It is worth observing that in suggesting the hallucination theory one steps out of the historical and into the philosophical arena. As we have seen, the postmortem appearance accounts are straightforward: the disciples and others claim to have seen Jesus alive after his death, and there is no *historical* reason whatsoever to gainsay them. There is, of course, nothing wrong with psychological consideration—but again, it is worth asking whether the attempt to undermine these historical accounts as hallucinations belies a biased assumption of naturalism.

Much could be said about the hallucination theory, but several obstacles render it implausible.[23] First, as we have seen, the appearances were taken to be *physical in nature*. Recall that the disciple Thomas initially did not believe those who claimed to have seen the risen Lord, yet he came to believe after *touching* Jesus. Could this, as well as sharing meals with him, be possible if Jesus's appearances were really hallucinations? Second, the *number and nature of the witnesses* do not comport with hallucination. Clinical psychologist Gary Sibcy explains, "I have surveyed the professional literature . . . written by psychologists, psychiatrists, and other relevant healthcare professionals during the past two decades and have yet to find a single documented case of a group hallucination, that is, an event for which more than one person purportedly shared in a visual or other sensory perception where there was no external referent."[24] In other words, individuals—not groups, much less groups of 500 or more!—experience particular hallucinations. Additionally, even if the disciples were all individually primed to hallucinate, we have

---

23. Gary Habermas, "Explaining Away Jesus's Resurrection: The Recent Revival of Hallucination Theories," *Christian Research Journal* 23, no. 4 (2001): 26–31, provides a succinct and helpful treatment.
24. Quoted in Licona, *Resurrection of Jesus*, 484.

already seen that the notion of a dying and rising Messiah was absolutely foreign to them (making a *resurrection* hallucination far-fetched). Besides, neither James nor Paul was a follower of Jesus at the time of their appearance experiences. This means that neither had any predilection to hallucinate a risen Jesus, much less to come to believe him to be the Messiah. Finally, the hallucination theory cannot explain why Jesus's tomb was, in fact, empty. As with previous naturalist explanations, if the disciples, James, Paul, and others each hallucinated appearances of a risen Jesus and on that basis began spreading the Christian gospel, then even if none of them thought to confirm an empty tomb, the Jewish leadership surely would have been all too happy to squash the movement by producing the body of Jesus. In short, the hallucination theory cannot adequately explain the postmortem appearances or the disciples' belief in the resurrection.

Figure 7.1 — Attempted Naturalist Explanations of:	
Empty Tomb	*Postmortem Appearances and Disciples' Belief*
1. Disciples stole the body.	1. Hallucination theory
2. Jewish leaders stole the body.	
3. Jesus was not actually dead.	
4. Women went to the wrong tomb.	

Beauty and Brilliance of the Resurrection

So, who was right: Paul or Aeschylus? Is Jesus's resurrection fact or fiction? We have seen that Jesus's tomb was indeed found empty, that Jesus did make multiple appearances following his death, and that the disciples' (and others') faith cannot be explained apart from their coming to believe in the resurrection; these are well-attested historical facts. Given the implausibility of alternative explanations, the resurrection account is seen to explain the facts in a way that no competing theory can match.

Beyond the case for its historicity, take a moment to consider afresh the meaningfulness of this event. By resurrecting Jesus from the dead, God in dramatic fashion vindicates the life and teachings of Jesus. Anyone can make audacious claims (including to be divine), but as the saying goes, the proof is in the pudding. Having pronounced approval at the launch of his earthly ministry at Jesus's baptism (Matt 3:13–17), God bookends Jesus's ministry by underscoring that approval in raising Jesus from the dead; the resurrection is, as Richard Swinburne puts it, God's signature on the life and teachings of Jesus.[25] What a beautiful picture!

The resurrection is why the gospel story matters—why the gospel is *alive*. And therein lies its brilliance: the resurrection is not a random anomaly of history, but rather an integral element of God's intentional plan for redemption. Without the resurrection there could be no atonement and redemption would remain unrealized. Coupled with his incarnation, Jesus's resurrection therefore brilliantly makes redemption possible. In fact, it's impossible to exaggerate the significance of the resurrection to Christian thought, not least because it fortifies the hope we have in Christ—hope that all who are in Christ shall likewise be resurrected; that Scripture's pervasive theme of "making new" (the believer's eternal state as well as the creation generally) is far from forgotten; and that because of resurrection, death has lost not only its victory but even its sting! Resurrection in God's brilliant plan is indeed, as J. R. R. Tolkien aptly puts it, "eucatastrophic." That is, it's the happy ending—a sort of "good catastrophe"—of the story of the incarnation that denies universal final defeat:

> This story begins and ends in joy. It has pre-eminently the "inner consistency of reality." There is no tale ever told that men would rather find was true, and none which so many sceptical men have accepted as true on its own merits. For the Art of it has the supremely convincing tone of Primary Art, that is, of Creation. To reject it leads either to sadness or to wrath.[26]

25. Richard Swinburne, *Was Jesus God?* (New York: Oxford University Press, 2008), 85–87.
26. J. R. R. Tolkien, "On Fairy Stories," in *The Tolkien Reader* (New York: Ballantine Books, 2001), 89.

Assignments

Assignment 7-1: Making Gospel Connections

Ask your nonbelieving friend what difference it would make if Jesus really was resurrected from the dead. What are his or her reasons for denying the historicity of this event? Try to answer these reasons in light of the three facts presented in this chapter.

Assignment 7-2

Discuss why people would deny the resurrection before even considering the evidence. What impact do philosophical presuppositions have, and what impact *should* philosophical presuppositions have on whether one accepts the historicity of the resurrection of Jesus?

Assignment 7-3

Answer the following questions:

1. What do you consider the strongest supporting evidence for each of the three minimal facts?
2. Explain how variations between the Gospel accounts of Jesus's resurrection actually *strengthen* the credibility of those accounts.
3. Do you think the earliest Christians could've gotten away with fabricating the key details of the resurrection story (e.g., that *women* first found the tomb empty, or that 500 people saw the resurrected Jesus at once)?
4. How important is a literal resurrection to the Christian faith?

Suggested Reading

Copan, Paul, and Ronald K. Tacelli, eds. *Jesus's Resurrection: Fact or Fiction? A Debate Between William Lane Craig and Gerd Lüdemann.* Downers Grove, IL: InterVarsity Press, 2000.

Craig, William Lane. *The Son Rises.* Eugene, OR: Wipf & Stock, 1981.

Habermas, Gary, and Michael Licona. *The Case for the Resurrection of Jesus.* Grand Rapids: Kregel, 2004.

Wright, N. T. *The Resurrection of the Son of God.* Minneapolis: Fortress Press, 2003.

CHAPTER 8

Is Jesus the Only Way?

Most religious believers think their religious tradition is true and all others false where they disagree. An atheist of course thinks that *all* religious claims (those about God and salvation) are false. There is no God, and thus there is no ultimate salvation. It used to be common that one either held to a specific religious tradition or one was an atheist (or perhaps agnostic). There were clear disagreements, and everyone argued for their respective views. Today the situation is a bit more muddled. In fact, it is popular today to be a pluralist and claim that all (or most) religious beliefs are true or at least provide a way to God. This idea poses a challenge for any view that claims to provide the one and only way to God. In this chapter, we defend Christian exclusivism from the challenge of religious pluralism.

The Christians Are Taking Over—or Are They?

An early apologetic argument for Christianity was the so-called miracle of the church. The argument was that the Christian church had become a worldwide phenomenon and virtually universal, or so it seemed. Imagine the perspective of a fourth-century Christian. Jesus's life and ministry had taken place only about 300 years earlier. In this time, Christianity had gone from being a small, persecuted Jewish sect centered in Judea and surrounding points, to becoming the sole authorized religion of the Roman Empire. It seemed that the whole world was Christian, and the parts that weren't were well on their way. However, from today's perspective, especially with the rise of global technology, we know the world hasn't become Christian (and probably never was well on its way even in the fourth century). There was and still is a rich and varied diversity of religious traditions in the world.

This awareness of religious diversity has led many Christians to question whether salvation is found only in Christ. Many have gone on to challenge not the truth of Christianity as a whole, but just its exclusivity. This is the challenge of religious pluralism.

We will first define and defend Christian exclusivism. We will then turn to the challenge of religious pluralism.

Christian Exclusivism

What is Christian exclusivism? According to Alvin Plantinga, Christian exclusivism amounts to two claims:

1. The world was created by God, an almighty, all-knowing, and perfectly good personal being (one that holds beliefs; has aims, plans, and intentions; and can act to accomplish these aims).
2. Human beings require salvation, and God has provided a unique way of salvation through the incarnation, life, sacrificial death, and resurrection of his divine son.[1]

Though there are of course those who accept claim 1 but deny claim 2, these together comprise Christian exclusivism.

We have, throughout the course of this book, already provided a variety of reasons for believing claims 1 and 2. We have, for example, offered explicit arguments for God's existence (chapter 3) and Jesus's resurrection (chapter 7). The one term that we haven't explicitly argued for, thus far, is the term *unique*.

There are at least two reasons to think that Jesus is the unique and only way of salvation. The first is that Jesus himself and his apostles, in no uncertain terms, claimed that Jesus is the only way to God. In John 14:6, Jesus says: "I am the way, the truth, and the life. No one comes to the Father except through me." In Acts 4:12, the apostle Peter says: "There is salvation in no one else, for there is no other name under heaven given to people by which we must be saved."

---

1. Alvin Plantinga, "Pluralism: A Defense of Religious Exclusivism," in *The Philosophical Challenge of Religious Diversity,* ed. Philip L. Quinn and Kevin Meeker (New York: Oxford University Press, 2000), 173.

The second reason to believe that Jesus is the only way to God follows straightforwardly from the nature of the gospel itself. The gospel says that we all stand as sinners before God. No amount of works, religious or otherwise, can reconcile us to a holy God. It is the death and resurrection of Jesus Christ that paid the penalty for our sin. It is on the basis of his work on the cross that we may be saved. Given the radical claims here, it simply doesn't allow for some other way to God. If in Jesus, God sent his son to die on the cross for our sins, it seems to follow that salvation is in no one else. Christ's work on the cross is sufficient but also necessary for salvation. This is to say that the gospel, if true, by its very nature is exclusively true.

Religious Pluralism Defined

What, then, is religious pluralism? Religious pluralism is the view that there are many (i.e., a plurality of) ways to God—where "God" is broadly construed to mean any ultimate reality beyond the natural world—and that many (if not most or even all) of the religions of the world provide these ways. It follows from this that, for the pluralist, there is no one religion that is exclusively correct.

There are many ways to be a pluralist. Let's first look at what we will call *simple religious pluralism* (simple RP) according to which all or most religious views are literally correct. Though the view is simple and even somewhat naive, it is very common among students (and most Hollywood celebrities!). There is something attractive about simple RP in the sense that we never have to say someone's view is wrong. We never have to rain on anyone's religious parade. Everybody is right about everything!

Sounds great, right? Well, get your umbrella; it's about to rain. The problem with the view is it is logically incoherent!

Christianity says that God is trinitarian (three persons in one). Islam says that God is strictly unitary (no division at all). Buddhism says that there is no personal God. The obvious problem here is that, just as a matter of logic, these couldn't all be true. It couldn't be that God is trinitarian, strictly unitarian, and nonexistent.[2] If God is trinitarian, then this logically entails that God is not strictly unitary. If the Muslim is right that God is unitary,

---

2. If truth is relative, could all these be true of God? As we argued in chapter 2, relativism is deeply problematic and ultimately self-defeating.

then it follows that the Buddhist is wrong in thinking God does not exist. Each of these could perhaps be false (i.e., polytheism could be true), but they cannot logically all be true. In sum, simple RP is logically incoherent since religious traditions make mutually incompatible claims.

If this weren't bad enough, simple RP is also self-refuting. Suppose one had the religious view (as most Christians arguably do) that simple RP is false. Given the thesis of simple RP—that all religious views are true—this would mean that *it is true that simple RP is false* (let *that* sink in!). Thus the truth of simple RP would have the logically incomprehensible consequence of falsifying simple RP.

So, though simple RP is a common view, it is not a defensible view. The view literally collapses under its own logical weight.

But why do people hold this view? It is sometimes claimed that religious exclusivity is arrogant and that simple RP is a position of *tolerance*. But these claims are unsustainable as well. Exclusivism can't be thought arrogant merely because the exclusivist claims that his or her view is true. To see why, consider that pluralists also claim their view is true and would then also be arrogant. Moreover, it is difficult to understand what it means to say that a claim itself is arrogant. This seems to be a *category error*—this is where a property or attribute is ascribed to something that can't possibly possess that property or attribute (e.g., to say, "The color red is heavy"). Claims are either true or false. It is people (or, more specifically, the way people act) that are either arrogant or humble. Though one *may* defend exclusivism in an arrogant way, one may defend it with humility as well. The pluralist can also act arrogantly (or humbly). The views themselves are neither arrogant nor humble, and it is a category error to think they are.

How about tolerance? Is it intolerant to be an exclusivist and tolerant to be a pluralist? Tolerance has become something of a contemporary buzzword. It is often taken to mean that we are tolerant insofar as we believe all views are equally valid. That is, it is intolerant to claim that one view is true and the rest false. If this is how we understand tolerance, then of course the exclusivist is intolerant. However, is the pluralist tolerant in this sense? No, not even close. The pluralist claims our view, the view of Christian exclusivism, is false. It claims that all exclusivist views are false. Given that the pluralist disagrees, this makes the pluralist, by definition, intolerant as well.[3]

But this is not what tolerance really even means. A more sensible definition is the idea that even though we believe others have false beliefs, we respect their right to hold to and defend alternate beliefs (i.e., we do not silence them, inflict violence on them, unfairly tax them, etc.). We are all for this idea of tolerance, since it allows for meaningful discussion. But this definition assumes that we in fact disagree with (i.e., assert the falseness of) contrary views. After all, if we didn't disagree, then there wouldn't be a reason to tolerate them.

Sophisticated Religious Pluralism

There is a more sophisticated version of religious pluralism (henceforth RP). Here the view is that all religions are, strictly speaking, false. That is, all religions, insofar as they make specific claims about God and transcendent reality, are false regarding those specific claims. Now, this might sound like atheism. But the sophisticated religious pluralist thinks, unlike the atheist, that there is a reality to which the religions of the world point. Though they believe that the specific claims of specific religions are, in their literal sense, false, most religions do provide a way to reach, in some sense, this supernatural or transcendent reality. That is, each religion provides a valuable and helpful framework for approaching transcendent reality with none being *the* exclusively right way of approach. That Jesus died to secure our salvation with God, though literally false as *the* means of salvation, helps Christians approach this supernatural reality. Whereas, following the pillars of Islam, though not literally currying favor from Allah, is valuable for getting in touch with the ultimate reality for Muslims. And so on, for the religions of the world.

What reasons are there for thinking there is a plurality of ways to approach God? Even though the view is more sophisticated, the arguments for this thesis are not always very compelling. Consider Columbia University professor Paul Knitter's defense of RP, for example: "I suspect that one of the few things that all Christians—no matter what their denominational or theological colorings—would agree on is the recognition that God is a reality

---

3. The further problem is that it is again self-refuting. If no one has the right to claim their view is true, then the advocate of tolerance cannot claim his view is true.

that no human mind can fully grasp."[4] He quotes certain church councils and the likes of Thomas Aquinas and Paul Tillich where they each make the point, in effect, that "God will always transcend, always be more than, what human beings can know or what God can give them to know."[5] He goes on:

> Now, if this is what all Christians believe, if God for them can really be known but never fully be known, then it follows with both logical and theological necessity that there cannot be only one way to know God. Why? Because there is always more to know about God. To hold to only one way is to close oneself to knowing more of the depths of divine truth. The "more," the excess, the transcendence of the God of Jesus calls us, therefore, to be open to "more ways" to know God.[6]

In response, it's difficult to see premises here from which the claim "there are many ways to God" follows as a matter of *logical necessity* (there seems to be no theological necessity here either), much less a plausible argument. Logical necessity means, given the premises, the conclusion is the *only* logical possibility. But surely it is logically possible that God is not fully known by finite minds (with which we completely agree) and yet faith in Christ is the exclusive way to God. God's incomprehensibility doesn't even seem plausibly to suggest there are many ways to know God. It suggests that there are many other *truths* about God, but this says nothing about whether there are therefore many *ways* to know God.

John Hick

One of the foremost defenders of sophisticated RP in recent years was the late philosopher of religion John Hick. Having grown up in a largely nonreligious household, Hick, in his own words, "underwent a powerful evangelical conversion under the impact of the New Testament figure of Jesus" in his college years.[7] This conversion was so significant that he planned

---

4. Paul Knitter, "There Are Many Ways to God," in *Debating Christian Theism*, 511 (see chap. 3, n. 32).
5. Knitter, 511.
6. Knitter, 511. Knitter goes on to argue for RP on the basis of trinitarian doctrine; that is, since God is many, there must be many ways to God. Though Knitter is a very respected scholar, this argument is difficult to take seriously.
7. John Hick, *An Autobiography* (Oxford: Oneworld, 2002), 33.

to enter Christian ministry. As he began study in preparation for this ministry, he began drifting from his evangelicalism toward pluralism. He said:

> As I spent time in mosques, synagogues, gurudwaras and temples as well as churches something very important dawned on me. On the one hand all the externals were different. . . . And not only the externals, but also the languages, the concepts, the scriptures, the traditions are all different and distinctive. But at a deeper level it seemed evident to me that essentially the same thing was going on in all these different places of worship, namely men and women were coming together under the auspices of some ancient, highly developed tradition which enables them to open their minds and hearts "upwards" toward a higher divine reality which makes a claim on the living of their lives.[8]

What Hick found across a wide range of experiences is that religious devotees all sought some sort of transcendent reality. He conceded the "externals" (and languages, concepts, scriptures, and traditions) are incompatibly different. However, its structure, in its most basic form, he thought was the same. On the basis of this, Hick retained the belief that there is ultimate reality beyond the natural world. Is this God? No, not necessarily, as this would commit Hick to more descriptive content than he thought we can give for the supernatural. Instead Hick referred to this reality as the "Real." The Real cannot be literally understood or described. It goes beyond our concepts and our language. The Real is, for Hick, "transcategorial," which means that God is beyond our ability to apply categories and concepts. But every person is, in a way, aware of the Real. Each culture, in attempting to describe the Real, has given expression *as experienced* by them in their specific religious claims that they make. But these should be seen only as the Real-as-experienced and not the Real-as-it-truly-is. No religion or individual has access to supernatural reality as it is in itself, but only the phenomenological experience of the Real. We can experience it, but this experiential reality, for Hick, is ambiguous, in the sense that it can be explained and described in many different but equally valid ways. Notice these are *valid* descriptions and not

---

8. Hick, 160.

true descriptions. Again, he, along with other sophisticated pluralists, would say that all religious claims about the Real are literally false.

Now, when Hick said that claims about the Real are literally false, he didn't mean these claims are simply nonsensical or false in every sense. Though he believed religious claims are, in a literal sense, false, they may be true in a *mythological* sense. There are a variety of ways to understand the term *myth*. It is sometimes used to simply mean false or fictional. But this is not the way Hick used the term. What, for Hick, distinguished a literal truth from a mythological truth? He said, "The literal truth or falsity of a factual assertion . . . consists in its conformity or lack of conformity to fact: 'it is raining here now' is literally true if and only if it is raining here now. . . . A statement or set of statements about X is mythologically true if it is not literally true but nevertheless tends to evoke an appropriate dispositional attitude to X."[9]

Hick seemed to think of myth as something like a *metaphor*. We use metaphors to communicate not literal truths, but to communicate certain impressions and attitudes. Take, for example, when in Shakespeare's famous play, Romeo says of Juliet:

What light through yonder window breaks?
It is the east, and Juliet is the sun.[10]

We immediately understand, given the context of the assertion, that Romeo doesn't mean to claim that Juliet is a giant ball of burning gas! Rather he is, in a way, painting a picture in words of her radiance and beauty. We can almost *feel* what Romeo is pointing us to. Putting this in Hick's terms, the Shakespeare quote gives us the appropriate dispositional attitude toward the character and scene. Likewise, Hick thinks that when

9. John Hick, *An Interpretation of Religion* (New Haven, CT: Yale University Press, 1989), 348.

10. William Shakespeare, *Romeo and Juliet* (Ware, UK: Wordsworth Classics, 2000), act 2, scene 2.

a religious figure attempts to describe the Real, she is not saying something literally true, but only something that gives us the appropriate attitude and disposition toward that Reality.

What's the appropriate dispositional attitude toward the Real? Hick believed that what we see in each world religion is a move away from self-centeredness. He wrote:

> The great world faiths embody different perceptions and conceptions of, and correspondingly different responses to the Real from within the major variant ways of being human; and that within each of them the transformation of human existence from self-centeredness to Reality-centeredness is taking place. These traditions are accordingly to be regarded as alternative Soteriological "spaces" within which, or "ways" along which, men and women find salvation/liberation/ultimate fulfillment.[11]

So, the appropriate dispositional attitude toward the Real is becoming centered not on ourselves but on the Real. For Hick, any religion that takes the focus off ourselves is producing the appropriate dispositional attitude and, thus, is one of many appropriate religious frameworks.

Assessment of Hick's RP

Hick was not a universalist in the sense that *all* approaches to the Real are appropriate.[12] That is, his version of RP does not entail that all religious individuals are "saved." He seemed to think that only those whose religious beliefs evoke Reality-centeredness rather than self-centeredness are appropriate.

The first problem with Hick's RP is that many religious traditions seem to be fundamentally self-centered. That is, contrary to Hick's claim, it is not clear that all or even most religions are truly Reality-centered. Consider, for example, the traditions that make heaven (or paradise, or enlightenment, etc.) the ultimate goal in being religious. This seems to be fundamentally self-interested, and transcendent reality is simply a means toward that gain. A religious devotee of this sort is seemingly only in it for himself or herself.

---

11. Hick, *Interpretation of Religion*, 240.
12. Hick was a universalist in the sense that salvation is *available* in all religions, but presumably this entails that it is possible for some to be unsaved.

Second, Hick believed that the Real is indescribable and transcategorial, and yet he seemed to give descriptions of and categories for understanding the Real. In other words, why shouldn't we understand his account as providing categories for how to think of the Real? But if this is what he has done, then the Real is not transcategorial. We just have a new set of categories by which we understand the Real.

Third, there is a problem of intention. Romeo intended for his claim to be understood metaphorically and it, for this reason, can be said to be metaphorically true. If Romeo meant that Juliet was the sun in a literal sense (i.e., she actually was a massive ball of burning gas), it wouldn't be correct to call it a metaphor. He would not be saying something metaphorically true, because he was not using it as a metaphor. It seems to us that most religious people intend their claims quite literally. Abraham, Jesus, Muhammad, Siddhārtha Gautama, the Hindu guru, and religious people everywhere arguably intend a literal understanding of the claims they make. So these claims can't be mythologically true unless they are intended to be understood in a mythological sense.

Fourth, Hick believed that a claim is (mythologically) true insofar as it produces an *appropriate* disposition toward the Real. But given the fact that the Real is transcategorial, it seems one could not know what the appropriate disposition is. In other words, what's available to us that makes our disposition appropriate or inappropriate? Even if all religions do move us to be Reality-centered, why think this is the appropriate way to approach the Real? Maybe the self-interested religious terrorist is approaching the Real in an appropriate way by his mass killing. How could Hick say that he is not?

When it comes to metaphors (such as Romeo's description of Juliet), we know that the sun is an appropriate metaphor for a beautiful woman since we already know what it's like to see a beautiful sunrise. We could give a more or less literal description of a sunrise, and for this reason we know the metaphor is appropriate. However, if the Real is completely indescribable and completely beyond our ability to comprehend, then we really don't know if the specific (mythological) approach is appropriate or not.

Thus, it seems that Reality-centeredness as a fundamental moral of all religions is unwarranted. Even if we grant the rather dubious claim that all religious traditions move people from self-centeredness to Reality-centeredness, this doesn't seem to constitute a good reason to think that this is the path of salvation. If Hick wants to say that the Real is indescribable and transcategorial, then he has no good reason for thinking that becoming Reality-centered is the path of salvation. For all we know, the Real doesn't want us to be Reality-centered!

The Myth of Inclusivism

Perhaps the most attractive part of RP is its supposed inclusivism. Religions are not exactly known for coming together on almost anything. It appears all religions can come together under the big tent that is RP. However, this appearance is not quite right. In fact, we'll argue RP is no more inclusive than the Christian exclusivist! To see this, we should notice that the thesis of RP says that RP is true and everyone else is wrong—everyone else is *excluded* in that sense.

Imagine we were convinced that everything Hick says about RP is true and we begin to take his writing as prophetic and divinely inspired. We could even start calling ourselves Hickians. John Hick has, after all, shown us the true way to the Real. Imagine that we begin to meet regularly to study and discuss his writings, and even begin to hit the streets getting people to accept the "good news" of Hickianity.

What we should notice is that this is no more inclusive than any religious view. In fact, it is just another religious tradition with its views about ultimate reality and the way to reach it. If one doesn't accept the claims of Hickianity, then one is excluded from the view (i.e., we do not accept it). The point of this thought experiment is to show that RP is no less exclusive in the claims it makes than any other view about ultimate reality. If you disagree with the pluralist, she will say that you are wrong. The pluralist believes that it is only

she who has the full view of reality, and the rest of the world, both now and historically, is just flat wrong about what they believe religiously.

To see this even more crisply, RP is often illustrated by the children's story of the blind men and the elephant. In the story, a group of blind men come upon an elephant for the first time. Since they are blind, they each attempt to understand what is before them by feeling the elephant. The first feels the side of the elephant and takes it to be like a wall. The second happens upon the trunk of the elephant and takes it to be long like a snake. The third touches the tusk and thinks an elephant is like a spear. The fourth feels the leg of the elephant and takes elephants to be like tree trunks. The fifth feels the ear and thinks elephants are like fans. And the sixth thinks an elephant is like a rope, given that he feels the tail.

What we are supposed to learn is that though different religious accounts may seem extremely different and contradictory, they are unknowingly approaching the same reality. Each of the views is, on the whole, literally wrong—an elephant is not very much like a snake or spear—but these are all getting at what an elephant, or at least parts of an elephant, is like.

Indeed, this nicely illustrates RP, especially its exclusivism! To see this we should, first, notice that each religious tradition is described as being *blind*. If one is religious, one might find this more than a little insulting. Each religious tradition only has a small, mostly false piece of the puzzle. But notice who we're told *isn't* blind, namely, the religious pluralist. The pluralist, it seems, can see reality as it really is. Whereas the rest of us are blind and inaccurately describing one small piece of what the Real is like, the pluralist has the full picture.

As it turns out, inclusivity is impossible. This is a consequent of the nature of a truth claim. Whenever we make a claim, we are claiming that it is true, and this implies that its contraries are all false. One can try to be perfectly inclusive, but it will always exclude someone. Imagine we assert the following view: "Everyone, no matter what they believe, is right." If anything is inclusive, this is it. But wait: doesn't this exclude everyone who says there are only some who are right? This extremely inclusive statement excludes all those who disagree (which, by the way, is almost everyone on the planet, since hardly anyone believes that everyone is right about everything). The claim, though it seems inclusive, actually excludes almost everyone! Anyone who makes a truth claim, given the nature of truth, is an exclusivist. Thus, if being exclusive is a problem, it is a problem for everyone!

But there's no reason to think that being exclusive, all by itself, is a problem. Indeed, there seems to be no way to have meaningful dialogue without it.

Religious Disagreement

We began the chapter pointing out that RP has grown in popularity given the rich and varied diversity of religious traditions in the world. We've argued that RP suffers from many challenges and should therefore be rejected. But there is still the radical diversity in the world. Can we claim that Jesus is the only way to God even though most of the world does not believe this? It is sometimes objected that the radical diversity and disagreement in the world makes Christian exclusivism unjustified.

What's the objection? The first point is there seem to be adherents of other faiths who are our *epistemic peers*. What is an epistemic peer? According to Thomas Kelly, epistemic peers, as it relates to a specific question, are "equals with respect to their familiarity with the evidence and arguments which bear on that question."[13] It is also often added that peers are, on the whole, equals in terms of intellectual ability. The Christian's epistemic peer is one who has considered all the same evidence, is equally intelligent, and yet rejects the truth of Christianity. The objection to Christian exclusivism, then, is that given the radical disagreement among epistemic peers, the evidence for Christianity is not compelling. If epistemic peers are looking at the same evidence and coming to radically different views, then the evidence must not be definitive. The Christian exclusivist has a broad set of defeaters, then, for her claims. What are the defeaters? The defeaters are all the inumerable epistemic peers of the world!

In response, it is important to point out that the diversity of opinion is not simply a phenomenon of religious inquiry. There is incredible diversity among epistemic peers in disciplines, such as philosophy, science, economics, morality, politics, and so on. The diversity here is not often seen as reason to deny any specific view in these disciplines. Why should it be different for religious topics? Moreover, one will be hard-pressed to find beliefs for which

---

13. Thomas Kelly, "The Epistemic Significance of Disagreement," in *Oxford Studies in Epistemology*, vol. 1, ed. Tamar Szabo Gendler and John Hawthorne (New York: Oxford University Press, 2005), 174.

there is no dissent from some epistemic peer somewhere. For example, suppose that Smith believes that white supremacy is false and a morally abhorrent view. Let's say that Smith has arrived at this view as a matter of careful reflection and it is a matter of strong conviction. However, suppose one points out that there are white supremacists out there, some of whom are presumably epistemic peers. Should this diminish Smith's conviction that white supremacy is false? He might (like us) be at a loss to understand why someone would find white supremacy plausible. But it would seem to be intellectually irresponsible of Smith to lessen his conviction on the mere fact that there is peer disagreement. Thus, the mere fact that there is disagreement does not seem to constitute a defeater for one's belief.

It is also unclear that all participants in the discussion have the same evidence available to them. It is our experience that unbelievers have often not fully appreciated the arguments the Christian exclusivist makes. There are some who have carefully and thoughtfully considered the evidence, but these are few and far between. The writings of the new atheists strike us as a good example of this. In fact, Michael Ruse (keep in mind he is an atheist) has said:

> I have written that *The God Delusion* made me ashamed to be an atheist and I meant it. Trying to understand how God could need no cause, Christians claim that God exists necessarily. I have taken the effort to try to understand what that means. Dawkins and company are ignorant of such claims and positively contemptuous of those who even try to understand them, let alone believe them. Thus, like a first-year undergraduate, he can happily go around asking loudly, "What caused God?" as though he had made some momentous philosophical discovery. . . . There are a lot of very bright and well informed Christian theologians. We atheists should demand no less.[14]

The point here is not to return the favor and merely ridicule Dawkins and company. It is to say that there are few who take the time and care to

---

14. Michael Ruse, "Dawkins et al Bring Us into Disrepute," *Guardian*, November 2, 2009, https://www.theguardian.com/commentisfree/belief/2009/nov/02/atheism-dawkins-ruse.

understand the opposing view, and this makes it less plausible that everyone in the discussion is an epistemic peer.

But there are some who thoughtfully reject Christian exclusivism. These seem to have carefully considered the case for Christianity and they have rejected it. But are they truly epistemic peers? It seems not, at least, in a strict sense. This is *not* to say that unbelievers are epistemically inferior to Christians. Rather, the point is that there is so much that goes into forming our fundamental beliefs that it is at least plausible that we do not share a strictly identical epistemic situation with anyone, even other Christians. To see this, we should first emphasize our limitations as knowers. There is only so much one can carefully consider in a lifetime. Also, arguments are almost always complex, with important subtleties that must be appreciated to see the full force of the argument. It is just not possible to fully consider every argument relevant to one's view. In addition to this, we make subtle but important decisions about logic, arguments, and evidence that bear on the conclusions we reach.

There are also many non-epistemic factors that affect our belief formation. We are not mere logic machines. In fact, this is sometimes used as an argument for pluralism. Hick said, "It is evident that in some ninety-nine percent of cases the religion which an individual professes and to which he or she adheres depends upon the accidents of birth. Someone born to Buddhist parents in Thailand is very likely to be a Buddhist, someone born to Muslim parents in Saudi Arabia to be a Muslim, someone born to Christian parents in Mexico to be a Christian, and so on."[15]

This, it seems, is true, but the question is, what follows from it? Should we be inclined to think that Christian exclusivism is false just because we were born in a country in which Christianity is common? It seems not, so long as we have carefully considered the case for Christianity vis-à-vis other views. Plantinga has responded to this claim, saying, "For suppose we concede that if I had been born in Madagascar rather than Michigan, my beliefs would have been quite different. . . . But of course the same goes for the pluralist. Pluralism isn't and hasn't been widely popular in the world at large; if the pluralist had been born in Madagascar, or medieval France, he

---

15. Hick, *Interpretation of Religion*, 2.

probably wouldn't have been a pluralist. Does it follow that he shouldn't be a pluralist?"[16] This would be a bad reason to reject pluralism just as it would be a bad reason to reject a specific religious view.

But still, our upbringing and prior experiences certainly figure in to our belief formation, as do our hopes, fears, and desires. Atheist philosopher Thomas Nagel has said:

> I speak from experience, being strongly subject to this fear myself: I want atheism to be true and am made uneasy by the fact that some of the most intelligent and well-informed people I know are religious believers. It isn't just that I don't believe in God and, naturally, hope that I'm right in my belief. It's that I hope there is no God! I don't want there to be a God; I don't want the universe to be like that. My guess is that this cosmic authority problem is not a rare condition and that it is responsible for much of the scientism and reductionism of our time.[17]

Now we don't think that Nagel is irrational in his atheism. He still presumably holds to his atheism on the basis of evidence. But the point is, we don't share his desire for atheism to be true. It looks as if his approach to the world is very different from ours.

Where does this leave us? It is our view that given the subtlety of the evidence and the way we bring our desires and background to bear on what we believe, there are no *identical* epistemic peers. We might be equals in our general ability to discover truth, but this need not mean that we are identical epistemic peers. Rather, it seems we all have a limited but nonidentical view of the world.

The point of all of this is to say that we can do no better than doing our level best to believe in accord with our evidence. After careful inquiry and reflection, we should believe those things that are best supported by the evidence that we have. If our best evidence points to atheism, then we should be atheists. If our best evidence points to Christian exclusivism, then we should so believe. The radical diversity of the world should, it seems to us, foster an attitude of intellectual humility in the realization that we may

---

16. Plantinga, "Pluralism," 187–88.
17. Thomas Nagel, *The Last Word* (New York: Oxford University Press, 1997), 130–31.

be wrong about some of what we believe. However, it is an overcorrection to think we cannot rationally believe something in the face of disagreement.

Concluding Thoughts

In closing, there is one piece of evidence that the Christian claims to have that the unbeliever does not. It is part of Christian doctrine to believe the Christian has something available to her that is unavailable to the unbeliever. This is the fact that Christ has revealed himself to the Christian through the ministry of the Holy Spirit as we have found our rest in him. If this is right, then Christian believers and unbelievers are never epistemic peers since the evidence for the genuine Christian is necessarily different. As we mentioned in chapter 2, "Truth, Knowledge, and Faith," we think of the testimony of the Holy Spirit as evidence. But it is not evidence that is sharable in a public defense of Christianity. However, this is not a discussion about the defense of Christianity. It is a discussion of the epistemology of Christian belief. In that sense, the fact that Christ has revealed himself to the Christian constitutes a very good reason to believe that Christianity, on top of the rest of the evidences we have, is true even in the face of radical disagreement.

Assignments

Assignment 8-1: Making Gospel Connections
Ask an unbeliever whether Jesus would be the only way to God if the gospel were true. The point is to explain the exclusiveness of the gospel itself.

Assignment 8-2
Discuss Christian exclusivism. What does a Christian exclusivist believe? How is the logic of simple RP flawed? How is simple RP also self-refuting?

Assignment 8-3
Answer the following questions:

1. What is Christian exclusivism?
2. Is Christian exclusivism inherently arrogant and intolerant?
3. What is sophisticated religious pluralism?
4. Do you think that there is a common element to all religious views?
5. What does John Hick mean by the term *transcategorial*? Why does he think this term applies to the Real?
6. Why is it said that inclusivism is a myth?
7. Explain the story of the elephant and the blind men. Do you think this story illustrates pluralism?
8. What do you think follows from the fact that many equally smart people disagree about religious matters?

Suggested Reading

Beckwith, Francis J., and Gregory Koukl. *Relativism: Feet Firmly Planted in Mid-Air.* Grand Rapids: Baker, 1998.

Copan, Paul. *True for You, But Not for Me: Overcoming Objections to Christian Faith.* 2nd ed. Bloomington, MN: Bethany House, 2009.

Hick, John. *An Interpretation of Religion: Human Responses to the Transcendent.* 2nd ed. New Haven, CT: Yale University Press, 2004.

Netland, Harold A. *Encountering Religious Pluralism: The Challenge to Christian Faith and Mission.* Downers Grove, IL: InterVarsity Press, 2001.

Okholm, Dennis L., and Timothy R. Phillips, eds. *Four Views on Salvation in a Pluralistic World.* Grand Rapids: Zondervan, 1996.

Quinn, Philip, and Kevin Meeker, eds. *The Philosophical Challenge of Religious Diversity.* New York: Oxford University Press, 1999.

CHAPTER 9

The Problem of Evil

You may not have heard of the name Kevin Carter, but you've probably seen the famous picture he took during the 1993 famine in Sudan. The picture is horrific. A starving child crawls through the bush toward a feeding station. A few yards away, a vulture longingly awaits its soon-to-be-dead prey.[1] This picture captures in a powerful way the reality, horror, and intensity of the suffering and cruelty found in this world. For Carter, the picture won him a Pulitzer Prize. He had risen to the summit of his profession by capturing images of pain and suffering. A few months after winning the Pulitzer, Carter committed suicide. In a note he explained, "The pain of life overrides the joy to the point that joy does not exist."[2] He had come face-to-face with evil and could not cope with its sting.[3]

The reality of pain and suffering—evil—raises at least three pressing questions for the Christian. First, does the reality of evil in the world show that God doesn't (or probably doesn't) exist? Many thoughtful people look at the distribution or amount of evil in the world and conclude on that basis that there is no God. Thus, our first challenge is to consider the strength of the case for atheism given the existence of evil. Second, assuming God does exist, why does he allow pain and suffering? Finally, how does one cope with the reality of evil?

Before we begin, understand that these questions are often regarded as intractable because of a failure to ask preliminary questions. In other words, there is a prior question to our questions, one percolating beneath the surface

---

1. See 100 Photos, Time.com, accessed February 9, 2018, http://100photos.time.com/photos/kevin -carter-starving-child-vulture.
2. Scott Macleod, "The Life and Death of Kevin Carter," *Time*, June 24, 2001, http://content.time. com/time/magazine/article/0,9171,165071,00.html.
3. Thanks to Professor Garrett DeWeese for bringing the story of Kevin Carter to our attention.

for the men and women on the streets. The prior question has to do with the nature of happiness. Most today, without much reflection, think of happiness as sensual fulfillment or pleasure. On this understanding of happiness, man's greatest need is the elimination of pain and suffering (i.e., the opposite of pleasure), and this is found through progress and the ultimate savior: technology. But this "answer" to the problem of pain does not go deep enough. It does not address man's greatest need. Nor is it really an answer; rather, it is a denial of the problem. Biblically, happiness is not *hedonistic*, but *edenistic*.[4] That is, happiness is best understood as a kind of human flourishing where we each become the kind of person God wants us to be (morally and intellectually virtuous) and experience life the way it was meant to be (in intimacy with God and harmony with others) as we live out his purposes. But if true happiness is a kind of human flourishing, then humanity's greatest need isn't merely the elimination of pain. The problem goes much deeper—to the core of our being. For humanity is flawed, cracked, broken—to use the old word, *sinful*—and our deepest need is redemption and restoration. Technology can't even scratch the surface of our deepest need. An understanding of the nature of happiness and God's role in such happiness locates the problem of evil— and it *is* a problem—within its proper context, a context we'll revisit at the end of the chapter. Now, let's consider our three pressing questions.

The problem associated with our first pressing question deals with what is called the *intellectual problem of evil*.[5] The intellectual problem of evil is concerned with providing a rational explanation of the coexistence of God and evil and comes in two versions. The first version, the *logical problem of evil*, argues that the existence of an omniscient, omnipotent, and wholly good God is incompatible with the reality of evil. If successful, such an argument would show, assuming that evil exists, that God's existence is *impossible*. A second version of the intellectual problem of evil, the *evidential problem of evil*, tries to show that the coexistence of God and evil are highly *improbable*.

In addressing the issues pertinent to the evidential problem, our second pressing question comes into focus: what, if any, are the reasons for God to

---

4. This is one of the central ideas of David Naugle's *Reordered Loves, Reordered Lives: Learning the Deep Meaning of Happiness* (Grand Rapids: Eerdmans, 2008).

5. For more on the different versions of the problem of evil as outlined in this paragraph and the next, see Craig, *On Guard*, 152–154 (see chap. 1, n. 6). We follow Craig's lead in characterizing the problem of evil as we do here and in figure 9.1.

allow pain and suffering? Moreover, can we know God's reasons for some or all instances of evil? Our third pressing question deals with what has been called the *emotional problem of evil* and concerns how to comfort someone who is experiencing evil. By clearly distinguishing the kinds of questions asked with respect to pain and suffering, it will become easier to identify the root cause of someone's unbelief. It could be, as William Lane Craig suggests, that for most people their unbelief is born out of a rejection of God in the face of intense personal suffering rather than a refutation of God via intellectual argument.[6]

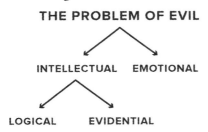

FIGURE 9.1   The Different Versions of the Problem of Evil

If so, then a more pastoral response would be in order. If, on the other hand, the root cause of the unbelief is intellectual, then the response will be more philosophical. We begin by exploring the logical problem of evil.

The Logical Problem of Evil

A set of statements is logically inconsistent when it is impossible for them all to be true at the same time. For example, consider the following statements:

(1) Jim Bob is a bachelor

and

(2) Suzy is married to Jim Bob.

Given the meanings of the words "bachelor" and "married," these two statements are clearly inconsistent, assuming "Jim Bob" refers to the same guy at the same time. However, the inconsistency isn't always obvious, or at least it isn't for those who don't understand what the words "bachelor" and

---

6. Craig, *On Guard*, 135. As an example, consider the case of Charles Darwin. It is perhaps commonly thought that Darwin rejected belief in God due to evolution—a refutation of the evidence—but in reality, his unbelief was born out of the intense emotional pain experienced by the death of his daughter, Anna, at age ten. For Darwin's story, see James Moore, *The Darwin Legend* (Grand Rapids: Baker, 1994), 38.

"married" mean. Sometimes the contradiction needs to be made explicit. To do so, what is needed is some other statement—a statement that is necessarily true—that entails, along with a statement from the original pair, the denial of the other statement from the original pair. The following statement should do the trick:[7]

(3) A bachelor is an unmarried male.

The conjunction of (1) and (3) renders (2) impossible.

Historically, many atheists have argued that there is a similar logical inconsistency between the statements

(4) God is omnipotent, omniscient, and wholly good
and
(5) There is evil in the world.

Given the obvious reality of evil in the world, statement (5) is exceedingly difficult to deny. Thus, if there is a logical inconsistency between (4) and (5), and (5) is clearly true, then (4) must be false. Thus, we will have found a proof that God doesn't exist. In the case of Jim Bob and Suzy, we didn't really need to go to the trouble of proving that (1) and (2) are logically inconsistent because we can just see that they are, given the widely understood notion of what it means to be a bachelor. With respect to (4) and (5), the inconsistency is not obvious. Thus we must find some additional statement or statements that render the contradiction apparent.

One of the most prominent proponents of the logical problem of evil was J. L. Mackie, who suggested the needed additions "are that good is opposed to evil, in such a way that a good thing always eliminates evil as far as it can, and that there are no limits to what an omnipotent thing can do."[8] Following Mackie, we might add:

(6) A good being always eliminates evil as far as it can,
and
(7) There are no limits to what an omnipotent being can do.

---

7. Notice that statement (3) is necessarily true, where a statement is necessarily true if it is true in all possible circumstances. In this case, (3) is necessarily true by virtue of the meaning of the word "bachelor."

8. J. L. Mackie, "Evil and Omnipotence," *Mind* 64, no. 254 (1955): 201.

As long as (6) and (7) are necessarily true, it seems we have found our inconsistent set, for the conjunction of (4) with (6) and (7) renders (5), the reality of evil in the world, impossible. The result for the believer in God is catastrophic: either deny the obvious truth of (5) or surrender commitment to (4).

The problem when considering Mackie is that neither (6) nor (7) is necessarily true, and thus the logical problem of evil fails. As Alvin Plantinga points out in his free will defense, (6) is not necessarily true since a wholly good being might have a morally sufficient reason to permit evil to occur. Further, (7) is not necessarily true because the reality of human freedom might make it impossible for God to bring about a world as morally good as this world without the presence of evil. As Plantinga puts it:

Alvin Plantinga

> A world containing creatures who are sometimes significantly free (and freely perform more good than evil actions) is more valuable, all else being equal, than a world containing no free creatures at all. . . . To create creatures capable of *moral good*, therefore, he must create creatures capable of moral evil;[9] and he cannot leave these creatures *free* to perform evil and at the same time prevent them from doing so. God did in fact create significantly free creatures; but some of them went wrong in the exercise of their freedom: this is the source of moral evil. The fact that these creatures sometimes go wrong, however, counts neither against God's omnipotence nor against his goodness; for he could have forestalled the occurrence of moral evil only by excising the possibility of moral good.[10]

As a result of Plantinga's influential work, the prospect of proving a logical incompatibility between the reality of an omnipotent, omniscient,

---

9. In the next section we'll distinguish moral evil from natural evil. For now, moral evil is all the evil brought about by the misuse of creaturely freedom.

10. Alvin Plantinga, *The Nature of Necessity* (Oxford: Clarendon Press, 1974), 166–67.

and wholly good God and the reality of evil in this world is significantly diminished, if not entirely hopeless.[11]

Before setting the logical argument aside, let's examine a popular reply to Plantinga's free will defense: *Couldn't God create free but morally perfect individuals, individuals who always choose the good?*[12] The suggestion is that since God is omnipotent, he can create any world he wants, including a world where people always freely choose the good. Unfortunately, even an omnipotent God cannot create any world he wants (e.g., God cannot create a world full of married bachelors). If people have free will, they may refuse to cooperate with God. Thus, there are a number of worlds that God cannot create because people in them wouldn't comply with God's desires. In fact, for all we know, it's possible that there are *no* worlds in which free creatures always do what God wants. If so, then there are no worlds with free but morally perfect individuals, and the "free but perfect" objection fails.[13]

---

11. Consider the following summary statements regarding the current status of the logical problem of evil. William Rowe (atheist): "It is reasonable to conclude that the logical form of the problem of evil is not much of a problem for theism," in *Philosophy of Religion* (Belmont, CA: Thomson Wadsworth, 2007), 117; Paul Draper (atheist/agnostic): "Logical arguments from evil are a dying (dead?) breed. . . . For all we know, even an omnipotent and omniscient being might be forced to allow [evil] for the sake of obtaining some important good. Our knowledge of goods and evils and the logical relations they bear to each other is much too limited to prove that this could not be the case," from "The Skeptical Theist," in *The Evidential Argument from Evil*, ed. Daniel Howard-Snyder (Bloomington: Indiana University Press, 1996), 176–77; Peter van Inwagen (theist): "It used to be widely held that evil. . . was incompatible with the existence of God: that no possible world contained both God and evil. So far as I am able to tell, this thesis is no longer defended," from "The Problem of Evil, the Problem of Air, and the Problem of Silence," in Howard-Snyder, ed., 151; and Brian Leftow (theist): "If you think that evil currently provides any very strong argument against the existence of God, you have not been paying attention. Purely deductive ('logical') versions of the problem of evil are very widely conceded to be 'dead', killed off by Plantinga's free-will defense. . . . The debate has shifted to 'evidential' versions of the problem of evil," Leftow, *God and Necessity* (Oxford: Oxford University Press, 2012), 547.

12. This objection was raised forcefully by Mackie in his 1955 article, and more recently by the atheist philosopher Alex Rosenberg in a debate with Christian philosopher William Lane Craig in *Is Faith in God Reasonable? Debates in Philosophy, Science, and Rhetoric*, ed. Corey Miller and Paul M. Gould (New York: Routledge, 2014), 35.

13. For more detailed discussions of the "Free but Perfect Objection," including the notion of what is often called "transworld depravity," see Daniel Howard-Snyder, "God, Evil, and Suffering," in *Reason for the Hope Within*, ed. Michael Murray (Grand Rapids: Eerdmans, 1999), 91–92; and Plantinga, *The Nature of Necessity*, 184–90.

> **Figure 9.2 — Freedom and Determinism**
>
> Plantinga's free will defense relies on a conception of freedom called *incompatibilism* (it is also called, more positively, libertarian freedom): freedom is incompatible with being determined. Thus, as a libertarianly free creature, I am the ultimate source of my actions and decisions and often (if not always) I have genuine alternate possibilities from which to choose. Alternatively, *compatibilism* holds that freedom is compatible with being determined: even if my actions and decisions are determined by either the laws of nature and the initial conditions of the universe (physical determinism) or God (theological determinism), as long as I am not coerced, I am free.

The Evidential Problem of Evil

That there is pain and suffering in the world is beyond dispute. What is at issue, however, is how a wholly good God could allow pain and suffering in the world. Upon reflection, it is not too difficult to discern a good reason for *some* suffering. I suffer the pain of the dentist so that my teeth can stay healthy. A child is allowed the possibility of falling and scraping her knees while learning how to ride a bike so that one day she may be able to ride without the aid of training wheels. Even in the Bible, it is clear that in this world Christians can expect trials, temptations, and suffering. Often, God uses such suffering to grow our character and bring others (or ourselves) closer to him. As C. S. Lewis so eloquently stated, "God whispers to us in our pleasures, speaks in our conscience, but shouts in our pain: it is His megaphone to rouse a deaf world."[14] So, some of the suffering we find in the world is compatible with a wholly good God. But there is much suffering and pain in the world that seems, from our perspective, to be absolutely pointless. And if it is pointless, we have evidence that God does not exist, since a wholly good God would not allow pointless evil.

We can formulate this evidential argument from evil as follows:

(8) If God exists, pointless evil does not exist.

(9) Probably, pointless evil exists.

(10) Therefore, probably, God does not exist.

---

14. C. S. Lewis, *The Problem of Pain* (San Francisco: HarperCollins, 2001), 91.

In responding, the theist has three options: (a) affirm the reality of pointless evil (and argue for the falsity of premise [8]), (b) deny the reality of point-less evil and provide a *theodicy* (and argue for the falsity of premise [9]), or (c) deny the reality of pointless evil and endorse *skeptical theism* (and again, argue for the falsity of premise [9]).

If you think God is wholly good and providentially in control of the world, then you will be inclined, as we are, to deny the reality of pointless evil and accept (8). Given his moral goodness and strong providential hand, it is *impossible* for God to allow an *all-things-considered* pointless evil. That is, God allows particular instances of evil only if it would result in some (all-things-considered) good that would outweigh the evil or, if prevented, some other evil at least as bad would result.[15]

With respect to premise (9), the key question is whether it is *rational* to believe all the horrendous evils that occur daily in our world are such that if God were to prevent them, he would have to forfeit some outweighing goods. A fawn is horribly burned in a forest fire and suffers terribly for days before death; a five-year old girl is brutally beaten, raped, and killed.[16] The atheist asks, "Is there really some great good that an omnipotent being could bring about only by permitting such evils? Further, even if so, is it true that *all* the instances of intense human and animal suffering occurring daily in our world lead to greater goods in such a way that even an omnipotent, omniscient being could not have achieved *any* of those goods without per-mitting the instances of suffering that supposedly lead to them?" As athe-ist philosopher William Rowe concludes, "It is the enormous amount of apparently pointless, horrendous suffering occurring daily in our world that grounds the claim in [premise 9]."[17]

The theist will respond, "God is wholly good; he would not allow a pointless evil to occur. Thus, God has a morally justified reason for allowing

---

15. What we say here is consistent with the possibility that a particular instance of evil *in itself* is not necessary to secure some outweighing good, but that some evil equally bad or worse may be necessary to secure the outweighing good. Or as Ross Inman puts it, "an instance of evil may be token-gratuitous without being type-gratuitous," in Inman, "Gratuitous Evil Unmotivated: A Reply to Kirk R. MacGre-gor," *Philosophia Christi* 15, no. 2 (2013): 437. That evils may not be *singularly* necessary to secure a greater good in no way establishes that such evils are *all-things-considered* pointless, which is what would be required to show the falsity of premise (8).

16. These two widely cited examples are from William Rowe, "An Exchange on the Problem of Evil," in *God and the Problem of Evil*, ed. William Rowe (Malden, MA: Blackwell, 2001), 126.

17. Rowe, 128.

all (or any particular) evil." To support this claim (and deny premise 9), the theist has two options, each having many historical and contemporary proponents:

Option #1: Provide a morally justified reason why God allows all (or any) evil.

Option #2: Argue that there is a morally justified reason for all (or any) evil, but this will often remain unknown.

NO POINTLESS EVIL: TWO OPTIONS

THEODICY: *"Here is the reason."*

SKEPTICAL THEISM: *"We can't know God's reason in all cases, but there is one."*

FIGURE 9.3 Two Possible Responses

We shall consider each option in turn.

Those who follow option #1 are seeking to provide a theodicy. A theodicy is an attempt to provide God's morally justified reason for allowing evil. Daniel Howard-Snyder details some of the most popular theodicies offered by Christians over the years. Among them, he lists the *punishment theodicy* (God is justified in punishing evildoers and suffering is a result), the *freewill theodicy* (being free requires that it is within one's power to do both good and evil), the *natural consequences theodicy* (a consequence of our ancestors turning from God is separation from God and the introduction of evil as a means to finding God again), the *natural law theodicy* (in order to have a world where creatures can choose freely, the world must be governed by predictable laws, but a by-product of such laws is harm to human and non-human animals alike), and the *higher-order goods theodicy* (certain goods such as mercy, compassion, and generosity to the sick require evil).[18]

How are theodicies supposed to show that there is no pointless evil? To see how, imagine that the following circle represents all of the evil in the

18. Howard-Snyder, "God, Evil, and Suffering," 86–101. See also Alvin Plantinga's "Supralapsarianism, or 'O Felix Culpa'" in *Christian Faith and the Problem of Evil*, ed. Peter van Inwagen (Grand Rapids: Eerdmans, 2004), 1–25, where it is argued that the best possible worlds are worlds with divine incarnation and atonement, and thus evil and suffering. For Plantinga, God allows evil because, given his perfect love and goodness, he wanted to create one of the best of all possible worlds, and such worlds require sin and evil.

world. Some of the evil is a result of natural disasters and the like (call it "natural evil"), and some is the result of
moral choices of free creatures (call
it "moral evil"). Next imagine a
bag containing sheets of paper
that list each possible theodicy.
Here is a three-step process for how
to employ theodicies to show that
there is no pointless evil (and that
premise 9 is false):[19]

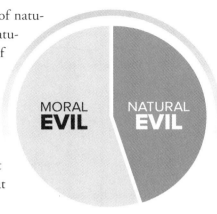

FIGURE 9.4 The World's Evil

FIGURE 9.5 The Theodicy Bag

Step 1: Reach into the "theodicy
bag" and pick a theodicy.

Step 2: Apply the theodicy to
instances of evil.

Step 3: Ask, has all the apparently
pointless evil been explained? If yes,
then the evidential problem of evil
is solved (i.e., premise 9 is shown
false). If there are still cases of unexplained evil, repeat the process until
a positive answer is obtained.

Suppose we reach into our theodicy
bag and pick out the *freewill theodicy*, which runs as follows.[20] In order for
genuine freedom to be obtained, it is required that it be within one's power
to do both right and wrong, to be both good and evil. If we lacked such
freedom, then we would not be responsible for our actions or our character.

---

19. This three-step process is further unpacked in Howard-Snyder's "God, Evil, and Suffering."
20. As explained by Howard-Snyder in "God, Evil, and Suffering," 88.

Since significant freedom is such a great good and requires that humans have the real possibility of doing wrong or developing a vicious character, we have found a reason that would justify God permitting evil. Evil is the result of the misuse of creaturely freedom. God provides the possibility of evil, but we humans actualize the reality of evil when we do wrong.

Assume the freewill theodicy is fundamentally correct. Does this explain why God permits *all* instances of evil? It does seem to account for much, perhaps all, of the moral evil in the world. But it is not clear that the freewill theodicy explains why God permits natural evil—suffering that results from earthquakes, hurricanes, famines, and the like—and if not, then there are still instances of evil left unexplained.[21]

Not to worry: the defender of theodicies can reach into the "theodicy bag," pick out another, and say, "Here is the reason why God permits natural evil." Perhaps we'd try the *natural law theodicy*, which runs as follows.[22] Human freedom requires that our actions are predictable. If, when hiking on the edge of a cliff, Smith intends to stop and ponder the view, then, all things being equal, the effect of his intention will be to stop and ponder the view. If, instead, the effect of his choice results in his doing a back flip off the cliff, then how things come out will be completely out of his control and, in this case, of deadly consequence. In short, if the world did not operate in a regular, lawlike way, we would not be able to predict the effects of our choices, and our freedom would be violated. So, predictability of the effects of our actions requires regular laws

The free will theodicy accounts for the moral evil in the world

MORAL **EVIL**   NATURAL **EVIL**

FIGURE 9.6   Free Will Theodicy and the World's Evil

---

21. It is open to the freewill theodicist to argue that all natural evil, too, is the result of a misuse of creaturely freedom, possibly non-human beings (Satan and his cohorts). See, for example, Plantinga, *The Nature of Necessity*, 192.

22. As explained by Howard-Snyder, "God, Evil, and Suffering," 94–95.

of nature. But the very same laws that allow us to choose freely also, as a by-product, produce harm. The same laws that enable us to walk on this earth also cause a rock to fall and hit a squirrel, or a stubbed toe. The very same laws that are conducive to life also bring about, as a by-product, disease, disaster, defects, and all kinds of natural evils. As C. S. Lewis eloquently puts it, "If matter has a fixed nature and obeys constant laws, not all states of matter will be equally agreeable to the wishes of a given soul."[23] Hence, if the natural law theodicy succeeds, God is justified in allowing natural evils since regular laws of nature are a requirement for creaturely freedom.

It's tempting at this point to think that the natural law theodicy can therefore account for all of the natural evil in the world, and God is vindicated (i.e., the freewill and natural law theodicies together provide the reason for why God allows evil, or again, they show that there is no pointless evil).

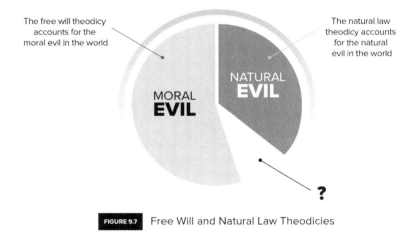

The free will theodicy accounts for the moral evil in the world

The natural law theodicy accounts for the natural evil in the world

MORAL **EVIL**

NATURAL **EVIL**

?

FIGURE 9.7 Free Will and Natural Law Theodicies

But upon reflection, things aren't so simple. The aforementioned theodicies can help us understand why God would be justified in allowing much evil; still, questions can always be asked: why *this* evil or this *type* of evil or *so much* evil? In the end, theodicies seem to fall short of providing a completely satisfying explanation for evils in all cases. The theodicies we just sketched (and we could keep reaching into our "bag" for more; we don't think it

---

23. Lewis, *The Problem of Pain*, 23.

would make a difference) don't *require* God to allow *as much* evil instead of less or *this* instance of evil or *that* kind of evil. If not, it is not clear that we have found God's morally justified reason for permitting evil in all cases.[24]

The reality is that we just don't seem to know, in all cases, God's reasons for allowing certain things to occur. It's hard to see how a particular instance of suffering or pain can bring about some good, or how so much evil could be morally justified by God. Scripture is clear that we are not always able to understand God's reasons for acting. As the apostle Paul rhetorically asks in the doxology of Romans 11, "For who has known the mind of the Lord? Or who has been his counselor" (v. 34)?[25] The obvious answer is, "No one." At the same time, the biblical account of God's nature is clear: God is good, and all that he does is good.[26] This suggests another route for making sense of pain and suffering.

Recall, we are looking for ways to refute premise (9). The theist maintains that since God is good, there is no pointless evil. Two popular strategies have been employed to show this. The first, providing a theodicy, while helpful is ultimately unsuccessful. This naturally leads to a consideration of option #2 (i.e., God has a morally justified reason for allowing evil; we just don't always know it). This route seems to hold much promise and has received a lot of attention as of late.[27] Theists who endorse such a claim are sometimes called *skeptical theists*, not because they are skeptical of God's existence, but rather they are skeptical of our ability to understand God's reasons for allowing evil.

To see how this argument is supposed to go, ask, "Why do you think there is pointless evil in the first place?" The atheist typically will employ what Howard-Snyder calls the "noseeum argument": since we are not able to discern God's reason for allowing evil (whether a particular instance or the overall amount of evil), there must not be one. Since we cannot "see-um," there isn't one.[28]

---

24. Howard-Snyder, "God, Evil, and Suffering," 101.

25. See also Job 38:1–4; 42:2–3; Isa 55:8–9.

26. See, for example, Ps 25:8; 34:8; 119:68; 145:9; Luke 18:19; Acts 14:17; and James 1:17.

27. For an excellent introduction to some of the important literature in this area, see Howard-Snyder, ed., *The Evidential Argument from Evil* (see n. 11 of this chapter). See especially the articles by Rowe, Alston, and Wykstra.

28. For more, see Howard-Snyder, "God, Evil, and Suffering," 103–5.

What can be said in response to the noseeum argument? Sometimes the inference involved in this kind of thinking is reasonable. The general form of the noseeum inference is: "So far as we can tell, there is no *x*; so, there is no *x*."[29] If I (Paul) am in an empty twelve-by-twelve-foot room, I can reasonably infer that no one else is in the room with me. However, there are other instances where the noseeum inference is not appropriate. For example, looking out the window of a small plane flying over a wheat field, the fact that, so far as I can tell, there are no mice, hardly makes it the case that there are none. The crucial question is, what distinguishes the reasonable noseeum inferences from the unreasonable ones? Daniel Howard-Snyder suggests, "A noseeum inference is reasonable only if it is reasonable to believe that we would very likely see (grasp, comprehend, understand) the item in question if it existed."[30] In the cases already discussed, it is reasonable for me to think I would see another person in an otherwise empty room but not a mouse on a field from the sky, given the way my sensory apparatus is equipped. If I had the perceptive apparatus of a hawk, then perhaps the inference would be valid. But human eyesight is simply not equipped (without the aid of an instrument) to see mice in fields from high in the sky. On the other hand, we are equipped (under normal circumstances) to see medium-sized objects—people—in small rooms, and thus if we do not see one, it is likely that there isn't one.

Applied to the problem of evil, is it reasonable to think that we would very likely see or comprehend a reason for evil, if there were one? There are reasons to doubt that we would very likely see God's reason for evil. And if so, then the noseeum inference is not a reasonable one when applied to the problem of evil. As finite persons, our perspective and knowledge are severely limited. We occupy a tiny slice of time, a mere vapor, from a radically limited perspective located on a speck of a speck, relative to a massive universe of events through which God is working to accomplish his plans and purposes. Our cognitive powers and imagination are such that we simply do not have the big picture before us in the way that God does. An all-knowing and eternal God, on the other hand, sees all of history, including the future, and providentially orders the events of the world so that his purposes are

---

29. Howard-Snyder, 103.
30. Howard-Snyder, 105.

ultimately achieved. Arguably, such a being will have reasons for acting that are beyond our ability to grasp. Thus, we should not expect to understand the complex connections between various events, including events of pain and suffering, allowed by God as he accomplishes his purposes.

The debate boils down to the question of which is more reasonable to believe: the reality of pointless evil or a wholly good God who has reasons for evil of which we are unaware. If, as we've argued, the skeptical theist is right, then it is not reasonable to think there is pointless evil. On the other hand, as we've shown in the chapter on God's existence, there are good reasons to think a maximally perfect God exists. It's not much of a fair fight. If a maximally perfect God exists, there is no pointless evil, even if we are not privy to God's reasons for permitting evil. This much theists of any variety—Jewish, Christian, Muslim—can affirm. But Christianity can go a step further than this mere theism. For in Christ, we find *God's answer* to the problem of evil, and we find the only remedy to cope with its sting. We turn now to a discussion of the emotional problem of evil.

The Emotional Problem of Evil

When staring into the face of evil—utter, pure evil—human nature is quickly laid bare. It is natural to cry out to God for help. "Why *this* suffering, God? Why *this much* suffering, God?" Yet often in these moments of suffering great and small, God seems distant, silent, and unconcerned. What to do?

It seems that there are only two options: *rest* and *trust* in God or *revolt* and *reject* God; a turning toward or a turning away; an opening of self or a closing of self.[31] But in revolting and rejecting God, how does one deal with pain and suffering? It seems there are two options here, as well: either deaden the pain by swimming in a sea of pleasure (i.e., by embracing *epicureanism*), or grit one's teeth and bear the pain as bravely as possible in a godless world (i.e., by embracing *stoicism*).[32] Consider two case studies:

---

31. Rest and trust need not be immediate. This turning to God allows for the believer to wrestle with God, to lean into God with doubts, and to work through emotions of anger and disappointment. This process might not be so restful, but it is moving toward rest and trust. It is often the only path to rest and trust.

32. See Ravi Zacharias, *Can Man Live Without God* (Nashville: W Publishing Group, 1994), 67.

The Plague in Athens. It was during the second year of the Peloponnesian war, in 430 BC, that the plague struck Athens. As the deadly disease rampaged through the packed city, killing over one-third of the population, the historian Thucydides reported that everyone began to live for the pleasure of the moment since they were going to die anyway. "No one held back in awe, either by fear of the gods or by the laws of men: not by the gods, because men concluded it was all the same whether they worshipped or not, seeing that they all perished alike; and not by the laws, because no one expected to live till he was tried and punished for his crimes."[33]

The Jewish Holocaust. As a young teenager, Elie Wiesel was a faithful, God-fearing Jew. But as he and his family, along with his fellow Jews, were deported from their homes and brought to Auschwitz in 1945, his life took a drastic turn for the worst. On his first night in the death camp, he came face-to-face with utter evil . . . yet God remained silent, and he turned away from God. "For the first time, I felt revolt rise up in me. Why should I bless His name? The Eternal, Lord of the Universe, the All-Powerful and Terrible, was silent. What had I to thank Him for?"[34] Wiesel walked away from God, and never looked back.

In each case, *hope* is dashed on the rocks of fate, and man's problem of pain and suffering remains unanswered. Man attempts to drown out the silence of God by a kind of closing of self, a turning of the soul away from God. But *toward* what? One is reminded of Bertrand Russell's quip: if atheism is true, then all we can do is build our lives on the "firm foundation of unyielding despair."[35] This is the atheist's problem of evil: there is no answer, no solution whatsoever. With atheism, all we can do is survive suffering and evil since it is all and only pointless.

---

33. Thucydides, *The History of the Peloponnesian War*, in *The Landmark Thucydides: A Comprehensive Guide to the Peloponnesian War*, trans. Richard Crawley, ed. Robert B. Strassler (New York: Touchstone, 1998), 2.53.

34. Elie Wiesel, *Night* (New York: Bantam Books, 1982), 31.

35. Bertrand Russell, *Why I Am Not a Christian* (New York: Touchstone, 1967), 107.

There is an answer to the problem of human suffering. It requires an opening of self, not a closing; a turning of one's soul toward God. For in doing so, we are led not to an answer, but to the Answerer.

What is God's answer to the problem of man's suffering? It is a person—Jesus—on a cross. Christ on the cross—that is God's answer to the problem of pain and suffering.[36] He has opened himself up to evil, and ultimately has taken it all upon himself on the cross. At the cross, God defeated pain and suffering, sin and darkness, and one day, for those who trust in Jesus, all of it will be washed away. Moreover, the cross provides the means for human flourishing and fulfillment, both in this life and in the next. In the end the world will be made right again: the broken healed, the bent straightened, the fallen redeemed and restored. If evil is, as one noted atheist describes it, "an ought-not-to-be,"[37] then one day all will be made as it should be, and those who trust in Jesus will experience the ultimate fulfillment of their natures—true happiness—for all of eternity with God.

This does justice to the problem, does it not? For the problem of suffering is more than just a philosophical problem (it is no less)—it is something we all deal with at the level of our lives. As such, it demands an existential response. As the late Harvard theologian Arthur C. McGill put it, "If the existence of Christians is oriented *toward* Christ as the life and light of God, it is in movement *away from* evil and death and darkness. In other words, the Christian is *on the way* from evil to good, from death to life, from darkness to light. He finds himself in a state of pilgrimage."[38] But it is a pilgrimage toward and with Christ. It is an invitation to experience the inner life of the triune God expressed in self-giving love to others. And it is the only way to make sense of pain and suffering in a world of violence.

---

36. Peter Kreeft, *Making Sense out of Suffering* (Ann Arbor, MI: Servant Books, 1986), chap. 7.

37. Richard Gale, "Evil as Evidence for God," in Moreland, Meister, and Sweis, eds., *Debating Christian Theism*, 197 (see chap. 3, n. 32).

38. Arthur C. McGill, *Suffering: A Test Case of Theological Method* (Eugene, OR: Wipf & Stock, 1982), 26.

Assignments

Assignment 9-1: Making Gospel Connections

Ask your nonbelieving friend what he or she thinks will bring happiness. Explore his or her understanding of happiness and draw connections to the problem of pain and suffering in the world. Try to discern whether your friend's objection to God with respect to evil is intellectual or emotional (or both). Respond accordingly.

Assignment 9-2

Discuss how the reality of evil in our world is a problem for the atheist. Specifically, discuss the *grounding problem* (what grounds objective evil?) and the *meaning problem* (how can we make sense of evil?), given atheism.

Assignment 9-3

Answer the following questions:

1. Which version of the problem of evil do you struggle with the most: the intellectual or the emotional?
2. Why do you think the problem of evil is so difficult for modern man? Does the contemporary view of happiness as sensual pleasure have anything to do with it?
3. Discuss the response offered in the text to the "free but perfect objection." Do you agree that God cannot create a world where free creatures always do good?
4. Which theodicy seems most compelling to you? Why?
5. Do you agree or disagree with the claim that we are just not in a position to know in all cases what God's morally justified reason for permitting evil is?
6. How is, paradoxically, God the only solution to the problem of evil?
7. Discuss how God's answer to the problem of evil is the only possible answer that is ultimately satisfying.

Suggested Reading

Kreeft, Peter. *Making Sense out of Suffering.* Ann Arbor: Servant Books, 1986.

Lewis, C. S. *A Grief Observed.* New York: HarperOne, 1994.

———. *The Problem of Pain.* New York: HarperOne, 2001.

Plantinga, Alvin. *God, Freedom, and Evil.* Grand Rapids: Eerdmans, 1974.

CHAPTER 10

Counterfeit Gospels: World Religions

By the late 1960s, many sociologists were predicting the death of God by the end of the twentieth century. The idea was that culture would become secular as man comes of age and throws off the shackles of religion. A curious thing happened, however. Religion has not gone away. In fact, as many sociologists now admit, we live in a post-secular age.[1] We inhabit, as Stephen Prothero puts it, a "furiously religious planet."[2] Religion is poised, in the twenty-first century, to play a dominant role in society. In America, where large swaths of the country feature churches on every corner, it is natural to think that the main player in religion is Christianity. But the Christian religion is not the only game in town. Many of our neighbors are Muslim, Jewish, Buddhist, Hindu, Mormon, Jehovah's Witnesses, and more.

Many books on apologetics spill a great deal of ink helping combat the challenge of atheism. That challenge is real, and it is important to help others learn how to show atheism and/or naturalism to be false. It is much more likely, however, that you will meet a religious person when doing evangelism and apologetics (recent studies show, for example, that only 7 percent of American adults are atheist or agnostic).[3] For that reason, we have included in this book two chapters dealing with other religions. In this

---

1. Douglas Jacobsen and Rhonda Hustedt Jacobsen, "Postsecular America: A New Context for Higher Education," *The American University in a Postsecular Age*, ed. Douglas Jacobsen and Rhonda Hustedt Jacobsen (Oxford: Oxford University Press, 2008), 10.

2. Stephen Prothero, *God Is Not One* (New York: HarperOne, 2010), 4.

3. For a nice summary of recent statistics on atheism in America, see Michael Lipka, "10 Facts about Atheists," Pew Research Center, June 1, 2016, http://www.pewresearch.org/fact-tank/2016/06/01/10-facts-about-atheists/.

chapter we shall deal with four major world religions, showing how they
differ and addressing common questions that often arise in interreligious
dialogue. In the next chapter, we'll consider a couple of home-grown religions, the so-called cults of Christianity that began in America and are now
rapidly expanding throughout the world.

It is vogue in our culture to paint all religions with the same broad brush,
minimizing their differences and accentuating their similarities. The New
Atheist cries out, "Religion poisons everything," heaping guilt on all religions
and all religious people without distinction.[4] The religious pluralist cries out,
"All religions are equally valid," leveling all religions even as they are relegated
to the realm of private and subjective beliefs. But all religions are not equal
in any interesting sense. Each religion is different: identifying a different fundamental human predicament and solution, employing different techniques
to connect with the divine, and following different exemplars of the faith. In
this chapter we shall consider the problem, solution, techniques, and exemplars of Islam, Judaism, Hinduism, and Buddhism.[5] While this discussion
will be introductory, our hope is that you will understand the basic differences between the world religions and be better prepared to point to the truth
of Christianity in the face of these counterfeit gospels.

Figure 10.1	Islam	Judaism	Hinduism	Buddhism
Problem	Self-sufficiency	Exile	Samsara	Suffering
Solution	Submission	Return	Moksha	Nirvana
Technique	Five Pillars of Islam	Law of Moses	Ritual, knowledge, or devotion	Noble Eightfold Path
Exemplar	Muhammad	Moses	Brahmin priests, Hindu holy man, or the everyday man	Buddha

4. This is the subtitle to the late Christopher Hitchens's book *God Is Not Great: How Religion Poisons Everything* (New York: Hachette, 2007).

5. This approach to understanding religions is from Prothero, *God Is Not One*. Prothero discusses eight rival religions, highlighting their individual differences with respect to problem, solution, technique, and exemplars.

Islam

With more than 1.6 billion followers, Islam is the second-largest religion (to Christianity's 2.3 billion followers) in the world. For many, given the near-daily threat of Islamic terrorism from suicide bombers, the Taliban, al-Qaeda operatives, and ISIS, Islam inspires fear. Yet chances are, the typical Muslim will be peaceful, insisting that Islam is a religion of peace and devotion to Allah, the one true God. What exactly is Islam?

The Arabic word *Islam* means "submission" or "surrender," and this signifies the key human problem identified by Islam.[6] Man's fundamental problem is not sin (Muslims reject the doctrine of original sin); rather, man's fundamental problem is pride and self-sufficiency. The solution to this self-sufficiency is submission to Allah. Submission will bring peace in this life and paradise in the next.[7] The core practices that take one from self-sufficiency to submission, from striving to peace, are the five pillars of Islam. These five pillars represent essential practices for all faithful Muslims and include confession (*shahada*), daily prayer (*salat*), fasting (*sawm*), giving (*zakat*), and pilgrimage to Mecca at least once (*hajj*) if possible.[8]

The most fundamental confession in Islam, the *shahada* affirms the exclusive worship of the one unitarian God, Allah, and obedience to the prophet of God, Muhammad: "I testify that there is no god but God, and Muhammad is the messenger of God."[9] Muhammad, born in AD 570, is the founder of Islam and the greatest prophet of Allah. He is the key exemplar of the Islamic religion. At age forty, this illiterate merchant reportedly received messages from Allah through the angel Gabriel from AD 610 until his death in 632. These messages have been codified within the Qur'an (which means "recitation"), which is considered the very word of God, and along with the Hadiths (a collection of informal sayings and other deeds of Muhammad), constitute the authoritative writings of Islam.

Three key issues to understand when engaging Muslims in evangelism are (1) the charge that the Trinity amounts to polytheism, (2) the Muslim

---

6. Prothero, 27.
7. Prothero, 32.
8. For a nice discussion of each of the five pillars, see Winfried Corduan, *Neighboring Faiths*, 2nd ed. (Downers Grove, IL: InterVarsity Press, 2012), 118–25.
9. Prothero, *God Is Not One*, 33.

denial of the incarnation of Christ, and (3) the claim that Old Testament Yahweh wars are just like Islamic jihad. Regarding the Muslim teaching on the Trinity, the Qur'an explicitly states the doctrine is blasphemous:

> The Messiah, Jesus the son of Mary, was no more than God's apostle and His Word which He cast to Mary: a spirit from Him. So believe in God and His apostles and do not say: 'Three.' Forbear, and it shall be better for you. God is but one God. God forbid that He should have a son! (Qur'an 4:171)[10]

God is a unity. God is one. The Christian doctrine of the Trinity is, according to Islam, the idea that God is not a unity, not one. Rather, Christianity is a form of polytheism, worshipping three gods: Father, Son, and Holy Spirit. In reply, it is important to point out that Christianity is not polytheistic. Christianity is monotheistic. The Christian doctrine of the Trinity endorses the claim that God is three persons and one divine substance. If there were three persons and three divine substances, then polytheism would be true. But that is not how Christians understand the Trinity.[11]

The Muslim Jesus was born of the virgin Mary, was a prophet of Allah, and a miracle worker.[12] Muslims do believe (in one sense) in Jesus and revere him as an important prophet. What Muslims deny, however, is that Jesus is divine. Jesus is not the incarnate, preexisting eternal Son.[13] God has no equals, and he cannot become less than God: "Say: 'God is One, the Eternal God. He begot none, nor was He begotten. None is equal to Him'" (Qur'an 112:1–4). Thus, to worship the man Jesus, as Christians do, is to commit idolatry. In reply, we should point out that Christians worship God—the eternal Son—who is revealed in the one man Jesus. According to the orthodox understanding of Christ set out at the Council of Chalcedon in AD 451, Jesus is fully God, fully man, one person, with two—a divine

---

10. All references to the Qur'an are from *The Koran: With Parallel Arabic Text*, trans. N. J. Dawood (London: Penguin Books, 1994).

11. For an accessible discussion of how Christians traditionally have understood the Trinity, see Thomas V. Morris, *Our Idea of God: An Introduction to Philosophical Theology* (Vancouver: Regent College Publishing, 2002), chap. 9.

12. For more on the Muslim understanding of Jesus, see David B. Capes, Rodney Reeves, and E. Randolph Richards, *Rediscovering Jesus: An Introduction to Biblical, Religious and Cultural Perspectives on Christ* (Downers Grove, IL: InterVarsity Press, 2015), chap. 10.

13. Nor did Jesus die on the cross since Allah would never abandon a great prophet of God.

and human—natures. While this is, at the end of the day, mysterious, there is nothing obviously incoherent about the Christian understanding of the incarnation, nor is it idolatrous to worship the divine Son of God, who has taken on an additional (human) nature in the incarnation.[14]

Finally, how can Christians condemn Muslim jihad given the violence of Yahweh in the Old Testament? The idea is that the Christian God is just as violent as Allah, and if Christians are going to condemn Allah, they should also condemn Yahweh in the Old Testament. Is the comparison between Muslim jihad and Old Testament wars fair? For at least two reasons, this is a poor comparison. First, *the Old Testament war commands are limited to a specific time and place in God's unfolding plan of redemption and blessing to all, whereas the Qur'an war commands are open-ended and ongoing.*[15] For example, according to Gen 15:13–16, God waited more than 400 years before he pronounced judgment on the Canaanites and ordered them driven out of the land. God's command was both a judgment on a wicked people group and part of his ongoing redemptive plan to bring blessing to all nations through Israel (Gen 12:1–3). In contrast, the Qur'an issues enduring commands to war against non-Muslims. These commands to violence are not divine judgments on evil actions (as in the case of the Canaanites) but religious persecution of anyone who fails to believe in Allah, for the Muslim is "the noblest" (Qur'an 98:7) while the unbeliever is "the vilest" (Qur'an 98:6) of all creatures. Thus, the Muslim is to "make war on [the unbelievers] until idolatry shall cease and God's religion shall reign supreme" (Qur'an 8:40). This command to jihad is ongoing and open-ended, whereas the command to war in the Old Testament is limited and localized to the land in Palestine. Second, *the trajectory of Islam is one of domination, whereas the trajectory of Christianity is one of grace.*[16] During his lifetime, the once-peaceful Muhammad carried out more than eighty-six

---

14. For a nice discussion of how to make sense of these claims, see Thomas D. Senor, "The Incarnation," in *The Routledge Companion to Philosophy of Religion*, ed. Chad Meister and Paul Copan (New York: Routledge, 2007), 556–65; and Thomas Morris, *The Logic of God Incarnate* (Ithaca, NY: Cornell University Press, 1986).

15. For more see Paul Copan and Matthew Flannagan, *Did God Really Command Genocide?* (Grand Rapids: Baker, 2014), chap. 21.

16. Nabeel Qureshi, *Answering Jihad: A Better Way Forward* (Grand Rapids: Zondervan, 2016), 123–24.

military campaigns.[17] Just before his death, after conquering the Arabian Peninsula, Muhammad told his followers, "I was ordered to fight all men until they say, 'There is no God but Allah.'"[18] Early Muslims followed their leader's example, conquering over one-third of the known world 150 years after his death.[19] The Islamic conquest that marked the life of Muhammad and early Islam has continued unabated to the present day. Contrast this trajectory with the ethic of patience and love embodied by Yahweh in the Old Testament and by Jesus in the New Testament. As Nabeel Qureshi summarizes, "Old Testament warfare is not meant to be an example that Christians model their lives around today. The trajectory in Christianity is not from peaceful to violent, but vice versa."[20]

Judaism

Central to Judaism is the belief in one God, who has called for himself a people—the Jewish people—to be his representatives on earth and a blessing to all. Being chosen by God brings with it great responsibility. God has provided the law—rules for right conduct—so that the Jewish people can demonstrate that living according to God's plan is both possible and good for the world. The problem is that something has gone wrong: the world is not as it should be. The first couple—Adam and Eve—disobeyed God and were exiled from the garden of Eden. The world is broken. Humanity is alienated from God. Repair of this world is needed. By walking humbly with God (Mic 6:8), this repair can be achieved. While Judaism affirms a belief in the afterlife, this is not of primary concern. Salvation is primarily this-worldly and attainable through good works as the Jewish people prepare the way for the Messiah and, ultimately, the restoration of all things.

There are roughly 14 million Jewish people worldwide today. This relatively small group has exerted an inordinate amount of influence in the world: many famous actors, writers, composers, politicians, and businesspeople are Jewish. To understand contemporary Judaism, one must first understand the history of the Jewish people and their relationship to the

---

17. Copan and Flannagan, *Did God Really Command Genocide?*, 280.
18. Sahih Bukhari, 1.2.25, as quoted in Copan and Flannagan, 279.
19. Qureshi, *Answering Jihad*, 50.
20. Qureshi, 125.

land and the temple. According to Winfried Corduan, early Judaism can be understood in terms of two eras: (1) the first commonwealth, from the time of Moses's reception of the law, around 1450 BC, until the destruction of the first temple and the subsequent exile of the Jews into Babylon, ending in 541 BC; and (2) the second commonwealth, beginning with the rebuilding of the temple after the Babylonian exile, around 515 BC, extending through the destruction of the second temple by the Romans in AD 70.[21] With the destruction of the temple in AD 70, as we noted in chapter 5, the world of Judaism changed dramatically. The Jews were driven from the land, and many of the sects of Judaism were destroyed (including the Sadducees, the Zealots, and the Essenes). The only surviving party of the Jews were the Pharisees, whose rabbinic spiritual descendants shaped Jewish thought and life for the next two millennia.[22]

The three main branches of contemporary Judaism understand themselves in relation to the rabbinic law, which now includes the Jewish Scripture (the Old Testament) and the Talmud, a mammoth collection of rabbinic interpretations of the law (called the Mishnah) and a collection of narratives illustrating application of the law (called the Gemara): Orthodox Jews adhere to the law, Reform Jews focus on the ethical core of the law, and Conservative Jews focus on Jewish tradition embodied within the law (the latter two branches are more recent attempts to maintain Jewish identity within a constantly changing contemporary culture).[23] With the establishment of the nation of Israel in 1948, some speak of a third Jewish commonwealth.[24] The temple, however, has not been rebuilt. In its place stands the Dome of the Rock, the second most holy site (the *Kaaba* in Mecca is considered the holiest site) of Islam.

The fundamental problem, according to Judaism, is exile, "distance from God and from where we ought to be." The solution is return, "to go back to God and our true home."[25] The main exemplar of Judaism is Moses. The technique of Judaism is right living: following the law of Moses, the 613 *mitzvot* (commandments) described in Jewish Scriptures and expounded in

21. Corduan, *Neighboring Faiths*, 63.
22. Corduan, 69.
23. Corduan, 78.
24. Corduan, 86–87.
25. Prothero, *God Is Not One*, 253.

the Talmud. While belief is important in Judaism (e.g., the *Shema*, "Listen, Israel: The LORD our God, the LORD is one" [Deut 6:4] has been recited for centuries at Jewish worship services), it is primarily a religion of *practice* (even the Shema points beyond doctrine to practice, beginning in 6:5 with "Love the LORD your God with all your heart, with all your soul, and with all your strength" and continuing on through verse 9 with prescriptions for right living).[26] Until the Messiah comes, "it is the job of the Jewish people to make things ready and to make things right—to 'repair the world' and put an end to exile."[27]

When sharing the gospel with your Jewish acquaintances, remember they too need the Messiah, Jesus. Remind them that Jesus was Jewish. Encourage them that if they become Christian, they do not need to leave their Jewish identity behind. Tell them that God's plan for restoring the world (*tikkun olam*) begins by transforming individual hearts and lives. Show them how Jesus fulfilled all the Old Testament prophecies about the coming Messiah (e.g., from the seed of Abraham [Gen 18:18], born in Bethlehem [Mic 5:2], a suffering servant [Isaiah 53], etc.). Encourage them to read the Gospel of Matthew, written to show Jewish people that Jesus is the Messiah.[28] Point them to Christian organizations that specifically reach out to Jewish people, such as Jews for Jesus.[29] The good news is that all—Jews and Gentiles—can find shalom—forgiveness of sins, right relationship with God, a way "home" through the shed blood of Christ on the cross. This is good news indeed!

Coda: Do Muslims and Jews Worship the Same God as Christians?

In December 2015, controversy exploded when Wheaton College professor of political science Larycia Hawkins posted to her Facebook page the following statement: "I stand in religious solidarity with Muslims because they,

---

26. Prothero, 251–52.
27. Prothero, 254.
28. "Matthew intends for his audience to be well versed in all the ways Jesus speaks and acts to fulfill Scripture, both prophetically and typologically. The better you know the Old Testament—the Bible of Jesus and Matthew—the better you will be able to understand Matthew's Jesus and his significance. . . . Matthew's Jesus is the consummate teacher, a prophet like Moses who is superior to Moses in every way." Capes, Reeves, and Richards, *Rediscovering Jesus*, 48, 52.
29. Found online at www.jewsforjesus.org.

like me, a Christian, are people of the book. And as Pope Francis stated last week, we worship the same God."[30]

Wheaton's administration put Professor Hawkins on leave over concerns regarding the theological orthodoxy of her "same God" claim. Not surprisingly, heated debate ensued. Yale Divinity School theologian Miroslav Volf, in an essay published in the *Washington Post*, argued that Hawkins's suspension was not over issues of theology, but was a result of anti-Muslim bigotry.[31] Notable philosophers and theologians published opinion pieces, blogs, and essays, either in support of the "same God" claim (e.g., Baylor's Frank Beckwith, Notre Dame's Michael Rea) or against it (e.g., Tyndale University's Rich Davis, Southern Seminary's president Albert Mohler).[32] For some it seems obvious that Muslims and Christians worship the same God. For

------

30. A summary of the issues and events surrounding Hawkins's claim can be found in Bob Smietana, "Wheaton College Suspends Hijab-Wearing Professor After 'Same God' Comment," *Christianity Today*, December 15, 2015, http://www.christianitytoday.com/gleanings/2015/december/wheaton-college-hijab-professor-same-god-larycia-hawkins.html.

31. Miroslav Volf, "Wheaton Professor's Suspension Is about Anti-Muslim bigotry, Not Theology," *Washington Post*, December 17, 2015, https://www.washingtonpost.com/news/acts-of-faith/wp/2015/12/17/wheaton-professors-suspension-is-about-anti-muslim-bigotry-not-theology/.

32. For a nice roundup of many of these essays (pro and con) for the "same God" thesis, see Frank Beckwith's blog post "Muslims, Christians, and the Same God: Round-Up with Advice to Volf and Clark (with Addendum)," *Return to Rome*, January 2, 2016, http://romereturn.blogspot.com/2016/01/muslims-christians-and-same-god-round.html?m=1.

others, it seems equally obvious they do not. Is the "same God" thesis true? Do Muslims and Christians worship the same God?

The question is complicated by the fact that Muslims and Christians believe many of the same things *about* God. They both believe God is eternal, one, necessary, omnipotent, omniscient, and the Creator of the world. This common philosophical conception of God was believed, as Frank Beckwith points out, by the great medieval thinkers of the Abrahamic religions—Saint Thomas Aquinas (Christian), Moses Maimonides (Jewish), and Avicenna (Muslim)—and is affirmed by many Christians, Muslims, and Jews today.[33] But, it is argued, if Muslims and Christians (and Jews) share the same common philosophical conception of God, then they *believe in* the same God. We think this is mistaken.

"Believing that" something is the case is different from "believing in" something or someone. "Belief in" adds the idea of trust or reliance upon. It is more robust than mere "belief that." To "believe in" God is to believe (1) that God exists and has the character he has and (2) to trust in God (i.e., the God who is believed to exist and have the character he has).[34] But Christians believe God is essentially triune and incarnate, whereas Muslims believe God is essentially non-triune and non-incarnate. Thus, when we move from the common philosophical conception of God to what Christians and Muslims actually believe about the God they trust and rely upon, the beliefs are quite different—even contradictory. Christians believe *in* a different God than Muslims do. Moreover, if the Christian God exists, then the Muslim God does not. If the Muslim God exists, then the Christian God does not. Thus, either way, we are not worshipping the same God.[35] Thus, while it is true that Muslims and Christians believe many of the same things *about* God, it is false that they believe *in*, and hence, worship the same God.

---

33. Francis J. Beckwith, "Why Muslims and Christians Worship the Same God," *The Catholic Thing* (blog), January 7, 2016, http://www.thecatholicthing.org/2016/01/07/why-muslims-and -christians-worship-the-same-god/.

34. For an excellent discussion of the notion of "belief in," see Jeroen de Ridder and Rene van Woudenberg, "Referring to, Believing in, and Worshiping the Same God: A Reformed View," *Faith and Philosophy* 31, no.1 (2014): 46–67.

35. As de Ridder and van Woudenberg put it, "Worship of God . . . requires belief in God. And there can be no adequate belief in God unless there is reference to God. And there can be no reference to God, unless God exists" (59).

Does this mean, by parity of reasoning, that the Jews in the Old Testament did not worship the same God as Christians? This would be odd given Jesus's claim to make God the Father (i.e., the same God believed in by the Jews in the Old Testament) known (John 17:25–26). In response, as Nabeel Qureshi notes, "the Trinity is an elaboration of Jewish theology, not a rejection. By contrast, [Islam is the] categorical rejection of the Trinity, Jesus's deity, and the fatherhood of God, doctrines that are grounded in the pages of the New Testament and firmly established centuries before the advent of Islam."[36] Thus, the God of the Old Testament is the same God Jesus proclaimed and revealed as triune in the New Testament. The Jews of the Old Testament believed in and worshipped the same God as Christians do today. The same cannot be said of modern Jews given their rejection of God's progressive revelation of Jesus. Worship of and belief in God do not require that our concept of God match the determinate reality of God perfectly, but it does require that our beliefs not be fundamentally mistaken, as is the case with Islam and, now that God has revealed himself most clearly in his Son, the Jewish faith today.

Hinduism

With more than 900 million followers, Hinduism is the third-largest religion (behind Christianity and Islam) in the world today. It is also, given its diversity and lack of dogma, one of the most difficult to understand. As Winfried Corduan notes, the main criterion for a religious group to count as Hindu is to fit within the traditional culture of India, most importantly in accepting the caste system.[37] Interestingly, Hinduism makes almost no restrictions on personal belief. As Prothero puts it, "Hinduism is what Hindus do and think, and what Hindus do and think is almost everything under the sun."[38]

Despite this diversity, there are broad practices and beliefs that are in common across the world of Hinduism. There are three major phases to Hinduism: Vedic Hinduism (beginning around 1500 BC), Advaita Vedanta Hinduism (beginning around 500 BC), and Bhakti Hinduism (beginning around 200 BC). Each new version of Hinduism builds on and exists (often

---

36. Qureshi, *Answering Jihad*, 115.
37. Corduan, *Neighboring Faiths*, 267.
38. Prothero, *God Is Not One*, 135.

in tension) with earlier versions. Common to all phases of Hinduism is the problem of *samsara*, which refers to the endless and unsatisfactory cycle of life, death, and rebirth. The solution is to achieve *moksha*, release from the endless cycle and spiritual liberation.

The caste system and the professional priest-hood are products of the earliest phase of Hinduism. The Vedic religion takes its name from the Hindu holy books, the Vedas, a collection of prayerful hymns, mantras, chants, and incantations for priests to follow in carrying out their duties.[39] The caste system, which has its roots in Vedic Scriptures, pro-vides a blueprint—like Plato in *The Republic*—of the ideal society. The priestly class, the Brahmins, are at the top, followed by the soldier class (the Kshatriyas), the merchant

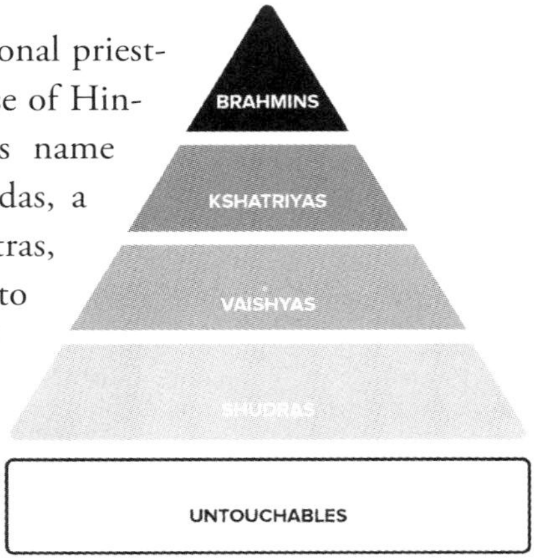

FIGURE 10.2   The Hindu Caste System

class (the Vaishyas), and the servant class (the Shudras). Outside the caste system are the "outcastes" or "untouchables," such as the Dalits, a perse-cuted and dejected people group existing on the fringe of Hindu society.[40] While it is not possible to switch castes or marry someone from another caste, through reincarnation one can die and be reborn as another being at a higher (or lower) caste. Whether or not one reincarnates at a higher or lower caste depends on one's *karma*: good actions produce good karma and reincarnation to higher levels of being, while bad actions produce bad karma and reincarnation to lower levels of being. Under Vedic Hinduism, release (*moksha*) from the cycle of reincarnation can be achieved through obedience to all the ritual obligations and total submission to the priests.[41]

---

39. Corduan, *Neighboring Faiths*, 271–72.

40. According to a 2011 census, there are more than 200 million Dalits in India. If you add to this number Christian and Muslim Dalits, there are more than 300 million people, a quarter of India's 1.2 billion citi-zens, who are Dalits. See a summary of the census published on the website of the International Dalit Sol-idarity Network, March 29, 2013, http://idsn.org/india-official-dalit-population-exceeds-200-million/.

41. Corduan, *Neighboring Faiths*, 279.

In the sixth century BC, a revolt against the Brahmins took place that sought to replace an empty ritualism with a belief system of mystical contemplation.[42] The result is Advaita Vedanta Hinduism, captured in a group of writings called the Upanishads. Central to this intellectual Hinduism is the idea that "Atman is Brahman." Atman, each individual soul, is identical to Brahman, the infinite and distinctionless soul of the world. The belief in distinctions (right and wrong, good and evil, body and soul, knower and thing known) are *maya*, illusion. Moksha, according to Advaita Vedanta Hinduism, is not achieved through external ritual but from within, by realizing and experiencing the Atman-Brahman identity.

The more philosophical Advaita Vedanta Hinduism appealed to the elites of India, but it offered little for the common person. Consequently, a second revolt against established Hinduism took place in the middle of the first millennium AD.[43] This third phase of Hinduism focused on devotion to a particular god of one's own choosing from the pantheon of gods.[44] Much of contemporary Hinduism fits into this third phase, known as Bhakti, or "devotional," Hinduism. Under Bhatki Hinduism, moksha is achieved not through ritual or knowledge, but through devotion to, and the mercy of, one's chosen god.[45]

Given the diversity of thought within Hinduism, it is important, when sharing the gospel with Hindus, to listen and discern what they actually believe. Of central importance will be your defense of the exclusivity of Christianity (see chapter 8). Jesus is not one more God that can be added to the pantheon of deities (Bhatki Hinduism) or one more illusion within the vast ocean of infinite being that exists without distinction (Advaita Vedanta Hinduism). According to Christianity, there are real distinctions in the world, the most fundamental of which is the distinction between the Creator and creature. Help them understand that truth, which obtains when one thing (a thought, belief, or statement) corresponds to another thing (reality, the world), is exclusive (see chapters 2 and 8). If Christianity

42. Corduan, 279.
43. Corduan, 281. Corduan notes that the seeds of this third phase of Hinduism were planted much earlier, around 200 BC, when the Bhagavad-Gita was written.
44. While it is often said that there are more than 330 million Hindu gods, this is certainly an exaggeration. For more, see Corduan, 282–83.
45. Major deities include Brahma (the creator god), Vishnu (the preserver god), and Shiva (the destroyer god). For more on the pantheon of Hindu gods, see Corduan, 282–93.

is true, then Hinduism, in any of its phases, is false at those points where it contradicts Christianity.

Finally, Hindus already believe in a moral universe. They already believe that their actions matter—that they have eternal consequences for good or ill. Help them see that the truth behind the belief in karma is that there is a moral law, and this moral law gives us reason to think there is a moral law giver (see chapter 3). Lovingly point out to them that man's fundamental problem is not that we are caught on an unending wheel of suffering, death, and rebirth, but rather that we are sinful creatures who fall short of the moral law and are in need of grace and forgiveness. In short, help them understand who Jesus is (see chapter 6) and to see the gospel as the only hope for finding genuine "release"—not from an unending cycle of suffering, but from the sin and guilt that hamper life and weigh us down.

Buddhism

According to legend, the founder of Buddhism, Siddhartha Gautama, was born a prince in India around the sixth century BC.[46] Within days of giving birth, his mother died, and Siddhartha was raised by his father, who wished him to become a great king. His early life was a utopian experience of pleasure and provision devoid of suffering, all within the palace walls. He married and had a son, yet still he grew curious about the surrounding world.

One day Siddhartha asked his father if he could explore the countryside. His father reluctantly agreed and proceeded to remove all evidence of suffering from the planned path of Siddhartha's chariot. However, as he explored the countryside, Siddhartha was exposed to four troubling states of affairs: a sick person, an old person, a corpse, and a holy man living a life of renunciation. Returning to the palace, Siddhartha could no longer enjoy the comfort and pleasure of his sheltered life. He resolved to live as a religious man and at age twenty-nine left his wife and son to embark on a spiritual journey seeking enlightenment.

After six years of wandering, he finally found enlightenment while sitting under a fig tree. He had become the Buddha, the "Awakened One." For

---

46. The life of Gautama Buddha is sometimes listed as 563–483 BC, but the exact dates are not known. See Prothero, *God Is Not One*, 174.

the rest of his life, he taught others the way of enlightenment, dying at the age of eighty after eating a spoiled piece of meat given to him as an offering.

The problem the Buddha discovered while sitting under the fig tree is that life is full of suffering. This is why reincarnation is considered a bad thing within all Eastern religions. The goal, then, is to reach nirvana, a state of bliss beyond description, where there is no suffering or attachment. The path to nirvana is the Noble Eightfold Path. By deliberately cultivating the right view, intention, speech, action, livelihood (becoming a monk), effort, mindfulness, and concentration, one can find release from the attachments of life and attain nirvana, either in this life or the next.[47]

Today there are roughly 450 million Buddhists in the world.[48] While there are two main branches of Buddhism, Theravada Buddhism and Mahayana Buddhism, in reality, the Buddhist religion is incredibly diverse, making it difficult to identify a basic core. Upon Buddha's death, his teachings, canonized by a council of his followers into a collection called the *Tripitaka*, spread rapidly throughout India.[49] Theravada Buddhism is largely a religion centered on the monks (*bikhus*), who alone can attain nirvana and are the focus of religious practice. The laity, according to Theravada Buddhism, exist to support the monks and maintain the temple. In doing so, the laity can build up merit for a better incarnation and the possibility of future enlightenment.

Mahayana Buddhism arose around 200 BC, offering the possibility of nirvana to all, not just the monks. Adopting new scriptures, such as the Lotus Sutra or the Heart Sutra, the Mahayanists championed a new exemplar called the *bodhisattva* or "Buddha-in-the-making."[50] By living a life of compassion, every human being could now become a "Buddha-in-the-making" and eventually attain nirvana. Moreover, laypeople can receive merit from many Buddhas and bodhisattvas in exchange for their devotion, lending further aid to those on the path toward nirvana.[51]

---

47. For a more detailed description of the Noble Eightfold Path, see Corduan, *Neighboring Faiths*, 320–21.

48. According to Prothero, *God Is Not One*, 175. Corduan estimates a much lower 376 million worldwide in *Neighboring Faiths*, 313.

49. The remainder of this paragraph summarizes the discussion of Theravada Buddhism found in Corduan, *Neighboring Faiths*, 321–25.

50. Prothero, *God is Not One*, 188.

51. Prothero, 190.

When sharing the gospel with Buddhists, it is important, given the enormous range of diversity in belief and practice, to focus on some of the characteristics common to all versions of Buddhism, including their fundamental negative attitude toward this life and their hope that Buddha (however understood) points to a solution.[52] Buddhism tells us to *extinguish* our desires, whereas Christianity encourages us to *redirect* our desires. According to Buddhism, desire is the source of all suffering. Thus, to eliminate suffering we must eliminate all desire. But this stance is self-defeating. To eliminate desire, it seems we must first desire to eliminate desire.[53] It is better to acknowledge the universal human desires for goodness, truth, and beauty and to identify their source in Jesus.

Christians ought to help Buddhists see that the self is real and in need of salvation. Fundamental reality is not, as Buddhism claims, the void. The self really does exist. The "I" that desires, thinks, perceives, and wills is real. Moreover, according to Christianity, Jesus entered into human history—a publicly verifiable event—so that we could be made whole again. Jesus did not come to extinguish the soul or lead others to a spiritual state of amorphous bliss. Encourage Buddhists to consider the claims of Jesus as recorded in the Gospel accounts. The hope is that they would see Jesus not as a spiritual guru on par with Buddha or a bodhisattva, but as the Lord and Savior of all, offering eternal life, forgiveness for sin, objective meaning in this life, and everlasting joy in the next.

Three Ways to Live

It is typically thought, as Timothy Keller reminds us, that there are two ways to live: the religious way and the irreligious way.[54] The religious way says, "I can earn my own salvation through good works." The irreligious way says, "I don't need God to find my own salvation." Both the religious and the irreligious way of life are strategies of "self-salvation."[55] Each of the world religions catalogued in this chapter are such self-salvation strategies:

---

52. Corduan, *Neighboring Faiths,* 352–53.
53. Dean C. Halverson, "Buddhism," in *The Compact Guide to World Religions*, ed. Dean C. Halverson (Minneapolis: Bethany House, 1996), 64.
54. Timothy Keller, *Gospel in Life: Study Guide* (Grand Rapids: Zondervan, 2010), 15–29.
55. Keller, 15.

follow the Five Pillars of Islam, or the Law of Moses, or the way of ritual, or the Noble Eightfold Path, and you can find salvation/release/nirvana. But Christianity offers a third way: the gospel way. The gospel way is the way of grace. It says, "I am a sinner saved by the gift of God." This is why Christianity is unique in the face of the world religions. All of the religions we've considered, and we could add more, are fundamentally the same in this sense: you must *work* to become righteous or enlightened. Christianity alone offers a better way. It offers Jesus. It offers grace. The good news is that when you get Jesus and the grace he offers, you get everything you need for life and godliness. May we all come "to grasp how wide and long and high and deep is the love of Christ" (Eph 3:18 NIV) as we share the gospel with those from other religions.

Assignments

Assignment 10-1: Making Gospel Connections

Talk to a friend or neighbor who belongs to one of the faith traditions discussed in this chapter. What did you learn? How did the conversation progress? Were you able to point out key differences between that person's religion and Christianity? Were you able to clear up any misunderstandings regarding Christianity?

Assignment 10-2

Discuss why it is popular to think that "all religions are basically the same." Why do you think Christians are often called intolerant? How might you respond to the charge that you are intolerant for believing that Christianity is the one true religion?

Assignment 10-3

Answer the following questions:

1. Why is the view that "all religions are equal" so popular today?
2. Do you think Islam is a religion of peace or of violence? Is this an important question?
3. How would you explain the Trinity to a Muslim or Jew? How would you explain the incarnation?
4. Do Christians and Muslims worship the same God? What about Christians and Jews?
5. What would Jesus say about the caste system in Hinduism?
6. How are Jesus and Buddha similar? Different?
7. What was most surprising to you in this brief study of some of the world's major religions?
8. How is Christianity unique among all the world religions?

Suggested Reading

Corduan, Winfried. *Neighboring Faiths: A Christian Introduction to World Religions*. 2nd ed. Downers Grove, IL: InterVarsity Press, 2012.

Halverson, Dean C., ed. *The Compact Guide to World Religions*. Minneapolis, MN: Bethany House, 1996.

Prothero, Stephen. *God Is Not One*. New York: HarperOne, 2010.

CHAPTER 11

Counterfeit Gospels: Mormons and Jehovah's Witnesses

The dawn of the nineteenth century saw Lewis and Clark leading their expedition into the unexplored west of North America (1803–1806)

and Napoleon crowning himself emperor of France (1804). Such events signaled a period of rapid change and innovation, including the appearance of new religious movements.[1] With the first publication of the Book of Mormon in 1830, roughly ten years after Napoleon's death and one year before Alexis de Tocqueville's historic visit to America, Joseph

Joseph Smith

Smith launched Mormonism (later named the Church of Jesus Christ of Latter-day Saints). Some four decades later, on the heels of the American Civil War and roughly thirty years before the Wright brothers achieved flight, Charles Taze Russell founded the movement

Charles Taze Russell

1. Ian J. Shaw, *Churches, Revolutions, and Empires: 1789–1914* (Fearn, UK: Christian Focus, 2012), chap. 15, provides a helpful summary and discussion of these movements.

now known as the Jehovah's Witnesses (1870s). Whereas the religions treated in the previous chapter are straightforwardly alternatives to Christianity, both Jehovah's Witnesses and Mormonism are sometimes thought to be expressions of Christianity. Having argued for the truth of traditional Christianity in earlier chapters, our thrust in this chapter is to identify certain of these religions' key points of departure from Christianity, safeguarding the truth of Christianity from these counterfeit gospels.

As the religious landscape in America continues to change, the immediacy of interreligious dialogue becomes increasingly pronounced. According to the Pew Research Center's 2015 Religious Landscape Survey, some 1.6 percent of American adults are Mormons (that is, just over 4 million) while 0.8 percent are Jehovah's Witnesses (that is, roughly 2 million).[2] These are the two largest homegrown religious traditions in America. Add to this the regular practice of both Mormons and Jehovah's Witnesses of door-to-door proselytizing, and the importance for Christians thoughtfully to engage the basic differences between these and Christianity is clear. Making the intentional decision to ignore many differences Christians are likely to find surprising and provocative—polygamy, refusal to celebrate birthdays, spirit babies, holy underwear, or disallowance to participate in politics, for example—this chapter focuses on four core differences between Christianity and Mormonism and Jehovah's Witnesses: Scripture, understanding of God, identity of Jesus Christ, and salvation. Despite important differences of belief between Mormons and Jehovah's Witnesses, because these groups differ from Christianity in similar ways, we have organized this chapter according to points of disagreement rather than by religion.

Scripture

According to traditional Christianity, the Bible alone is the holy Word of God given to humankind. That is to say, the Bible is God's revelation and was given to humankind by the inspiration of the Holy Spirit. As 2 Tim 3:16 says, "All Scripture is inspired by God and is profitable for teaching, for rebuking, for correcting, for training in righteousness." Second Peter 1:21

2. The full survey findings are available in Pew Research Center's report titled "America's Changing Religious Landscape," released May 12, 2015, http://www.pewforum.org/files/2015/05/RLS-08-26-full-report.pdf.

similarly tells us that "no prophecy was ever borne of human impulse; rather, men carried along by the Holy Spirit spoke from God" (NET). Christians believe the entire Bible to be the very words of God written down by men who were moved by the Holy Spirit.[3] Moreover, Christians are generally agreed that the canon of Scripture is closed—that is, there are to be no additions to or subtractions from the canon.

Christians also believe that the Bible alone is sufficient to know the way of salvation and obedience to God. We therefore do not need anything in addition to the Bible to tell us these things. As 2 Tim 3:15 says, "from infancy you have known the sacred Scriptures, which are able to give you wisdom for salvation through faith in Jesus Christ." The Bible, therefore, is the ultimate and final authority in matters of faith and practice. Since God cannot be mistaken, then the Scriptures as he gave them to us cannot contain mistakes. There is no need for God to provide further revelation in order to "complete" the Bible's teaching on faith and practice, and any alleged additional revelation from God must agree with the Bible. As the Westminster Confession of Faith summarizes, "The whole counsel of God, concerning all things necessary for His own glory, man's salvation, faith and life, is either expressly set down in Scripture, or by good and necessary consequence may be deduced from Scripture: unto which nothing at any time is to be added, whether by new revelations of the Spirit, or traditions of men."[4] This, of course, is an incomplete presentation of what Christians believe regarding Scripture, but it gets on the table key aspects of this belief that conflict with the beliefs of Mormons and Jehovah's Witnesses.[5]

Both Mormons and Jehovah's Witnesses accept the Bible as the written Word of God, frequently appealing to the Bible in sharing their convictions

---

3. As is well known, Protestants recognize the sixty-six books of the Old and New Testaments as comprising the entire canon of Scripture, whereas Catholics include the Apocrypha in the biblical canon. Historical context for this disagreement is helpfully given in F. F. Bruce, *The Canon of Scripture* (Downers Grove, IL: InterVarsity Press, 1988), esp. chaps. 5–7. Paul D. Wegner, Terry L. Wilder, and Darrell L. Bock compellingly argue that the Apocrypha are not properly part of the biblical canon in Wegner, Wilder, and Bock, "Do We Have the Right Canon?" in *In Defense of the Bible*, 393–428 (see chap. 5, n. 23).

4. In John H. Leith, ed., *Creeds of the Churches*, 3rd ed. (Louisville: John Knox Press, 1982), 195.

5. Nathan D. Holsteen, Michael J. Svigel, and others provide an accessible, fuller discussion in Holsteen and Svigel, eds., *Exploring Christian Theology: Revelation, Scripture, and the Triune God* (Minneapolis: Bethany House, 2014), 25–77.

with others. "The Bible," according to Jehovah's Witness teaching, "is a gift from God, one for which we can be truly grateful."[6] The Bible "is a book to be read, studied, and loved. Show your gratitude for this divine gift by continuing to peer into its contents. As you do so, you will gain a deep appreciation of God's purpose for mankind."[7] Likewise, according to their articles of faith, Mormons "believe the Bible to be the word of God. . . . "[8] Taken at face value, Christians would readily endorse these claims. A closer look, though, reveals important differences.

One important difference involves the *sufficiency* of Scripture. To complete the above quotation, Mormons "believe the Bible to be the word of God as far as it is translated correctly; we also believe the Book of Mormon to be the word of God."[9] In fact, the four "standard works" recognized by Mormons as scripture include the Bible (King James Version), the Pearl of Great Price, the Doctrines and Covenants, and the Book of Mormon. As we have seen, Christians believe that in the Bible God has made known everything needed to know the way of salvation and obedience to God. In attributing to extrabiblical works equal status with the Bible, Mormons in effect deny the sufficiency of Scripture. Joseph Smith, in fact, after claiming to have acquired the golden plates containing the text of the Book of Mormon from an angel (allegedly written in "reformed Egyptian" and translated by Smith[10]), said: "I told the brethren that the Book of Mormon was the most correct of any book on earth, and the keystone of our religion, and a man would get nearer to God by abiding by its precepts, than by any other

---

6. Watchtower Bible and Tract Society of New York, *What Does the Bible Really Teach?* (Brooklyn: Watchtower Bible and Tract Society, 2005), 18. Note: Jehovah's Witness literature does not identify individual authors, preferring anonymous publication by the Watchtower Bible and Tract Society.

7. Watchtower, 26.

8. Articles of Faith, no. 8, in Church of Jesus Christ of Latter-day Saints, *The Pearl of Great Price* (Salt Lake City: Church of Jesus Christ of Latter-day Saints, 1981), 60; hereinafter simply, Pearl of Great Price; cf. Craig L. Blomberg and Stephen E. Robinson, *How Wide the Divide?* (Downers Grove, IL: InterVarsity Press, 1997), 55ff.

9. Articles of Faith, 60.

10. Book of Mormon 9:32; cf. Pearl of Great Price, 56. "Reformed Egyptian is an undocumented language never seen by any leading Egyptologist or philologist who has ever been consulted on the problem." Walter Martin, *The Kingdom of the Cults* (Minneapolis: Bethany House, 2003), 201, n. 15.

book."[11] Influential Mormon teacher Bruce McConkie likewise teaches the necessity of adding the Book of Mormon to Scripture.[12]

Jehovah's Witnesses similarly oppose the sufficiency of Scripture. Freely repudiating traditional Christian interpretations of Scripture, Jehovah's Witnesses insist that to understand God's Word, individuals must also follow the teaching of the Watchtower Bible and Tract Society. Witnesses "must adhere absolutely to the decisions and scriptural understanding of the Society because God has given it this authority over his people."[13] Indeed, "unless we are in touch with this channel of communication that God is using, we will not progress along the road to life, no matter how much Bible reading we do."[14]

Mormons and Jehovah's Witnesses also diverge from Christian thinking about the integrity of the text of the Bible. While Christians agree that correct translation of the Bible is essential for correct understanding thereof, both Mormons and Jehovah's Witnesses take the further step of insisting that today's Bible is inaccurate or incomplete. While Mormons "believe the Bible to be the word of God as far as it is translated correctly," they also believe the text of the Bible to be corrupted. The Book of Mormon declares, "Wherefore, thou seest that after the book hath gone forth through the hands of the great and abominable church, that there are many plain and precious things taken away from the book, which is the book of the Lamb of God" (1 Nephi 13:28). Thus the need for further "testament" to God's Word: to confirm "true" biblical teaching. The loss of "many plain and precious things" from the Bible is expanded upon in various places by key Mormon leaders.[15] Although Jehovah's Witnesses countenance the King James Version of the Bible, they strongly prefer the New World Translation (NWT),

---

11. Joseph Smith, *Teachings of the Prophet Joseph Smith* (Salt Lake City: Deseret, 1976), 194.

12. Bruce McConkie, *Mormon Doctrine*, 2nd ed. (Salt Lake City: Bookcraft, 1966), 99; Ezra Taft Benson, "A New Witness for Christ," *Ensign*, November 1984, 7.

13. *Watchtower*, May 1, 1972, 272. Cf. the pages noted from the following *Watchtower* issues: November 1, 1961, 668; January 15, 1983, 22, 27; October 1, 1967, 587; February 15, 1981, 19.

14. *Watchtower*, December 1, 1981, 27. See Anthony Hoekema's *Jehovah's Witnesses* (Grand Rapids: Eerdmans, 1963), 25–44, for fuller critique.

15. For example: Bruce McConkie, *The Millennial Messiah* (Salt Lake City: Deseret, 1982), 160–64; Orson Pratt, "The Bible and Tradition, Without Further Revelation, An Insufficient Guide" in Pratt, *Divine Authenticity of the Book of Mormon* (Liverpool: 1851); Robert J. Matthew, *"A Bible! A Bible!"* (Salt Lake City: Bookcraft, 1990), esp. 13, 74–75; Mark E. Petersen, *As Translated Correctly* (Salt Lake City: Deseret, 1966).

produced in 1950 by their own Watchtower Bible and Tract Society. Ostensibly produced "in an effort to purge the Bible of the many transmission and translation errors believed to have crept in over the centuries,"[16] the NWT is known for its rendering of verses in a manner favorable to Watchtower beliefs when these differ from orthodox Christianity.

It is clear that these rejections of the Bible's textual integrity each assume the corruption of the biblical text. In addition to the discussion in our earlier chapter on the Bible, we point readers to the extensive literature on textual criticism (that is, the branch of textual studies focusing on confirming the precise original wording of the biblical documents).[17] In short, experts have found the text of the Bible to be astonishingly well preserved, with no variant reading affecting common Christian doctrine. When it comes to the Book of Mormon and the NWT, however, no such confidence is justified. The former, for example, recounts the alleged rise and fall of ancient peoples in present-day North America—yet there is an utter absence of archaeological evidence to support this claim.[18] The latter has been widely dismissed as a legitimate translation of the Bible, with experts criticizing the NWT's habit of adding words, omitting words, and mistranslating verses in support of preconceived doctrinal positions.[19] Bruce Metzger, longtime professor of Bible at Princeton Theological Seminary and world-renowned expert on biblical manuscripts, for example, demonstrates the inadequacies of the NWT on multiple grounds.[20]

---

16. Leslie Howsam and Scott McLaren, "Producing the Text: Production and Distribution of Popular Editions of the Bible," in *The New Cambridge History of the Bible*, vol. 4, *From 1750 to the Present*, ed. John Riches (New York: Cambridge University Press, 2015), 81.

17. For example, Paul Wegner, "Has the Old Testament Text Been Hopelessly Corrupted?" and Wallace, "Has the New Testament Text Been Hopelessly Corrupted?," in *In Defense of the Bible*, chaps. 5–6 (see chap. 5, n. 23). See also Bruce, *The New Testament Documents: Are They Reliable?* (see chap. 6, n. 49), and Norman L. Geisler and William E. Nix, *From God to Us: How We Got Our Bible* (Chicago: Moody Press, 1974).

18. Ross Anderson, *Understanding the Book of Mormon* (Grand Rapids: Zondervan, 2009), chap. 7. See also Thomas J. Finley, "Does the Book of Mormon Reflect an Ancient Near Eastern Background?" and David J. Shepherd, "Rendering Fiction: Translation, Psuedotranslation, and the Book of Mormon," in *The New Mormon Challenge*, ed. Francis Beckwith, Carl Mosser, and Paul Owen (Grand Rapids: Zondervan, 2002), chaps. 10 and 11; and Bill McKeever and Eric Johnson, *Mormonism 101* (Grand Rapids: Baker Books, 2000), 104–21.

19. Robert M. Bowman Jr., *Understanding Jehovah's Witnesses* (Grand Rapids: Baker Books, 1991), 65–74.

20. Bruce M. Metzger, "The Jehovah's Witnesses and Jesus Christ: A Biblical and Theological Appraisal," *Theology Today* 10, no. 1 (April 1953): 65–85.

Figure 11.1	Christianity	Mormonism	Jehovah's Witnesses
Bible is God's Word?	YES	YES	YES
Bible is sufficient for knowing way of faith and practice?	YES	NO	NO
Contemporary biblical text hopelessly corrupt?	NO	YES	YES

God

Given that religions worshipping different deities are no more the same than buses, bicycles, and bulldozers are the same mode of transportation, it is important to note that both Mormons and Jehovah's Witnesses deny central elements of Christian belief about God. The worship of God as one being in three persons (i.e., the Trinity) has always been a touchstone of Christian belief, as is evident both in Christian praxis and Christian interpretation of the Bible. To be sure, Christians believe in the existence of only one God (monotheism), and this God is tri-personal; God the Father, God the Son, and God the Holy Spirit are distinct *persons* who share a common *being*.[21] This entails the rejection of any form of polytheism. Further, Christians believe God to be incorporeal rather than essentially physical. As Jesus says, "God is spirit" (John 4:24), and as spirit God is not limited spatially. God is the creator and sustainer of everything that exists. The Bible is clear about this: God created every existing thing that is not God, and everything continues to exist because of God. Consider the Bible's opening words: "In the beginning God created the heavens and the earth" (Gen 1:1). Not only do Christians believe God created the heavens and the earth, the Bible teaches that he did so *ex nihilo* (Lat., "out of nothing"). Whereas the demiurge in Plato's classic account of origins utilizes preexisting materials to "create," Christians affirm

---

21. See Gerald Bray, *The Doctrine of God* (Downers Grove, IL: InterVarsity Press, 1993); Gerald O'Collins, *The Tripersonal God* (New York: Paulist Press, 1999); and Fred Sanders and Klaus Issler, eds., *Jesus in Trinitarian Perspective* (Nashville: B&H Academic, 2007).

God's creation of all things from absolutely nothing.[22] As Heb 11:3 says, "By faith we understand that the worlds were prepared by the word of God, so that what is seen was not made out of things which are visible" (NASB). Christians also believe God is eternal and unchanging. This means God has always been God; there was never a time when God was not God. Psalm 90:2 proclaims, "Before the mountains were born, before you gave birth to the earth and the world, from eternity to eternity, you are God." Again, this summary is not meant to exhaust Christian belief about God, but it highlights key points of disagreement with Mormons and Jehovah's Witnesses.

Both Mormon and Jehovah's Witness conceptions of God differ significantly from that of Christians. All Jehovah's Witnesses and many Mormons forthrightly reject belief in God as Trinity. Regarding the doctrine of the Trinity, the Watchtower and Bible Tract Society's *Let God Be True* is unequivocal:

> God was not the author of this doctrine. . . . In the year 325 (A.D.) a council of clergymen met at Nice in Asia Minor and confirmed the doctrine. It was later declared to be the doctrine of the religious organization of "Christendom," and the clergy have ever held to this complicated doctrine. The obvious conclusion, therefore, is that Satan is the originator of the "trinity" doctrine.[23]

Jehovah's Witnesses elsewhere caricature the Christian doctrine of the Trinity as belief in three gods or as "confusing" and therefore unbelievable.[24] Monotheistic belief just is, one reads, the belief "that God is one Person—a unique, unpartitioned Being who has no equal."[25] On their view there is only one "Almighty God," but this is not regarded as incompatible with the existence of lesser gods.[26] This, as we have seen, simply begs the question against Christianity.[27]

---

22. Plato, *Timaeus*, 28b–31b. Cf. Paul Copan, "Creation Ex Nihilo or Ex Materia? A Critique of the Mormon Doctrine of Creation," *Southern Baptist Journal of Theology* 9, no. 2 (2005): 32–54.

23. Watchtower, *Let God Be True* (Brooklyn: Watchtower Bible and Tract Society, 1946), 82.

24. Watchtower Bible and Tract Society, *Should You Believe in the Trinity?* (Brooklyn: Watchtower Bible and Tract Society, 1989).

25. Watchtower, 13.

26. See, for example, Watchtower, *Let God Be True*, 35–36.

27. See Robert M. Bowman Jr., *Why You Should Believe in the Trinity: An Answer to Jehovah's Witnesses* (Grand Rapids: Baker Books, 1989); and Hoekema, *Jehovah's Witnesses*, 45–54.

For its part, Mormon teaching also denies the Trinity: "Many men say there is one God; the Father, the Son, and the Holy Ghost are only one God. I say that is a strange God anyhow—three in one, and one in three! It is a curious organization. . . . All are to be crammed into one God, according to sectarianism."[28] In fact, according to Mormon apostle Bruce McConkie, Father, Son, and Holy Spirit are actually distinct gods,[29] a notion supported in *The Pearl of Great Price* alongside a denial of the Christian understanding of creation.[30] Beyond the denial of the Trinity, Mormon teaching also denies God's eternal and unchanging nature. Joseph Smith taught that God is one of many gods who were once men. "God himself was once as we are now, and is an exalted man, and sits enthroned in yonder heavens!" Smith continues:

> I am going to tell you how God came to be God. We have imagined and supposed that God was God from all eternity. I will refute this idea, and take away the veil, so that you may see. . . . It is the first principle of the gospel to know for a certainty the character of God, and to know . . . that He was once a man like us; yea, that God himself, the Father of us all, dwelt on an earth, the same as Jesus Christ Himself did.[31]

This is echoed by Brigham Young: "How many Gods there are, I do not know. But there never was a time when there were not Gods and worlds."[32] Further differences remain, but enough has been said to make clear that the God of Christianity is not the god(s) of Mormonism.[33] In virtue of the fact that they clearly do not worship the God of Christianity, we must conclude that Mormonism and Jehovah's Witnesses are distinct from Christianity.

---

28. Joseph Smith, *Teachings of the Prophet Joseph Smith*, as quoted in McKeever and Johnson, *Mormonism 101*, 52.

29. McConkie, *Mormon Doctrine*, 319, 576. Cf. Ron Rhodes and Marian Bodine, *Reasoning from the Scriptures with the Mormons* (Eugene, OR: Harvest House, 1995), 243–46.

30. Book of Abraham 4–5, where the creative activity is done by "the Gods" (plural).

31. Smith, *Teachings of the Prophet Joseph Smith*, 345–46.

32. Brigham Young, *Journal of Discourses*, 7:333, accessed March 21, 2018, http://jod.mrm.org/7/331.

33. See chapters 5–8 in Beckwith, Mosser, and Owen, *The New Mormon Challenge*.

Figure 11.2	Christianity	Mormonism	Jehovah's Witnesses
Is God tri-personal?	YES	NO	NO
Is monotheism true?	YES	NO	NO

Jesus Christ

"Who do you say that I am?" (Mark 8:29). Jesus's question cuts sharply to the heart of matters, for it is the central question all must face. Why? Simply because "the one who has the Son has life. The one who does not have the Son of God does not have life" (1 John 5:12; see also John 3:36). Christians echo Peter's response: "You are the Messiah!" This Christian confession rests upon certain staggering truths about Jesus revealed in the Bible, beginning with the incarnation: that is, the belief that the eternal second person of the Trinity took on flesh (i.e., added to his divine nature a truly human nature). As John explains, "In the beginning was the Word, and the Word was with God and the Word was fully God. . . . Now the Word became flesh and took up residence among us. We saw his glory— the glory of the one and only, full of grace and truth, who came from the Father" (John 1:1, 14 NET). As the fourth-century church father Athanasius noted, "we were the purpose of his embodiment, and for our salvation he so loved human beings as to come to be and appear in a human body."[34] Jesus Christ is, uniquely, both truly God and truly human; compromising even slightly either his full deity or his full humanity moves one outside of orthodox Christianity. Having been born of the virgin Mary (Luke 1:30–35; 2:6–7), Jesus regularly and *intentionally* displayed both his divine and human natures.[35] That Jesus understood himself to be God is clear. As noted in chapter 6, he forgives the sins of others (Mark 2:5; Luke 7:47–48) and makes such claims as "The Father and I are one" (John 10:30) and "If you know me, you will also know my Father. From now on you do know

---

34. Athanasius, *On the Incarnation* (Crestwood, NY: St. Vladimir's Seminary Press, 1996), 53.

35. See the helpful discussion in Millard Erickson, *Christian Theology*, 3rd ed. (Grand Rapids: Baker, 2013), 623–58; cf. Robert M. Bowman Jr. and J. Ed Komoszewski, *Putting Jesus in His Place* (Grand Rapids: Kregel, 2007).

him and have seen him . . . The one who has seen me has seen the Father" (John 14:7, 9). That Jesus in each instance claimed to be God is a fact not lost on his hearers (Mark 2:6; John 19:7), who immediately accused Jesus of blasphemously claiming to be God (Mark 2:7; John 8:59).[36]

By denying that Christ, as the incarnate second person of the Trinity, is eternally God, both Jehovah's Witnesses and Mormons reject an essential tenet of orthodox Christianity. Staking out a position reminiscent of the fourth-century heretic Arius of Alexandria,[37] Jehovah's Witnesses explicitly deny the divinity of Jesus: "Thus, Jesus had an existence in heaven before coming to earth. But was it as one of the persons in an almighty, eternal triune Godhead? No, for the Bible plainly states that in his prehuman existence, Jesus was a created spirit being, just as angels were spirit beings created by God. Neither the angels nor Jesus had existed before their creation."[38] Jesus, in their view, is merely the preeminent of all Jehovah's creatures (being, in fact, the incarnation of the created archangel Michael).[39] As the Watchtower's *Aid to Bible Understanding* explains, "Since Jehovah is eternal and had no beginning . . . the Word's being with God from the 'beginning' must here refer to the beginning of Jehovah's creative works. . . . Thus the Scriptures identify the Word (Jesus in his prehuman existence) as God's first creation, his firstborn Son . . . [T]his Son was actually a creature of God.[40] In support of this belief, the NWT alters the text of Col 1:16–20 (adding the word "other" four times) to portray Jesus as part of the created order.[41] This denying of an eternally divine nature to Jesus is fundamentally incompatible with Christian belief.

Mormon teaching also denies that Christ is eternally God, holding instead that he *attained* the status of deity before coming to earth. As McConkie explains, "by obedience and devotion to the truth . . . [Christ] attained that pinnacle of intelligence which ranked Him as a God."[42] This

36. Christian belief about Jesus is helpfully summarized in the Constantinopolitan creed, in Leith, *Creeds of the Churches*, 33.

37. D. Jeffrey Bingham, *Pocket History of the Church* (Downers Grove, IL: InterVarsity Press, 2002), 46–50.

38. Watchtower Bible and Tract Society, *Should You Believe in the Trinity?*, 14.

39. Watchtower, *Let God Be True*, 33–34.

40. Watchtower, *Aid to Bible Understanding* (Brooklyn: Watchtower Bible and Tract Society, 1971), 918.

41. Bowman, *Understanding Jehovah's Witnesses*, 66.

42. McConkie, *Mormon Doctrine*, 129, as quoted in Rhodes and Bodine, *Reasoning from the Scriptures with the Mormons*, 267.

is to be understood against the background of the Mormon conception of Christ's "preexistence." It is held that the Son of God originally ("spiritually") was born of God the Father in heaven: "Christ is the Firstborn. . . . All men lived in a pre-existent estate before they were born into this world; all were born in pre-existence as the spirit children of the Father. Christ was the Firstborn Spirit Child, and from that day forward he has had, in all things, the preeminence."[43] It was then that "Christ, the Word, the Firstborn, had, of course, *attained* unto the status of Godhood while yet in preexistence."[44] Not only is Christ's eternal deity denied, but Mormon belief regarding the physical body of the incarnate Christ bears striking similarity to the Christological heresy known as Apollinarianism. In the teaching of Mormon "prophets," the spirit called "Christ" came to inhabit a physical body produced for him by a literal sexual union between God the Father and Mary,[45] which undermines the genuine humanity of Jesus. The point is that these views line up remarkably well not with Christian orthodoxy but with Christian heterodoxy. This alone demonstrates both are fundamentally different from traditional Christianity. Differences abound between the Christian doctrine of Christ and that of both Mormons and Jehovah's Witnesses, but we must turn to our fourth and final core difference regarding the gospel.

Figure 11.3	Christianity	Mormonism	Jehovah's Witnesses
Is Jesus the incarnate second person of the Trinity?	YES	NO	NO
Is Jesus a creature?	NO	YES	YES

---

43. Bruce McConkie, *What the Mormons Think of Christ* (Salt Lake City: Church of Jesus Christ of Latter-day Saints, n.d.), 30–31; cf. *Doctrines and Covenants*, 93:21–23.

44. McConkie, emphasis added. Milton R. Hunter says much the same in *The Gospel through the Ages* (Salt Lake City: Deseret, 1945), 51.

45. See the compiled quotations in McKeever and Johnson, *Mormonism 101*, 43–45.

The Gospel

Do you remember the jailer from the story of Acts 16? Paul and Silas had been thrown into jail for preaching the good news of Jesus Christ. That evening an earthquake opened all the prison doors and released all the prisoners from their chains. Assuming all the prisoners to be escaping, the jailer was just about to kill himself when the apostle Paul intervened. Paul told the jailer that none of the prisoners had fled, and upon seeing that it was true the jailer asked Paul and Silas, "Sirs, what must I do to be saved?" (Acts 16:30).

Christians find in the Bible a plain answer to this momentous question. The Bible teaches that humans—every single one of us—are sinful. Early in Genesis we read that Adam disobeyed God. Romans 5:12, 17–18 tells us that as a result of Adam's sin, death entered the world. We all suffer as a result. The Bible also says that "all have sinned and fall short of the glory of God" (Rom 3:23). This means every one of us is sinful, and deep down we all recognize our imperfection against God's holy standard. For our violation of God's law, we face the condemnation of God as the holy and righteous Judge—and the deserved penalty is death (Rom 6:23). That is bad news, but the Bible teaches that God loves us even though we are sinful. Indeed, "God proves his own love for us in that while we were yet sinners, Christ died for us" (Rom 5:8; cf. John 3:16). Jesus Christ died for the purpose of paying our deserved penalty for us; Jesus died to make the salvation of sinners possible. As we have seen (chapter 7), Jesus did not remain dead: he was resurrected (1 Cor 15:3–5)! On this basis anyone—*anyone*—can be redeemed from their sins, if only they will place their faith and trust in Jesus Christ. That's the good news that is the gospel!

What surprises many people when they hear what Jesus did for them is that it is a *free* gift. Ephesians 2:8–9 says, "You are saved by grace through faith, and this is not from yourselves; it is God's gift—not from works, so that no man can boast." This is the good news of Jesus Christ: that when we were dead in our sins (Eph 2:1), he died to save us. We have been offered something we have not and indeed cannot earn. "What must I do to be saved?" The Christian answer is simple: "Believe in the Lord Jesus, and you will be saved" (Acts 16:31). "The one who believes in the Son has eternal life, but the one who rejects the Son will not see life; instead, the wrath of God remains on him" (John 3:36). Unfortunately, both Jehovah's Witnesses and Mormons disagree with the Christian understanding of the gospel.

Whereas the Bible emphasizes that salvation is by grace alone, Mormonism holds that one must do certain other things in addition to placing one's faith in Jesus to obtain salvation. This includes, for example, being baptized: "And he commandeth all men that they must repent and be baptized in his name, having perfect faith in the Holy One of Israel, or they cannot be saved in the kingdom of God" (2 Nephi 9:23). Although Christians affirm it as an important step in the Christian life, they deny any salvific necessity to baptism. Joseph Smith, however, insisted, "Many talk of baptism not being essential to salvation; but this kind of teaching would lay the foundation of their damnation. I have the truth, and am at the defiance of the world to contradict me, if they can."[46] Further, the Book of Mormon avers that "we know that it is by grace that we are saved, after all we can do" (2 Nephi 25:23). There is the potential for confusion here, because Eph 2:8 proclaims it is "by grace you have been saved" (NIV). Although similar, the added phrase ending 2 Nephi 25:23 is conspicuous. The ending of Eph 2:8 reads, "this is not from yourselves; it is God's gift"; contrary to Smith and the Book of Mormon, the Bible adds neither baptism nor anything else to the atoning work of Christ as essential for salvation. What is meant by "after all we can do"? "The phrase 'after all we can do' teaches that effort is required on our part to receive the fullness of the Lord's grace and be made worthy to dwell with him."[47] Ezra Taft Benson, Mormon president from 1985 until his death in 1994, elaborates:

> What is meant by "after all we can do"? "After all we can do" includes extending our best effort. "After all we can do" includes living His commandments. "After all we can do"; includes loving our fellowmen and praying for those who regard us as their adversary. "After all we can do" means clothing the naked, feeding the hungry, visiting the sick and giving "succor [to] those who stand in need of [our] succor" (Mosiah 4:15)—remembering that what we do unto one of the least of God's children, we do unto Him. . . .

---

46. Smith, *Teachings of the Prophet Joseph Smith*, 361.
47. Church of Jesus Christ of Latter-day Saints, *True to the Faith: A Gospel Reference* (Salt Lake City: Intellectual Reserve, 2004), 77.

"After all we can do" means leading chaste, clean, pure lives, being scrupulously honest in all our dealings and treating others the way we would want to be treated.[48]

Christians do affirm the importance of such "good works," but not as contributions to one's own salvation. Mormon leader James Faust, however, is unambiguous: "Many people think they need only confess that Jesus is the Christ and then they are saved by grace alone. We cannot be saved by grace alone, 'for we know that it is by grace that we are saved, after all we can do.'"[49] It is clear, then, that Mormon teaching denies the Christian belief in salvation by grace through faith alone.

For their part Jehovah's Witnesses also deny that salvation is by grace through faith alone. The Watchtower Bible and Tract Society's book *You Can Live Forever in Paradise on Earth* presents several "requirements" God makes "of those who want to become subjects of his government," including learning the "knowledge needed," exhibiting "righteous conduct," and being "loyal *spokesmen* or *proclaimers* of God's kingdom."[50] Later, in a chapter titled "What You Must Do to Live Forever," the same book reiterates that "more than faith is needed. There must also be works to demonstrate what your true feelings are about Jehovah" in order to gain eternal life.[51] The necessity of these added "requirements" for salvation is restated across Watchtower literature, including, for example, being "*associated with God's channel*, his organization," that is, the Watchtower society.[52] A convert must "persevere in doing God's will and continue to adhere to all of God's requirements for the rest of his life. Only then will he be saved to eternal life."[53] Jehovah's Witnesses also say that "to have real value in the eyes of our heavenly Father," one must undergo baptism—indeed, "not just the act of getting baptized, but everything associated with the baptismal arrangement is essential for salvation."[54] Undergoing baptism, it is held, accrues to one a "good con-

---

48. Ezra Taft Benson, *The Teachings of Ezra Taft Benson* (Salt Lake City: Bookcraft, 1988), 354.

49. James E. Faust, "The Atonement: Our Greatest Hope," *Ensign*, November 2001, 18.

50. Watchtower Bible and Tract Society of New York, *You Can Live Forever in Paradise on Earth* (Brooklyn: Watchtower Bible and Tract Society, 1989), 127–33.

51. Watchtower Bible and Tract Society of New York, 250.

52. *Watchtower* magazine, February 15, 1983, 12, 15.

53. *Watchtower*, December 15, 1989, 30.

54. *Watchtower*, May 1, 1980, 12.

science," and "as long as he maintains that good conscience he is in a saved condition."[55] Although Witnesses frequently describe salvation as a matter of grace, it is evident they mean something much different than do Christians.

Figure 11.4	Christianity	Mormonism	Jehovah's Witnesses
Is salvation by grace alone?	YES	NO	NO

Distinguishing Faiths

Both Mormons and Jehovah's Witnesses share certain traits with Christianity, but as we have seen, their rejection of essential tenets of the Christian faith are telltale signs of counterfeits. Such counterfeit faiths are, like the world religions considered in the previous chapter, recognizable alternatives to Christianity. Admittedly, many find it difficult to accept the scandalous Christian belief that salvation is—indeed, can only be—the *free* gift of God offered to sinners. Surely, they think, sinners must be expected to defray the cost of their salvation! Here it must be remembered what distinguishes Christianity from such "religious ways" to live: we must accept the beauty and brilliance of the Christian gospel! This is the way of grace, the way of accepting that salvation is readily but exclusively found in a relationship with the Jesus of the Bible.

---

55. *Watchtower*, May 1, 1980, 13.

Assignments

Assignment 11-1: Making Gospel Connections

Mormons and Jehovah's Witnesses are quite willing to meet. Consider inviting them for a discussion with the goal of asking clarifying questions about Scripture, God, Jesus Christ, and the gospel. Try to establish points of disagreement in order to share the true gospel.

Assignment 11-2

Summarize the Christian view of the Bible, God, the identity of Jesus, and the gospel. What is the best way to communicate this view to Mormons? To Jehovah's Witnesses?

Assignment 11-3

Do you agree that it is wise, when engaging in interreligious dialogue, to focus on the main issues presented in this chapter? Why?

Assignment 11-4

Explain why Christians regard the understanding of salvation as by grace through faith alone to be essential.

Suggested Reading

Beckwith, Francis, Carl Mosser, and Paul Owen, eds. *The New Mormon Challenge*. Grand Rapids: Zondervan, 2002.

Bowman, Robert Jr. *Why You Should Believe in the Trinity: An Answer to Jehovah's Witnesses*. Grand Rapids: Baker Books, 1989.

Geisler, Norman, ed. *The Counterfeit Gospel of Mormonism*. Eugene, OR: Harvest House, 1998.

Hoekema, Anthony. *Jehovah's Witnesses*. Grand Rapids: Eerdmans, 1963.

McKeever, Bill, and Eric Johnson. *Mormonism 101*. Grand Rapids: Baker Books, 2000.

Rhodes, Ron. *Conversations with Jehovah's Witnesses*. Eugene, OR: Harvest House, 2014.

CHAPTER 12

Standing Firm and Going Out

Throughout the book, we've attempted to provide reasons for believing that Christianity is true and that Christianity is satisfying. We've made a case for Christianity both in giving positive reasons and by addressing what we take to be some of the strongest objections against Christianity. Yet what we've presented here is really only the tip of the iceberg, and you should also know, it's a big ol' iceberg! There truly is a staggering number and variety of arguments and evidences that have been offered for Christianity. There are also brand-new arguments being developed, and new evidence is being discovered.[1] There are even some arguments that have fallen out of use throughout the centuries and are being, in a way, rediscovered.[2] Unlike many views, the case for Christianity has only gotten better throughout its history. There also seems to be no end to the ways in which Christian faith speaks to our deepest longings. This is truly an inexhaustible fount!

But there are also many other objections that may be raised against the Christian view that we haven't addressed. Worldview discussions, thoughts about God, and the claims of Christianity are big issues and can get really complicated. It is perfectly normal to encounter a challenge or objection one has not (yet) considered. We'd like to provide some suggestions about *how* to encounter new ideas and challenges.

---

1. At the time of writing this book, there were announcements of discoveries of manuscripts of portions of the New Testament that had been extracted from ancient mummy masks. We have been told in personal correspondence with Craig Evans that a fragment of Mark's Gospel has been discovered that is being dated to the first or second century. This will be the earliest fragment of Mark's Gospel to date.

2. See, for example, Lydia McGrew's *Hidden in Plain View: Undesigned Coincidences in the Gospels and Acts* (see chap. 5, n. 18).

The Value of Doubt

You will likely face challenges to your faith. With the rise of New Atheism and the growth of the religiously "none," there is a great likelihood that you have faced hostility directed at your faith (if not, you will). More important, you will likely have questions about God, Jesus, theology, the Bible, and so on, that will constitute a challenge to your faith. A normal reality of faith is having doubts, from time to time.

We'd like to suggest a somewhat controversial thesis. We think that doubting one's faith can be a very valuable experience. When we doubt our faith, it is certainly not an altogether enjoyable experience. And doubts can turn into an unhealthy skepticism. However, we think having and asking deep and difficult questions about our faith is valuable since, if treated properly, it can and should lead one to truth, knowledge, and a greater faith. Think about it. When we press our faith with hard questions, we determine the reasonableness of our beliefs. So if the particular belief is no good, then it will not stand the test, and we'll get ourselves a better belief. However, if it is rationally grounded, then we will not only continue to believe it, but we will have an even greater faith. We believe Christianity is true. If it is true, we don't need to somehow rig the system to continue believing it. If it is true, we can confidently ask the deep and difficult questions.

Again, this is not always easy or enjoyable. Here are some suggestions.

The first thing to keep in mind is that the mere existence of a doubt or an objection one cannot (yet) address doesn't thereby defeat one's Christian beliefs. It is important to realize there can be objections to your faith, and it is perfectly reasonable to maintain your faith even if you do not know just how to answer the objection.

To see this, we offer an analogy. Most of us, from time to time, fly on airplanes. If we are honest, most of us don't really know how a craft largely made of metal and weighing in at about a million pounds (if it is a 747) can lift off the ground and literally cruise through the sky six miles off the planet! It's almost absurd if you really stop to think what happens when we fly. We could be sitting in the airport, discussing and struggling to know how this phenomenon is even possible. But here's the thing: Even if we were having this deep discussion about flight, when your seat section was called, we bet you would board the airplane! We would too. We all would. Unless we already struggle with a phobia of flying, we all know enough about airplanes and air travel to know that it is a very safe and reliable way to travel despite any questions and doubts we might have. Most of us have flown many times before and witnessed the safety and reliability of flight. We also undoubtedly know many people who have as well. We may even have heard the statistics about how safe it is to fly on an airplane. We may not know the physics of what makes flight possible, and we may have serious doubts about how this works, but we rationally get on the airplane. We could even be cruising at 30,000 feet, entrusting our very lives to the airplane, and continue to discuss and struggle with these questions. Our faith (despite the doubts) in the airplane is completely rational.

Likewise, if one has good reasons for taking Christianity as true, it is completely appropriate to ask deep and difficult questions about the truth of Christianity while entrusting one's life to its truth.

As we mentioned in chapter 2, we think most Christians have good reasons for believing in Christianity even before they do a study in Christian apologetics (remember the little old country grandma!). When one is not backed into a corner, most Christians can rattle off a number of excellent reasons for believing that Christianity is true. For instance, the world has clear and obvious design and order that's best explained by the existence of God. Perhaps you can also talk through some of the historical reasons for believing that Jesus rose from the dead and for trusting the reliability of Scripture. If you have reflected on the gospel, then you know that it addresses our deepest longings and makes sense of our fallenness. If you are a believer, we suspect you've seen your life changed by Christ, have seen God answer prayer, and heard incredible testimonies of these things along the way. If so, all of these constitute reasons for thinking that Christianity is true.

We, of course, think we should all improve our rational grounds for faith. Indeed, this is the point of the book. Even still, a typical Christian seems to have plenty of evidence to maintain rational belief in Christianity in the face of doubts.

So hang on! Don't jump ship just because you find an objection to Christianity plausible or can't answer what seems like a hard problem. Now, we don't want to stay in this place of doubt either.

Doubt Your Doubts

Once you've taken a deep breath, the second suggestion for treating doubt is to evaluate the doubts. Remember: doubts don't win by default, by their mere existence. It seems that the doubts should defeat our beliefs only if the doubts are more rational than our Christian beliefs. Thus, what one must do is attempt to raise objections to the doubts—here we are doubting our doubts—to see whether there is good reason to think that the doubts are sufficiently reasonable to defeat our beliefs.

There are two ways to doubt a doubt.

The first is to determine whether the claim we are finding plausible is genuinely a problem. This is where we ask "so what?" It's vital to determine whether there is a problem, if the claim is true, and to what degree it is a problem. Many ideas seem problematic at first glance, but turn out, as we evaluate them, to be completely harmless. And so, in evaluating our doubt, we need to determine whether the doubt, if true, would defeat any of our Christian beliefs.

To illustrate this, it is sometimes pointed out that there are many differences across the different Gospels. A paradigm case of this is the empty tomb accounts in the Gospels. One may be challenged with asking exactly which women came to the tomb that Easter morning.

> Matthew says, "Mary Magdalene and the other Mary went to view the tomb" (Matt 28:1).
>
> Mark says, "Mary Magdalene, Mary the mother of James, and Salome . . . went to the tomb" (Mark 16:1–2).
>
> Luke says, "Mary Magdalene, Joanna, Mary the mother of James, and the other women with them . . . [returned] from the tomb" (Luke 24:9–10).
>
> John says, "Mary Magdalene came to the tomb early" (John 20:1).

There are, in these passages, obvious discrepancies. It can be a bit surprising that each Gospel account has a different list of women. Let's suppose someone wonders whether this means that the text is unreliable on the basis of these discrepancies.

But let's ask the question, so what? So what if there are discrepancies like this? Does this mean that there are errors? To think that this means that there are errors seems to be too quick. As we reflect on this, we can see that discrepancies and differences of detail are not necessarily contradictions and errors if the differences can be reconciled.

Can the different lists of women be reconciled? This surely is not all that difficult. There is overlap with each list (e.g., Mary Magdalene is mentioned in each), and none of the accounts says that it was only the women specifically named that were there. This leaves open the possibility that these are all incomplete lists (perhaps Luke's is complete since it is the longest). John's account only mentions Mary Magdalene, but it never says she came all by herself when it easily could have. If it did, then we would have a genuine contradiction on our hands. But as it is, we can reconcile these accounts by understanding that a group of women came and discovered an empty tomb and each Gospel account gives a different but consistent representative subset of these women.

Why would the authors mention some and leave out the others? When describing a group of people, we too will very often mention a representative subset depending on who we are talking to and what our purposes are. Suppose the president of the United States and three of his Secret Service agents showed up to your house to discuss politics with you. After the experience, you'd likely phone a friend and blurt out that the president of the United States just came to your house. You are not intending to deceive your friend. It's just that the president is the person of prominence in that group, and you wouldn't likely mention the Secret Service agents. When the White House records the events of the president's day, it might mention everyone who was involved in coming to your house. Though these descriptions are different, they are truthfully and consistently describing the same event.

Look carefully at the tomb accounts we listed. There are differences but no contradictions. To say that Mary was there is perfectly consistent with saying that Mary and Salome were there and makes sense if, for example, Salome is unknown to, say, John's audience. Mary Magdalene is clearly the person of prominence in the list. She is always mentioned and always mentioned first.

So when we ask "so what?" we see that the mere fact that there are differences can be rationally accounted for. The problem seems to simply dissolve.

The second way to evaluate a doubt is to determine whether the doubt is reasonable. Here we ask, "Why think this claim is true?" For example, let's say that we hear a news report of the discovery of an ancient Palestinian ossuary that bears the name "Jesus, son of Joseph." The claim is made that they have discovered the bodily remains of Jesus Christ. Is this a problem if the bodily remains of Jesus have been found? You bet it is! It has been Christian orthodoxy from the beginning that Jesus rose *bodily* from the dead. If his bodily remains are found, then clearly this central claim is defeated.

But now we need evidence, because this tune has played before (usually around Easter time on public television), and let's just say it has not always been a hit! If the ossuary dates early and looks to be authentic, then it would of course be a genuine problem for Christian faith. If it turns out that there are compelling reasons to think the inscription is a modern forgery (as has often been the case with these sorts of claims), then the problem is dissolved. It is the evidence that matters here.

What's the Risk?

You might be thinking that encouraging doubts and questions sounds a bit risky. And you're right. Investigating and attempting to address a doubt does indeed open us to the possibility of our beliefs being false.

But ignoring doubts, it seems, is no less risky. Many folks walk away from the faith not so much because their doubts were abundantly rational, but because they never find any space or community to authentically think about and address their deep questions. This is so very tragic, since, there are, in our experience of asking the deep and difficult questions for decades, good answers to our questions. Christianity stands up to the hardest questions. What's more is that, as Christians, we stand in a rich tradition of taking the hardest objections to Christianity and offering thoughtful and honest responses.[3] Far too many folks walk away on the basis of doubts when

---

3. See, for example, the story of Augustine in chapter 1.

they haven't even considered the great heritage of answers to their questions from church history as well as in contemporary sources.

So there is risk on both sides, and our thesis is that there is great value in exploring our doubts. We're not saying to ignore the challenge. You'll need to address the problem. How's the best way to do this? In community . . . which leads to our next point.

There is (virtually) nothing new under the sun when it comes to objections and challenges. It is practically impossible that you will stumble on a problem that no one in the history of Christianity has ever worked on. You are not alone in this. We have sometimes found students struggling deeply with a challenge that has been so thoroughly addressed that most non-Christians don't even think it is a good argument. Or it is something that, say, Augustine thoroughly refuted sixteen centuries ago (fourth century).

So hang on. Be driven to your knees and simultaneously to your desks (or perhaps to the library). The point is that you begin to ask these hard questions about faith. You begin to wrestle with these deep and difficult issues, always one step at a time and always in community.

The Brilliance of the Gospel

The subtitle of the book is *Apologetics and the Brilliance of the Gospel*. We've attempted to argue for the rationality of Christianity and the attractiveness of the Christian gospel. We conclude the book by pointing directly at the brilliance of this gospel. In addition to thinking that Christianity is true, we think that Christianity is beautiful. Our thesis is Christianity, especially its most fundamental thesis of the gospel, is not merely rational to believe on an intellectual basis, but it is also incredibly attractive as well and meets us at the deepest parts of who we are. In short, the gospel is brilliant. It is both intellectually smart and also, at times, blindingly beautiful.

In closing, it would be helpful to summarize the gospel once again. Here is a brief summary:

God creates the world, not out of his own need, but out of love and for his glory. The gospel is decidedly not about us and what we can get out of it. Instead, *God is the end of our salvation*. The ultimate aim of all of reality is to bring glory to him.

However, humans freely sin. *Our sin results in the need of salvation.* Now, it is occasionally asserted that people are, on the whole, good. However, with only a little prodding, most will admit that despite our best intentions, everyone makes mistakes along the way, some of which have terrible consequences. This is the human predicament, and we spend a fortune and countless hours in therapy, on self-help tools, and even in religious efforts to correct this problem. We are, at our core, broken, unwhole, and fallen. In this state, we have chosen to knowingly go against God's holy law; we are thereby under the condemnation of God as the holy and righteous judge.

But—and here is the good news—Jesus Christ pays the penalty in our place on the cross and defeats sin by rising again! *Jesus Christ is the basis of our salvation.* God in his grace and mercy has provided a way of salvation, and this is precisely in the person and work of Jesus Christ. God's justice is perfectly satisfied, and his love and mercy for us is expressed. Jesus is the solution to the human predicament. He solves our sin problem.

Given this work, we are called to place our faith in Christ. *Faith is the means of our salvation.* This does not earn our salvation, since salvation has already been earned on the cross. It is simply coming to see that God is God, recognizing that he is the ultimate end, and repenting of the ways we have self-served. This, of course, means that, given our salvation, we seek to live in such a way that everything that we do is for him!

The result of salvation: we are rightly restored and properly oriented to bringing glory to God. Being rightly restored and properly oriented to God is, we claim, the avenue for true human flourishing. This is when we are truly complete.

Before we move on, we must confess that even though we have been thinking about these Christian ideas for decades, we still find ourselves in awe of their brilliance. Each of us works in philosophy and the history of ideas, and we are trained in the highest levels of academia. Part of this process is reading works of the greatest minds from ancient times until now. We each, for example, think that Plato was a genius. Alfred North Whitehead once reduced the entire Western philosophical tradition to "a series of footnotes to Plato."[4] Now, admittedly, this might be a bit overstated. True, Plato

---

4. Alfred North Whitehead, *Process and Reality* (New York: Free Press, 1979), 39.

is a towering figure in philosophy. However, Plato's philosophical ideas, as intriguing and interesting as they are, pale in comparison to the Christian gospel. We each find ourselves hearing this afresh and are forced to pause in wonder at the beauty and brilliance of the gospel.

Let's dig deeper.

The gospel is decidedly unexpected. That is, if this were man-made, we'd expect it to be aimed at us just like every other human creation. But this is not, at the end of the day, a humanistic gospel. We benefit massively, to be sure, but this is only through surrendering and giving over our lives to Christ as Lord. Jesus often spoke of this inversion. He spoke of the last being first (Matt 20:16; Luke 13:30) and said that whoever loses his life for Christ's sake will find it (Matt 16:25; Luke 9:24). Though unfortunately there are people who present the gospel as a kind of sales pitch, the gospel is not about us and our securing our spot within eternal bliss. There will be some kind of eternal bliss, but this is not what salvation is all about. Our enjoying eternity is something of a by-product of making Christ Lord of our lives and being properly oriented toward God. For other religions the ultimate focus is our enlightenment, or getting into paradise along with our seventy-two black-eyed virgins, or becoming a god. These religions seem to have as their aim our having an exalted status in eternity. After all who wouldn't want enlightenment? And who wouldn't want to be a god? And if we are honest, who wouldn't want every sensual delight? These are all seductive, in a way, but they all appeal to our base desires.

With the Christian gospel, by contrast, there's a sense in which we don't want the gospel because we have to lose ourselves. We admit that we are not the center of our universe and take our place in worshiping the One who is. The gospel may not be what we want, but it is exactly what we need, ultimately satisfying our deepest longings. We lose ourselves, indeed. But in so doing, we find our true selves! The gospel, it seems, perfectly fits our need and satisfies the human predicament. As we said, we are broken and fallen. We are in moral rebellion against God, and nothing we do is sufficient to solve this problem. We may want to do the good, we may even try to do good, but we never achieve the good.

Almost every worldview offers some sort of solution to this human predicament. We have canvassed some of these proposed solutions in previous chapters. What virtually every proposed solution has in common involves giving us something to do. But how can *doing something* possibly constitute a solution to the human predicament? Our problem in the first place was that we have a moral problem. We don't *do* what we are supposed to do in the first place. How does giving us a new list of things to do even sort of solve the problem?

To illustrate the problem here, suppose you have a nasty fall and break your leg. Let's say you go to the doctor and he tells you that you indeed have a fracture. Suppose the doctor says, "My prescribed treatment for your condition is to get up and *walk it off*." Wait—what? Precisely how is walking off a broken leg supposed to help with a broken leg? The problem, as it currently stands, is that you can't walk, and trying to walk will only exacerbate the problem. It would be at this point that we'd suggest getting a new doctor.

In the same way, no amount of attempting to live a good life, the life of a religious tradition, or even the life of a "good Christian," for that matter, will help our human predicament since our problem is precisely that we cannot live the way we are supposed to live in the first place. If your religion or denomination is merely telling you to do things to help your condition, then we'd suggest you get yourself a new religion or denomination.

Now, to be clear, we are not saying that religious performances are unimportant. But in the Christian view, doing things should be an expression of our faith, not a prerequisite for faith. Indeed, James says that our faith is literally dead without good deeds (2:17). But if salvation is predicated on living a certain moral lifestyle, then this thing is hopeless. If it is up to our performances, then we are doomed.

But here comes the beauty of the gospel. "For you are saved by grace through faith, and this is not from yourselves; it is God's gift" (Eph 2:8). There is perhaps no more profound truth to reflect on related to this topic than this statement. Just let that sink in for a moment. Our salvation is by grace. It is not by works. You can't earn this salvation. It is the gift of God to you. It is the work of the perfect man, God in the flesh, who has earned our salvation. It is accepting this gift through faith, venturing our trust in God rather than ourselves, that secures our salvation. This is amazing and wondrous in its implications!

You should know that this is *completely unique* to Christianity. There's not another religion in the history of the world that predicated salvation on grace by faith. Though this points us away from ourselves, we'd like to suggest that it is precisely the appropriate remedy for the human predicament. Indeed it is what makes us whole and makes us flourish. There's a certain beauty and brilliance to these profound truths that are so very attractive and, we think, ultimately points us to the divine.

From its beauty alone we don't conclude that it is therefore true. It is logically possible for something to be beautiful and yet false (e.g., good fiction or fairy tales). However, we've spent considerable time offering intellectual reasons for its truth in this book. What we conclude is that it is not only true, but it is also beautiful. We can be satisfied intellectually and in the deepest parts of who we are.

Assignments

Assignment 12-1: Making Gospel Connections

Ask an unbelieving friend what his or her greatest obstacles are to believing in Christianity. Make it clear that all you want to do is listen to his or her objections and learn from them. Then begin to study up on those questions, looking both to good books, as well as trusted mentors. Be sure to follow up with your friend to dialogue about his or her questions. Remember: don't be a gunslinger apologist! Have a conversation about how Christians address the challenges that he or she brought up.

Assignment 12-2

Answer the following questions:

1. Do you think that doubt can be valuable for faith?
2. What is the Christian gospel?
3. Describe the first time in your life that the gospel made sense. What about it attracted you?
4. Do you think that the gospel is beautiful? If so, how would you characterize its beauty?

Suggested Reading

Buechner, Frederick. *Telling the Truth: The Gospel as Tragedy, Comedy, and Fairy Tale*. New York: HarperCollins, 1977.

Ganssle, Gregory. *Our Deepest Desires: How the Christian Story Fulfills Human Aspirations*. Downers Grove, IL: InterVarsity Press, 2017.

Naugle, David. *Reordered Love, Reordered Lives: Learning the Deep Meaning of Happiness*. Grand Rapids: Eerdmans, 2008.

Bibliography

Aeschylus. *The Oresteia*. Translated by Robert Fagles. New York: Penguin Books, 1979.

Anderson, Ross. *Understanding the Book of Mormon*. Grand Rapids: Zondervan, 2009.

Anselm. *Proslogion*. Translated by Thomas Williams. Indianapolis: Hackett, 1995.

Aquinas, Thomas. *The Summa Theologica of Saint Thomas Aquinas*. Vol. 1, *Prima Pars, Q. 1–64*. Translated by Fathers of the English Dominican Province. Scotts Valley, CA: NovAntiqua, 2008.

Aristotle. *Aristotle: Selected Works*. 3rd ed. Translated and edited by Hippocrates Apostle. Grinnell, IA: Peripatetic Press, 1991.

Athanasius. *On the Incarnation*. Crestwood, NY: St. Vladimir's Seminary Press, 1996.

Audi, Robert. *Epistemology: A Contemporary Introduction*. 3rd ed. New York: Routledge, 2011.

Augustine. *Confessions*. Translated by Henry Chadwick. New York: Oxford University Press, 1991.

———. *The Trinity*. Translated by Edmund Hill. New York: New City Press, 2012.

Barrow, John D., and Frank J. Tipler. *The Anthropic Cosmological Principle*. New York: Oxford University Press, 1986.

Bartsch, Hans Werner, ed. *Kerygma and Myth*. New York: Harper & Row, 1961.

Bateman, Herbert W. IV, Darrell L. Bock, and Gordon H. Johnston. *Jesus the Messiah: Tracing the Promises, Expectations, and Coming of Israel's King*. Grand Rapids: Kregel Publications, 2012.

Bauckham, Richard. *Jesus and the Eyewitnesses: The Gospels as Eyewitness Testimony*. Grand Rapids: Eerdmans, 2006.

Beckwith, Francis. "Muslims, Christians, and the Same God: Round-Up with Advice to Volf and Clark (with Addendum)." Return to Rome, January 2, 2016, http://romereturn.blogspot.com/2016/01/muslims-christians-and-same-god-round.html?m=1.

———. "Why Muslims and Christians Worship the Same God," *The Catholic Thing*, January 7, 2016, https://www.thecatholicthing.org/2016/01/07/why-muslims-and-christians-worship-the-same-god/.

Beckwith, Francis J., and Gregory Koukl. *Relativism: Feet Firmly Planted in Mid-Air*. Grand Rapids: Baker, 1998.

Beckwith, Francis, J. P. Moreland, and William Lane Craig, eds. *To Everyone an Answer*. Downers Grove, IL: InterVarsity Press, 2004.

Beckwith, Francis, Carl Mosser, and Paul Owen, eds. *The New Mormon Challenge*. Grand Rapids: Zondervan, 2002.

Beilby, James K., and Paul Rhodes Eddy, eds. *The Historical Jesus: Five Views*. Downers Grove, IL: InterVarsity Press, 2009.

Benson, Ezra Taft. *The Teachings of Ezra Taft Benson*. Salt Lake City: Bookcraft, 1988.

Bingham, D. Jeffrey. *Pocket History of the Church*. Downers Grove, IL: InterVarsity Press, 2002.

Bird, Michael F. "Did Jesus Think He Was God?" In *How God Became Jesus,* edited by Michael Bird et al, 45–70. Grand Rapids: Zondervan, 2014.

Blomberg, Craig L. *The Historical Reliability of the New Testament: Countering the Challenges to Evangelical Christian Beliefs*. Nashville: B&H Academic, 2016.

Blomberg, Craig L., and Stephen E. Robinson. *How Wide the Divide?* Downers Grove, IL: InterVarsity Press, 1997.

Boa, Kenneth, and Robert M. Bowman. *Faith Has Its Reasons: Integrative Approaches to Defending the Faith.* 2nd ed. Downers Grove, IL: InterVarsity Press, 2006.

Bowman, Robert M. Jr., *Understanding Jehovah's Witnesses.* Grand Rapids: Baker Books, 1991.

———. *Why You Should Believe in the Trinity: An Answer to Jehovah's Witnesses.* Grand Rapids: Baker Books, 1989.

Bray, Gerald. *The Doctrine of God.* Downers Grove, IL: InterVarsity Press, 1993.

Bruce, F. F. *The Canon of Scripture.* Downers Grove, IL: InterVarsity Press, 1988.

———. *Jesus and Christian Origins Outside the New Testament.* Grand Rapids: Eerdmans, 1974.

———. *The New Testament Documents: Are They Reliable?* Grand Rapids: Eerdmans, 1962; Downers Grove, IL: InterVarsity Press, 1981.

Buechner, Frederick. *Telling the Truth: The Gospel as Tragedy, Comedy, and Fairy Tale.* New York: HarperCollins, 1977.

Capes, David B., Rodney Reeves, and E. Randolph Richards. *Rediscovering Jesus: An Introduction to Biblical, Religious and Cultural Perspectives on Christ.* Downers Grove, IL: InterVarsity Press, 2015.

Carrier, Richard. *On the Historicity of Jesus.* Sheffield, UK: Sheffield Phoenix Press, 2014.

Church of Jesus Christ of Latter-day Saints. *True to the Faith: A Gospel Reference.* Salt Lake City: Intellectual Reserve, 2004.

Conee, Earl, and Richard Feldman. *Evidentialism: Essays in Epistemology.* New York: Oxford University Press, 2004.

Copan, Paul. *True for You, But Not for Me: Overcoming Objections to Christian Faith.* 2nd ed. Bloomington, MN: Bethany House, 2009.

Copan, Paul, and Matthew Flannagan. *Did God Really Command Genocide?* Grand Rapids: Baker, 2014.

Copan, Paul, and Paul K. Moser, eds. *The Rationality of Theism*. New York: Routledge, 2003.

Copan, Paul, and Ronald K. Tacelli, eds. *Jesus's Resurrection: Fact or Fiction? A Debate Between William Lane Craig and Gerd Lüdemann*. Downers Grove, IL: InterVarsity Press, 2000.

Corduan, Winfried. *Neighboring Faiths: A Christian Introduction to World Religions*. 2nd ed. Downers Grove, IL: InterVarsity Press, 2012.

Cowan, Steven B., and Terry L. Wilder, eds. *In Defense of the Bible*. Nashville: B&H Academic, 2013.

Craig, William Lane. *The Kalām Cosmological Argument*. Eugene, OR: Wipf and Stock, 2000.

———. *On Guard*. Colorado Springs: David C. Cook, 2010.

———. *Reasonable Faith: Christian Truth and Apologetics*. 3rd ed. Wheaton, IL: Crossway, 2008.

———. *The Son Rises*. Eugene, OR: Wipf & Stock, 1981.

Craig, William Lane, and J. P. Moreland. *Philosophical Foundations for a Christian Worldview*. Downers Grove, IL: InterVarsity Press, 2003.

———., eds. *The Blackwell Companion to Natural Theology*. Malden, MA: Blackwell, 2009.

———. *Naturalism: A Critical Analysis*. New York: Routledge, 2000.

Davis, Stephen. *God, Reason and Theistic Proofs*. Grand Rapids: Eerdmans, 1997.

Davison, Andrew. *Imaginative Apologetics: Theology, Philosophy and the Catholic Tradition*. Grand Rapids: Baker, 2012.

Dawkins, Richard. *The Blind Watchmaker*. New York: W. W. Norton, 1986.

———. *The God Delusion*. New York: Houghton Mifflin, 2006.

———. *River out of Eden*. New York: Perseus Books, 1995.

Dembski, William A., and James M. Kushiner, eds. *Signs of Intelligence: Understanding Intelligent Design*. Grand Rapids: Brazos Press, 2001.

de Ridder, Jeroen, and Rene van Woudenberg. "Referring to, Believing in, and Worshiping the Same God: A Reformed View." *Faith and Philosophy* 31, no. 1 (2014): 46–67.

Dodd, C. H. *The Apostolic Preaching and Its Developments.* London: Hodder & Stoughton, 1936.

Draper, Paul. "The Skeptical Theist." In *The Evidential Argument from Evil*, edited by Daniel Howard-Snyder, 175–92. Bloomington, IN: Indiana University Press, 1996.

Dunn, James. "Prophetic 'I'-Sayings and the Jesus-Tradition: The Importance of Testing Prophetic Utterances within Early Christianity." *New Testament Studies* 24 (1977–78): 175–98.

Eddy, Paul Rhodes, and Gregory A. Boyd. *The Jesus Legend.* Grand Rapids: Baker Academic, 2007.

Ehrman, Bart. *Did Jesus Exist?* New York: HarperOne, 2013.

———. *Misquoting Jesus: The Story Behind Who Changed the Bible and Why.* New York: HarperCollins, 2005.

———. *The New Testament: A Historical Introduction to the Early Christian Writings*, 2nd ed. New York: Oxford University Press, 2000.

Erickson, Millard. *Christian Theology.* 3rd ed. Grand Rapids: Baker, 2013.

Eusebius. *The Church History*. Translated by Paul L. Maier. Grand Rapids: Kregel, 2007.

Evans, C. Stephen. *Natural Signs and Knowledge of God: A New Look at Theistic Arguments*. New York: Oxford University Press, 2010.

Flew, Antony. *God and Philosophy*. New York: Prometheus Books, 2005.

Ganssle, Gregory. "Making the Gospel Connection: An Essay Concerning Applied Apologetics." In *Come Let Us Reason: New Essays in Christian Apologetics*, edited by Paul Copan and William Lane Craig, 3–16. Nashville: B&H Academic, 2012.

———. *Our Deepest Desires: How the Christian Story Fulfills Human Aspirations*. Downers Grove, IL: InterVarsity Press, 2017.

Geisler, Norman, ed. *The Counterfeit Gospel of Mormonism*. Eugene, OR: Harvest House, 1998.

Geisler, Norman L., and William E. Nix. *From God to Us: How We Got Our Bible*. Chicago: Moody Press, 1974.

Geivett, Douglas, and Gary R. Habermas, eds. *In Defense of Miracles: A Comprehensive Case for God's Action in History*. Downers Grove, IL: InterVarsity Press, 1997.

Gettier, Edmund. "Is Justified True Belief Knowledge?" *Analysis* 23 (1963): 121–23.

Goetz, Stewart, and Charles Taliaferro. *Naturalism*. Grand Rapids: Eerdmans, 2008.

Green, Joel B. "Luke-Acts, or Luke and Acts? A Reaffirmation of Narrative Unity." In *Reading Acts Today*, edited by Steve Walton, Thomas E. Phillips, Lloyd Keith Pietersen, and F. Scott Spencer. New York: T&T Clark, 2011.

Groothuis, Douglas. *Christian Apologetics*. Downers Grove, IL: InterVarsity Press, 2011.

Gurry, Peter. "The Number of Variants in the Greek New Testament." *New Testament Studies* 62, no. 1 (2016): 97–121.

Habermas, Gary R., and Michael R. Licona. *The Case for the Resurrection of Jesus*. Grand Rapids: Kregel, 2004.

Halverson, Dean C., ed. *The Compact Guide to World Religions*. Minneapolis: Bethany House, 1996.

Hengel, Martin. *Crucifixion in the Ancient World and the Folly of the Message of the Cross*. Philadelphia: Fortress Press, 1977.

Hick, John. *An Autobiography*. Oxford: Oneworld, 2002.

———. *An Interpretation of Religion: Human Responses to the Transcendent*. 2nd ed. New Haven, CT: Yale University Press, 2004.

Hoekema, Anthony. *Jehovah's Witnesses*. Grand Rapids: Eerdmans, 1963.

Holsteen, Nathan D., and Michael J. Svigel et al. *Exploring Christian Theology: Revelation, Scripture, and the Triune God*. Minneapolis: Bethany House, 2014.

Howard-Snyder, Daniel. "God, Evil, and Suffering." In *Reason for the Hope Within*, edited by Michael Murray. Grand Rapids: Eerdmans, 1999.

Howard-Snyder, Daniel, and Paul K. Moser, eds. *Divine Hiddenness: New Essays*. New York: Cambridge University Press, 2002.

Howsam, Leslie, and Scott McLaren. "Producing the Text: Production and Distribution of Popular Editions of the Bible." In *The New Cambridge History of the Bible*. Vol. 4: *From 1750 to the Present*, edited by John Riches. New York: Cambridge University Press, 2015.

Hume, David. *An Enquiry Concerning Human Understanding*. Edited by Eric Steinberg. 2nd ed. Indianapolis: Hackett, 1993.

———. *The History of England*. Edited by W. B. Todd. Indianapolis: Liberty Classics, 1983.

———. *New Letters of David Hume*. Edited by R. Klibansky and E. C. Mossner. Oxford: Oxford University Press, 1954.

Hunter, Milton R. *The Gospel through the Ages*. Salt Lake City: Deseret, 1945.

Josephus. *The Life and Works of Flavius Josephus*. Edited and translated by William Whiston. Peabody, MA: Hendrickson, 1987.

Keller, Timothy. *The Reason for God*. New York: Dutton, 2008.

Kelly, Thomas. "The Epistemic Significance of Disagreement." In *Oxford Studies in Epistemology*, edited by Tamar Szabo Gendler and John Hawthorne, 167–96. Vol. 1. New York: Oxford University Press, 2005.

Koester, Helmut. *Introduction to the New Testament,* vol. 2: *History and Literature of Early Christianity*. Philadelphia: Fortress, 1982.

Köstenberger, Andreas J., and Michael J. Kruger. *The Heresy of Orthodoxy: How Contemporary Culture's Fascination with Diversity Has Reshaped Our Understanding of Early Christianity*. Wheaton, IL: Crossway, 2010.

Krauss, Lawrence M. *A Universe from Nothing: Why There Is Something Rather Than Nothing*. New York: Free Press, 2012.

Kreeft, Peter. *Making Sense out of Suffering*. Ann Arbor: Servant Books, 1986.

Kreeft, Peter and Ronald Tacelli. *Handbook of Christian Apologetics*. Downers Grove, IL: InterVarsity Press, 1994.

Larmer, Robert A. *The Legitimacy of Miracle*. New York: Lexington Books, 2014.

Leith, John H., ed. *Creeds of the Churches*. 3rd ed. Louisville, KY: John Knox Press, 1982.

Lennox, John. *God's Undertaker*. Oxford: Lion Book, 2009.

Lewis, C. S. *God in the Dock*. Edited by Walter Hooper. Grand Rapids: Eerdmans, 1970.

———. *A Grief Observed*. New York: HarperOne, 1994.

———. *Mere Christianity*. San Francisco: HarperOne, 2001.

———. *Miracles*. 2nd ed. New York: HarperCollins, 1947.

———. *The Problem of Pain*. San Francisco: HarperCollins, 2001.

———. *Studies in Medieval and Renaissance Literature*. Edited by Walter Hooper. New York: Cambridge University Press, 2013.

Licona, Michael R. *The Resurrection of Jesus: A New Historiographical Approach*. Downers Grove, IL: InterVarsity Press, 2010.

Litfin, Bryan. *After Acts: Exploring the Lives and Legends of the Apostles*. Chicago: Moody, 2015.

Loftin, R. Keith, ed. *God & Morality: Four Views*. Downers Grove, IL: InterVarsity Press, 2012.

Lüdemann, Gerd. *The Resurrection of Jesus: History, Experience, Theology*. Translated by John Bowden. Minneapolis: Fortress Press, 1994.

Maier, Paul L. *In the Fullness of Time: A Historian Looks at Christmas, Easter, and the Early Church*. Grand Rapids: Kregel, 1991.

Martin, Walter. *The Kingdom of the Cults*. Rev. ed. Minneapolis: Bethany House, 2003.

Matthew, Robert J. *"A Bible! A Bible!"* Salt Lake City: Bookcraft, 1990.

McConkie, Bruce. *The Millennial Messiah*. Salt Lake City: Deseret, 1982.

————. *Mormon Doctrine*. 2nd ed. Salt Lake City: Bookcraft, 1966.

————. *What the Mormons Think of Christ*. Salt Lake City: Church of Jesus Christ of Latter-day Saints, n.d.

McDowell, Sean. *The Fate of the Apostles*. Burlington, VT: Ashgate, 2015.

McGrew, Lydia. *Hidden in Plain View: Undesigned Coincidences in the Gospels and Acts*. Chillicothe, OH: DeWard Publishing, 2017.

McKeever, Bill, and Eric Johnson. *Mormonism 101*. Grand Rapids: Baker Books, 2000.

Menuge, Angus. *Agents Under Fire*. Lanham, MD: Rowman & Littlefield, 2004.

Metzger Bruce M., and Bart D. Ehrman. *The Text of the New Testament: Its Transmission, Corruption, and Restoration*. 4th ed. New York: Oxford University Press, 2005.

Moreland, J. P. *Christianity and the Nature of Science*. Grand Rapids: Baker, 1989.

————. *Consciousness and the Existence of God: A Theistic Argument*. New York: Routledge, 2008.

————. *Scaling the Secular City*. Grand Rapids: Baker, 1987.

Moreland, J. P., Chad Meister, and Khaldoun A. Sweis, eds. *Debating Christian Theism*. New York: Oxford University Press, 2013.

Morris, Thomas. *Our Idea of God*. Notre Dame, IN: University of Notre Dame, 1991; Vancouver, BC: Regent College Publishing, 2002.

————, ed. *God and the Philosophers*. New York: Oxford University Press, 1994.

Nagel, Thomas. *The Last Word*. New York: Oxford University Press, 1997.

Naugle, David. *Reordered Loves, Reordered Lives: Learning the Deep Meaning of Happiness*. Grand Rapids: Eerdmans, 2008.

Netland, Harold A. *Encountering Religious Pluralism: The Challenge to Christian Faith and Mission*. Downers Grove, IL: InterVarsity Press, 2001.

Newman, Randy. *Bringing the Gospel Home*. Wheaton, IL: Crossway, 2011.

Numbers, Ronald L., ed. *Galileo Goes to Jail and Other Myths about Science and Religion.* Cambridge, MA: Harvard University Press, 2009.

O'Collins, Gerald. *The Tripersonal God.* New York: Paulist Press, 1999.

Okholm, Dennis L., and Timothy R. Phillips, eds. *Four Views on Salvation in a Pluralistic World.* Grand Rapids: Zondervan, 1996.

Petersen, Mark E. *As Translated Correctly.* Salt Lake City: Deseret, 1966.

Plantinga, Alvin. *God, Freedom, and Evil.* Grand Rapids: Eerdmans, 1977.

———. *The Nature of Necessity.* Oxford: Clarendon Press, 1974.

———. "Pluralism: A Defense of Religious Exclusivism." In *The Philosophical Challenge of Religious Diversity*, edited by Philip L. Quinn and Kevin Meeker, 172–92. New York: Oxford University Press, 2000.

———. *Where the Conflict Really Lies.* New York: Oxford University Press, 2011.

Plato. *Plato: Complete Works.* Edited by John M. Cooper. Indianapolis: Hackett, 1997.

Pratt, Orson. *Divine Authenticity of the Book of Mormon.* Liverpool, UK: 1851.

Prothero, Stephen. *God Is Not One.* New York: HarperOne, 2010.

Qureshi, Nabeel. *Answering Jihad: A Better Way Forward.* Grand Rapids: Zondervan, 2016.

Reeves, Michael. *Rejoicing in Christ.* Downers Grove, IL: InterVarsity Press, 2015.

Reppert, Victor. *C. S. Lewis's Dangerous Idea.* Downers Grove, IL: InterVarsity Press, 2003.

Rhodes, Ron. *Conversations with Jehovah's Witnesses.* Eugene, OR: Harvest House, 2014.

Rhodes, Ron, and Marian Bodine. *Reasoning from the Scriptures with the Mormons.* Eugene, OR: Harvest House, 1995.

Rosenberg, Alex. *The Atheist's Guide to Reality: Enjoying Life without Illusions.* New York: W. W. Norton, 2011.

Sanders, Fred, and Klaus Issler, eds. *Jesus in Trinitarian Perspective*. Nashville: B&H Academic, 2007.

Shaw, Ian J. *Churches, Revolutions, and Empires: 1789–1914.* Fearn, UK: Christian Focus, 2012.

Sherwin-White, A. N. *Roman Society and Roman Law in the New Testament.* Oxford: Clarendon Press, 1963.

Smith, Joseph. *The Pearl of Great Price.* Salt Lake City: Church of Jesus Christ of Latter-day Saints, 1981.

———. *Teachings of the Prophet Joseph Smith.* Salt Lake City: Deseret, 1976.

Strauss, David F. *A New Life of Jesus.* London: Williams and Norgate, 1879.

Strobel, Lee. *The Case for Christ.* Grand Rapids: Zondervan, 1998.

Stump, Eleonore. *Wandering in Darkness: Narrative and the Problem of Suffering.* Oxford: Clarendon Press, 2012.

Swinburne, Richard. *The Christian God.* New York: Oxford University Press, 1994.

———. *The Existence of God.* 2nd ed. New York: Oxford University Press, 2004.

———. *Was Jesus God?* New York: Oxford University Press, 2008.

Thucydides. *The History of the Peloponnesian War.* In *The Landmark Thucydides: A Comprehensive Guide to the Peloponnesian War*, edited by Robert B. Strassler, translated by Richard Crawley. New York: Touchstone, 1998.

Tolkien, J. R. R. "On Fairy Stories." In *The Tolkien Reader*, 33–99. New York: Ballantine Books, 2001.

Twain, Mark. *Following the Equator.* New York: Dover, 1989.

Virgil. *Aeneid.* Translated by Frederick Ahl. New York: Oxford University Press, 2007.

Voltaire. *The Works of Voltaire: A Philosophical Dictionary.* Translated by William F. Fleming. Vol. 11. New York: E. R. DuMont, 1901.

Wallace, Daniel B., ed. *Revisiting the Corruption of the New Testament: Manuscript, Patristic, and Apocryphal Evidence.* Grand Rapids: Kregel, 2011.

Watchtower Bible and Tract Society. *Aid to Bible Understanding*. Brooklyn: Watchtower Bible and Tract Society, 1971.

———. *Let God Be True*. Brooklyn: Watchtower Bible and Tract Society, 1946.

———. *Should You Believe in the Trinity?* Brooklyn: Watchtower Bible and Tract Society, 1989.

———. *What Does the Bible Really Teach?* Brooklyn: Watchtower Bible and Tract Society, 2005.

———. *You Can Live Forever in Paradise on Earth*. Brooklyn: Watchtower Bible and Tract Society, 1989.

Wright, N. T. *The Challenge of Jesus*. Downers Grove, IL: InterVarsity Press, 2015.

———. *The New Testament and the People of God*. Minneapolis: Fortress Press, 1992.

———. *The Resurrection of the Son of God*. Minneapolis: Fortress Press, 2003.

———. *Simply Jesus*. New York: HarperCollins, 2011.

Yancey, Philip. *The Jesus I Never Knew*. Grand Rapids: Zondervan, 1995.

Scripture Index

Name Index

Subject Index